A CHILD'S STORY OF THE BOOK OF MORMON

A CHILD'S STORY OF THE BOOK OF MORMON

FOUR VOLUMES IN ONE

DETA PETERSEN NEELEY

Deseret Book Company
Salt Lake City, Utah

First printing as four volumes in one, September 1987

Library of Congress Cataloging-in-Publication Data

Neeley, Deta Petersen.
   A child's story of the Book of Mormon.

   Summary: Presents the deeds and adventures of the Book
of Mormon retold in simplified language.
   1. Book of Mormon stories. [1. Book of Mormon
stories] I. Book of Mormon.   II. Title.
BX8627.A2N4   1987   289.3′22   87-19903
ISBN 0-87579-101-8

Printed in the United States of America

10

Contents

Author's Preface

A *Child's Story of the Book of Mormon* is a sincere and prayerful effort to present the true spirit of the Book of Mormon to Latter-day Saint children. For the sake of the child's interest and understanding, the story is dramatized and told in simple language of today.

Great care has been expended to make the background upon which the facts of the story are woven geographically and historically correct. Since children's greatest interest is centered in the home and the family and they are more familiar with family life situations than any others, emphasis has been placed on this phase of the story. Being cognizant of the divinity of the origin of the Book of Mormon, I have made a conscious effort to present the facts of this most sacred book, free from personal interpretations.

This book is intended for children of all ages. Children who possess fourth-grade reading ability will be able to read the book for themselves, since the story is based upon a carefully selected vocabulary. Younger children will enjoy having the stories read to them.

The purposes of the book are threefold:
(1) To create in children deep and lasting interest in the Book of Mormon.
(2) To stimulate, through development of the text, an ap-

preciation for and recognition of the true values of life by picturing the deep satisfaction that comes through believing in God and keeping His commandments.

(3) To present a story of the Book of Mormon that children themselves can read and understand.

In this troubled world, the great truths of the Book of Mormon can be a mighty force in healing our doubts and clearing our vision. Children suffer greatly in times of insecurity and chaos, and they need the strength and peace of mind that comes from a knowledge of this book of scripture. *A Child's Story of the Book of Mormon* is a conscientious effort to meet this need by bringing the true spirit of the Book of Mormon within the range of children's comprehension.

—Deta Petersen Neeley

Publisher's Preface

This book combines into one volume the popular *Child's Story of the Book of Mormon,* which was originally published in four books. In this book, each of the former volumes is a separate part, and each tells a portion of the exciting story of the Book of Mormon.

Part 1, "The Journey to the Promised Land," tells how Lehi and his family leave Jerusalem and describes their trials in the wilderness. It also recounts their adventures as they cross the sea and finally arrive in the promised land.

Part 2, "The Precious Land of Promise," gives the details of Lehi's family and their adventures in the promised land. It continues for several generations, showing how Lehi's family splits into the Nephites and the Lamanites.

Part 3, "The Land of Their Inheritance," tells of wars and wickedness as well as periods of peace and faith in God. As the Lamanites and the Nephites quarrel with each other, they discover new peoples and renewed faith in God.

Part 4, "The Savior Comes to the Promised Land," describes how the descendants of Lehi are blessed to see Jesus Christ. But the peace they enjoy after this event is eventually shattered and the Nephites are subsequently destroyed.

PART 1
The Journey to the Promised Land

CHAPTER 1

L ong ago* and far away, in the great city of Jerusalem,
lived a man named Lehi, his wife, Sariah, and their
four sons, Laman, Lemuel, Sam, and Nephi.

Late one afternoon, as Sariah went about her work of
preparing the evening meal, there was a smile on her
gentle lips. She was thinking of her four strong sons. She
loved them all dearly, but in Nephi she found her greatest
joy. How much like his father he was—kind and gentle
and understanding. Even though he was still very young,
he was as strong and tall as a man.

When all the food had been placed on the table, she
sank gratefully into a chair. The sun had been burning
hot all day long, but although it was now sinking below
the western hills, the air had grown so still that the heat
seemed even worse than it had been earlier in the day.

From where she sat she could see the garden
through the open door. It was beautiful, just touched by
the rosy light of the setting sun. Soon Lehi would come
through the garden gate and she would run to meet him
just as she always did. How dear, how good he was. It
made her happy just to think of him. If only Laman and
Lemuel were more like their father—but they were in-
clined to be proud and selfish, rejoicing in the pleasures
of the great city of Jerusalem. Night after night, she had

---

*About 600 B.C.

3

lain awake worrying about her eldest sons. Sam and
Nephi seldom gave her any cause for worry.

At that moment, Lehi came through the garden gate
and up the path toward the house. As soon as Sariah
saw him she got up from her chair and started to meet
him but, as she reached the kitchen door, she stopped
abruptly and stood looking at him with wonder in her
eyes. Was something wrong? He was walking with his
head bowed; she had never known him to do that before. He always walked with his head so erect and his
shoulders so straight. Now he looked as if he carried the
weight of the world on his shoulders. At last he raised his
head and looked at her. His eyes were sparkling with a
strange light as if they were lit by a divine inner glow.

Smiling, she said, "Good evening, Lehi."

"Good evening," he answered.

"Is something wrong?" she asked with concern.

"No, my dear."

"But your face is so white and you are trembling. If
you are not ill what is it, then?" asked Sariah.

"Well, Sariah, something wonderful has happened."

Suddenly he stopped speaking and leaned against
the door. Sariah, seeing his weakness and thinking he
might fall, ran quickly to bring him a chair.

"I am very tired," he said, waving the chair away. "I
think I'll go to my room and lie down before I tell you
about all the wonderful things I've seen and heard today."

Sariah hurried ahead of him to open the bedroom
door and place the pillow as he liked it.

After supper, Lehi gathered his family around him,
saying, "I have something to tell you. A great and marvelous thing happened to me today."

"Did you strike it rich, Father?" asked Laman.

"No, my son, it is something far greater than riches."

"Go on, tell us about it," said Nephi, his eyes glowing with interest.

"Ever since Zedekiah became king of Judah, there have been prophets going throughout the land telling the people that they must repent or Jerusalem will be destroyed. Today I left the city and went into the hills to pray. I prayed long and earnestly for my people. While I was praying, a great pillar of fire came and dwelt upon the rock in front of me. I saw and heard many things, and because of what I saw and heard, I began to tremble and grow weak."

Lehi sighed deeply and stopped speaking. For several moments he sat in silence, lost in his thoughts. Sariah, for the first time since he had begun to speak, took her eyes from him and turned to look at her four sons. She hoped that they accepted his words with the same faith that she did. When she looked at Nephi and Sam she was reassured, for their eyes shone with devotion for their father and faith in his words, but when she looked at Laman and Lemuel she saw something quite different. There was disbelief mingled with amusement.

"The sun was very hot today, Father—probably it set your fire," said Lemuel, exchanging a mischievous glance with Laman.

"No, my boy, it was not the sun that started the fire. When the vision ended, I came home, but when I reached here I was so overcome that I lay upon my bed. As I lay there, I beheld another vision. All at once, I thought I saw the heavens open up. God was sitting on His throne and around Him were many angels, so many I couldn't count them. They were singing and praising God. As I watched, one of them began descending to earth. He shone brighter than any of the others. The light around him was brighter than the noonday sun.

Twelve other angels followed him and they came down and stood upon the earth. The first one came and stood before me and gave me an open book to read and I read of the wickedness of my people. Woe, woe unto Jerusalem."

"But why do you say, 'woe, woe unto Jerusalem'?" asked Laman angrily.

"Because of what I saw and heard. I saw Jerusalem destroyed and many of my people killed and many others carried away into Babylon. When I saw all these great and marvelous things I praised God."

Lehi turned and looked at Sariah. The moment their eyes met, he knew how true was her faith in God and how truly she loved him.

"But, Father, if you told the people what you saw, don't you think they would listen and repent?" asked Sam in a quiet, humble voice.

"Are you out of your mind, Sam?" asked Lemuel. "If Father goes about the city telling the people how wicked they are and that they are to be destroyed, they will laugh us all out of Jerusalem. If he—"

"Lemuel." Lehi's voice was so stern that Lemuel was silent—ashamed of himself. "Think well of what you do and say, son, for if you disobey God you may be destroyed, too. God has commanded me to go among the people and tell them all the great and marvelous things I saw and heard. I will plead with them to repent and be saved."

Lehi was true to the commandments the Lord had given him. He went among the people and told them what he had seen and heard, how Jerusalem would be destroyed and many of the people killed and many others carried to Babylon, and even of the coming of the Messiah. When he told them all these great and wonderful things, they made fun of his visions and laughed at him. But when he kept on telling them not to continue in their wicked ways, they grew very angry and sought to take his life.

To Sariah, who loved him, the rising anger of the Jews filled her heart with fear. Whenever he stayed away from home longer than she thought he should, she became so anxious about him that she was almost ill with worry.

One day Nephi returned home to find his mother waiting by the garden gate, white-faced and trembling. Tenderly he put his arm about her shoulders and said, "Has anything happened to Father?"

"No—that is, I don't think so. It is only that he should have been home before this."

"Don't worry, Mother. Father will be all right," said Nephi.

"But how can you say such a thing?" she asked. "You know there are many wicked men who want to take his life."

"God watches over those He has chosen, and He has chosen Father to carry His word to the Jews. As long as Father keeps His commandments, nothing can happen to him. He will even deliver him out of the hands of his enemies."

"Thank you, my son. I am ashamed to have doubted the mercy of God, and won't again."

CHAPTER 2

The summer was nearly gone. Days and nights had grown cooler and Sariah had found peace and happiness since her talk with Nephi, when he had reminded her of the goodness of God and how He watched over those who kept His commandments. Now, as she made honey cakes for supper, she sang softly to herself. She was so interested in what she was doing that she didn't notice Lehi come in. When she finally looked up, she saw him watching her thoughtfully.

"Oh, Lehi, you frightened me! How long have you been standing there?"

"I'm sorry I frightened you, my dear. There is something I must tell you."

"Come, Lehi, sit down. You look worried," said Sariah, kindly.

"Yes, I am. I have something to tell you that I'm afraid will make you very unhappy."

Sariah stopped stirring the honey cakes and asked fearfully, "Has anything happened to our sons?"

"No, my dear, it is only that we must leave this house and Jerusalem at once."

"Leave this house?" asked Sariah. "You must be joking. This is our home. Here are all the things we have worked so hard for. No place else could possibly be home."

"But if I stay here I'll be killed," said Lehi.

Now, Sariah liked her home, but she loved Lehi and her sons, so she said at once, "The first thing tomorrow morning I'll begin to get everything ready for us to leave. How long will I have?"

"Thank you, my dear. I'll help you. We must leave as soon as it is dark."

"Surely you don't mean we are to leave tonight? We couldn't possibly get ready. What makes you say we must go now?"

"God has commanded me to go. He spoke to me in a dream. He called me blessed for keeping His command-ments. But because I did as He commanded, my people plan to kill me. In my dream, He commanded me to leave Jerusalem at once."

Sariah was silent so long that Lehi turned to look at her. He saw great tears rolling down her cheeks.

"Very well," she said. "I will have these honey cakes made in a few minutes, then I will help to get things ready. There are still several hours before dark; even so, there won't be time for everything. We will have to leave some of our things, won't we?"

"Yes, I plan to take only provisions and tents."

"But surely you will take the gold and silver and pre-cious things?" questioned Sariah.

"No, we'll have no need for things like that in the wilderness."

For several minutes Sariah just stood motionless, thinking of all the comforts she would have to leave be-hind. It was bad enough to leave the house and the land, but to leave things they could just as well take with them—she couldn't understand it. And what about the boys? How would they take the news? Knowing her sons, she believed that Sam and Nephi would understand and would even help in the preparations—but with Laman and Lemuel it was different. They liked Jerusalem, their friends, and the good times they were used to having. They would hate to leave it all. They would quarrel with their father and perhaps even refuse to go. It was with a heavy heart that she went to bake the honey cakes.

When night came, all preparations had been made. Everything had happened just as she had thought it would. Sam and Nephi had understood and had eagerly entered into preparing for the journey. But Laman and Lemuel sat silent and angry. They had quarreled with their father and would have refused to go had not Lehi grown so stern with them that they dared not disobey.

When Lehi closed the door of the house for the last time, Sariah was glad it was dark so her family couldn't see the tears that rolled down her cheeks. The darkness had come more quickly than usual due to the bank of clouds that rolled up higher and higher in the western sky.

When they reached the shores of the Red Sea, they were all so tired they rested until morning. For three days they traveled along the shores of the sea until they reached a valley. Here Lehi pitched the tent and built an altar of stone to God and gave an offering.

A river ran through the little valley and emptied into the Red Sea; Lehi named it Laman. He called the valley Lemuel. He thought it would please Laman and Lemuel to have the valley and river named after them, but instead, their faces grew dark with anger and hatred. Seeing this, Lehi spoke to his sons, "Laman, my son, I wish you could be like this river, forever running into the sea of all goodness. And Lemuel, I wish you could be like the valley, strong, firm, and true to the commandments of God."

"Who wants to be named after an old river in the desert?" asked Laman in anger. "I know I don't. The only thing I wanted was to stay in Jerusalem with my friends where we had a house, land, gold, and silver."

"Friends?" questioned Lehi. "The Jews of Jerusalem were not our friends. They wanted to kill me, and when they had done that they would have destroyed you too, my son."

"And whose fault was that?" asked Lemuel. "If you hadn't gone about telling of your foolish visions and dreams, we could have stayed in Jerusalem."

"Foolish is right," agreed Laman. "How could you think, for a single minute, that a great city like Jerusalem would be destroyed? No wonder the Jews laughed at you. But you had to go on telling them about their wickedness and their evil doings, until at last they wanted to kill you. If you weren't my father I think I should want to kill you, too."

"Look at us now," complained Lemuel. "You have exposed us to the weather and all sorts of hardships. We freeze by night and burn by day, and when our food is gone, what will we do then, starve? And if we don't starve we'll probably be torn to pieces by a pack of wild animals. If you had no feelings for us, your children, you should have had for our mother. Why don't you admit that you were wrong and go back to Jerusalem and ask their forgiveness?"

They expected their father to become angry and shout at them, but instead, he stood quietly by, listening to them. When they were through he half closed his eyes and stood silently praying to God, asking His Spirit to guide him. When at last he looked at them, his eyes were so bright they looked like two burning balls of fire, and when he spoke, his voice was so powerful that it shook the bodies of Laman and Lemuel. Do what they would, they couldn't stop shaking. When he stopped speaking, they were too frightened to say anything to their father. They went away promising to obey him.

To Nephi, who stood nearby, it was like a miracle. He went out from the others and prayed that he might know the mysteries of God. While he prayed he was filled with the Spirit of God and he knew that all his father had told them was true. He found Sam and told him of his prayer. Sam believed what Nephi told him and had faith, but when he told Laman and Lemuel they were angry and turned away. With a sad heart Nephi prayed again to God to soften the hearts of Laman and Lemuel. Suddenly he heard the voice of the Lord saying: "Blessed art thou, Nephi, because of thy faith, for thou hast sought me diligently, with lowliness of heart. And inasmuch as ye shall keep my commandments, ye shall prosper, and shall be led to a land of promise; yea, even a land which I have prepared for you; yea, a land which is choice above all other lands. And inasmuch as thy brethren shall rebel against thee, they shall be cut off from the presence of the Lord. And inasmuch as thou shalt keep my commandments, thou shalt be made a ruler and a teacher over thy brethren. For behold, in that day that they shall rebel against me, I will curse them even with a sore curse, and they shall have no power over thy seed except they shall rebel against me also. And if it so be that they rebel against me, they shall be a scourge unto thy seed, to stir them up in the ways of remembrance." (1 Nephi 2:19-24.)

CHAPTER 3

Nephi walked slowly along the river's edge, winding in and out with the stream as it made its way down to the Red Sea. A short distance from his father's tent, he came to a willow tree. He stopped, looked about him with searching eyes, and then lay down in the cool shade of the little tree. He had been to this spot a number of times before. Here it was that he prayed in earnest to God for guidance and understanding. Here it was that he had heard God's voice and now, today, when his heart was troubled, he came here again to find peace and to renew his faith in God.

For a few moments he lay upon the ground, looking up into the sky and letting his thoughts drift with the clouds that sailed by overhead. Life in the wilderness was not easy; it had been especially difficult for his mother, who wasn't used to hardships. His father, his brothers, and he, too, had tried to help her in every way they could, but she had singled out Laman and Lemuel, giving them many tasks and keeping them as near her as possible. Nephi guessed the reason for this. He believed she thought that if she kept them near her and busy, they would not become bitter against their father and rebel because of the burden they had to bear.

Nephi's handsome face grew sad when he thought of his mother, who seemed so tired and worried. Yet in spite of all the hardships she had to bear, she never complained. Her fine courage and strength of character made him very proud of her.

Just at that moment a huge cloud sailed into view. All the other clouds had disappeared. As Nephi watched, he fancied this one to be a great white ship sailing on and on into the deep blue sea alone. Then the thought came to him that the ship was like his family, traveling all alone in the wilderness. Then suddenly, as he watched the cloud, an angry wind caught at it and sent it twisting and turning, at last tearing it apart into many pieces that went floating off alone. This, too, was like his family. The anger of Laman and Lemuel was like the angry wind, threatening to tear them apart and separate them. His mother understood this and that was what worried her.

Long after the last of the huge cloud had disappeared and other clouds had rolled up to take its place, Nephi lay still, lost in his troubled thoughts. What was to become of them all? It was hard enough to live in the wilderness, without quarreling with each other into the bargain. Then he remembered that God had told him that someday he would be ruler over his brothers. The thought was frightening. There would be so much for him to learn. First of all, he must seek wisdom. He knew that in his father he had a great teacher. His father's days were filled with good words and good deeds. With God's help he would strive to be like him.

There was a slight sound of movement in the bushes. Nephi stirred uneasily. Suddenly, he knew he was not alone. From somewhere in the bushes, eyes were watching him. For a moment, he felt the icy fingers of fear closing about his heart. Lying flat on his back, he knew he was easy prey for a hungry, wild beast. But Nephi had great courage and soon his fear was replaced by action. Slowly, very slowly, he moved his hand to his waist until his fingers closed about his hunting knife. Before he had time to draw it from his belt, there was a harsh, crackling sound in the bushes and instantly he sprang to his feet with knife in hand.

"Put your knife away, Nephi. It's only your brother."

"Oh, Laman," breathed Nephi with relief.

"I daresay you thought me a wild beast, ready to tear you to pieces."

"I didn't know what to expect," replied Nephi humbly.

"You're not very brave, are you, brother?" sneered Laman. "Or very ambitious?"

"What do you mean by that?" asked Nephi.

"Oh, only that while the rest of the family works, you lie in the shade and watch clouds drift by."

"I finished my work even before you started," said Nephi. "But if I can help with anything more I'll be glad to."

"No, I don't need your help. I came to tell you that Father wishes to see you."

"Do you know what Father wants me for?" inquired Nephi pleasantly.

"Yes, and knowing you for the great coward you are, I am sure you're not going to like what he has to tell you," said Laman.

Nephi felt the hot blood rush to his cheeks. Suddenly he was very angry, and he had every right to be, since Laman was going out of his way to be insulting and to pick a quarrel with him. Nephi turned and took a long look at the ugly sneer across Laman's face. Then he turned on his heel and went quickly back up the river.

When Nephi reached his father's tent, he was told to go inside. Coming from the bright sunshine outside into the dim twilight of the tent blinded him for a few seconds. He was forced to stand still until his eyes grew accustomed to it. When he could see again, he discovered his father sitting cross-legged on a fur robe on the floor. His father motioned for Nephi to come and sit down beside him on the robe.

"Did you send for me, Father?" asked Nephi politely.

"Yes, my son," answered Lehi, and then he was silent.

Nephi waited a long time for his father to speak. When at last he did, his voice was serious and troubled. "Nephi, my son, I had a dream today in which the Lord commanded me to send you and your brothers up to Jerusalem."

"Up to Jerusalem?" There was astonishment in Nephi's voice. But Lehi continued without heeding it.

"In Jerusalem there is a man named Laban. He has a record of the Jews and a genealogy of your forefathers. The Lord has commanded me to send you and your brothers to get them. They are records engraved on plates of brass. You and your brothers are to bring them back to me here in the wilderness. When I told Laman and Lemuel, they complained, saying it is a hard thing I ask of them. But I did not ask it of them; it was the Lord who commanded me."

Nephi could well imagine how his brothers would hate to go back to Jerusalem. It was such a hard journey and then, too, it would be dangerous. They had little or no faith in their father's visions and for that reason they would think it would be a foolish trip. But Nephi had always believed in his father's words and, since he had heard God's voice himself, he had real knowledge of his father's truthfulness.

"I will go up to Jerusalem and bring back the plates of brass as the Lord has commanded." There was quiet dignity in Nephi's voice.

"Thank you, my son. It will not be an easy task. You shall be favored of the Lord because you did not complain," said Lehi.

"I shall succeed because when the Lord gives a commandment to the children of men, he prepares a way for them to accomplish the things he asks of them," said Nephi.

"You have made me very happy," said Lehi, "for you are blessed of the Lord."

"How soon do you want us to start?"

"At dawn tomorrow. You will need tents and provisions for several days. I thought you could make the preparations today and be ready to leave early in the morning."

As Sariah helped the boys with their preparations, her heart was heavy and her eyes held a worried look. She was sad at the thought of parting with them and worried because of the danger they would encounter. And to add to her worry was the sight of her eldest sons going about their preparations silently and dark with anger. But when she looked at her two youngest sons, her heart was cheered, for they were talking merrily to each other. At dawn next morning, she watched with tear-dimmed eyes as her sons departed.

CHAPTER 4

Jerusalem! There's Jerusalem!" shouted Laman, pointing a dusty finger directly in front of him, where the great city of Jerusalem was clearly defined against the skyline.

"Jerusalem! There's Jerusalem!" echoed Lemuel.

Laman and Lemuel continued to shout for joy, slapping each other on the back, and even shaking Sam's and Nephi's hands. Finally they turned each other about so fast they fell into the sand.

Nephi and Sam looked at each other with amazement. What a wonderful change had come over their elder brothers! On the long journey across the desert, they had remained sullen and quarrelsome. At times they had even been cruel to Nephi and Sam, taking the best of their food and making them carry more than their share of the burden, and now they were wild with joy. Suddenly, Nephi grew worried. Could it be that they had forgotten why they had come to Jerusalem, or that they were not outcasts as well as their father, or that it would take expert planning to get the plates, to say nothing of the danger involved? He was about to remind them of these things when he thought better of it and decided there was time enough for that. Let them rejoice while they could.

After a while, when their excitement had passed away, Lemuel said, "I know where we are now. I have been here before. See that hill to the left of us? Up among the rocks, there is a little spring of clear blue water. We could go there and wash ourselves and rest until dark. It will be safer for us to enter Jerusalem at night."

Nephi was greatly relieved by Lemuel's words because they showed that at least he remembered why they had made the journey to Jerusalem. The brothers all agreed that it would be a good idea to wait until night, so they started at once to climb the hill. When they reached the top, Lemuel had little difficulty locating the spring. It was a wonderful place to rest because they could not be seen by passersby and yet they had a clear view of the surrounding country. After they washed, ate, and rested they all felt much better.

"I have a suggestion to make," said Sam seriously. "I think it is better for just one of us to go to the house of Laban. I believe he is more apt to open his doors for one stranger than for four."

"I agree with Sam," said Laman good-naturedly. "There's another reason, too, why just one of us should go. If Laban should become angry and capture or destroy us, it would be better that just one was captured or destroyed than all of us. In that event, the other three might come to the rescue. What do you think about it, Nephi?"

Nephi was so surprised at being asked a question that he hesitated for a second or two. Never once during the journey had they bothered to ask him anything. They had acted as if he weren't there. Now, to be asked a question of such importance was a great surprise.

Looking up, he saw Laman waiting for an answer, so he said, "I think it's a good idea, and I will go to the house of Laban if you would like me to."

"You're all right, Nephi," said Laman with real affection in his voice. "But we will do as Father would do in matters of this kind. We'll draw lots."

The brothers agreed and the lot fell upon Laman. Just as twilight was deepening into night, he set out on his dangerous mission.

When he reached the city streets he was dismayed because a full moon had risen and was flooding everything with its silvery light. It was almost as light as day. He turned into a narrow, crooked street that was empty except for an old, white-haired man. He stopped and inquired the way to Laban's house from the old fellow.

When he reached the house a servant took him in to Laban, who was eating meat and drinking wine. He invited Laman to sit down and wait while he finished his meal. A feeling of uneasiness came over Laman as he watched the great, angry mouth of Laban tear at the meat.

"Well, young man, what do you want with me?" asked Laban, getting up from the table and coming around to Laman.

Laman took a deep breath and came right to the point. "My father has told me that you have plates of brass upon which are engraved the records of the Jews."

"Yes, I have such plates," answered Laban. "Do you want to see them?"

"No," answered Laman honestly, "but I would like to take them to my father who dwells in the wilderness. Besides being a record of the Jews, these plates bear the genealogy of my father."

For a few minutes Laban was speechless with anger. The hot blood rushed to his face, dyeing it a deep purple. He drew his lips back, showing yellow teeth that looked like the fangs of an animal.

"You want to take my plates away to the wilderness!" he roared. "Why, you are a robber, and I will slay you." As he rushed for his sword, Laman fled from the house and back to his brothers. They were all very sorry to hear the bad news.

"Since we have done all we can to get the plates, we might as well return to our father and mother in the wilderness," said Laman.

"As God lives and as we live, we will not go back to our father until we have accomplished what the Lord commanded of us." Nephi's voice was so inspired that his brothers listened in silence. "Let us keep the Lord's commandments and try again to get the plates. We all know that, in Jerusalem, our father left gold and silver and all manner of riches. Let us go back and gather them together and take them to Laban and see if he will accept them in exchange for the brass plates. It is the wisdom of God that we should have these plates so that we can preserve the language of our fathers for our children. Besides, we must preserve the word of God as spoken by the prophets from the time the world began down to the present day. Let us do as the Lord has commanded, for we must have these records."

Nephi spoke so earnestly and with such inspiration that his brothers listened to what he had to say. When he had finished, they decided to go up to their father's house in Jerusalem.

The boys were overjoyed at being back in their father's house. They went about touching everything as though they had just discovered a great treasure.

"Let's see if Father's riches are still here," suggested Nephi.

They wandered through the house, gathering up all the valuable things they came across. When they piled up the gold, silver, and other precious things they were astonished.

"It must have taken courage to go away and leave all this behind," said Lemuel.

"It took something greater than courage," said Nephi. "It took great faith in God."

When they had gathered all the precious things, they set out for Laban's house.

He met them at the door and, seeing Laman, shouted loudly, "So you're back again?"

No sooner had he spoken than he saw the precious things they carried.

"Yes, I am back again and these are my brothers," said Laman.

With a sly look in his beady eyes, Laban said, "Please come in and let me serve you."

Laman hesitated for a moment, wondering if he should warn his brothers that Laban was full of tricks. Perhaps he had set a trap for them. Then he remembered that they must have the plates at any cost, so he turned and followed Laban into the house. Laban took them to the same room he had been in earlier that evening.

"My brothers and I have brought great riches and we would like to exchange some of them for the brass plates," said Laman.

"Some of them; why not all?" asked Laban.

"Because the gold and silver and precious things we have here are worth far more than the plates," said Laman.

"But not to you," teased Laban.

"Are we to understand that you are not interested in trading?" asked Laman.

"First, I must see your treasure. Spread it out so that I can see it," he said.

When everything was spread upon the floor, Laban licked his lips greedily. He was surprised to see the extent of their riches. Suddenly, he clapped his hands and servants appeared from everywhere. He ordered them to fall on the brothers and kill them, but the brothers ran from the house and back to their hiding place in the rocks. Their gold and silver and precious things fell into the hands of Laban.

CHAPTER 5

The deep, heavy breathing of the brothers told of the great effort they had made to escape from the wicked servants of Laban. But they were safe now, hidden away in the great black cave among the rocks. The moon had just set and dawn was beginning to break, changing the blackness of the cave to a deep gray, allowing the brothers to see each other in the half-light.

"That was a narrow escape," whispered Laman.

"We're safe now. They won't follow us here among the rocks. Besides, we could hold off twice the number in the mouth of this cave." Sam's voice held a quiet note of reassurance.

"Oh, they won't bother us now; they've got what they want. All our gold and silver and precious things are now in the hands of Laban." There was a rising note of anger in Laman's voice.

"That was a fine trap we fell into," said Lemuel, following Laman's lead as always.

"And whose fault was that?" snapped Laman.

"Oh, it's Nephi's, that nice little brother of ours," sneered Lemuel.

The two elder brothers talked on and on, working themselves into a fine rage. They remembered how

Nephi had persuaded them against their better judgment to go up to Jerusalem and gather together all their riches and take them to Laban. They remembered that their father was responsible for their journey and they called him a dreamer of bad dreams. Sam had been silent at first but, at last, he came to the defense of his father and Nephi. This so angered them that they fell on Sam and Nephi and struck them with a rod.

Suddenly, an angel stood before them and said, "Why do you strike your younger brother? Don't you know that God has commanded him to be your ruler because of your wickedness? Go back to Jerusalem and the Lord will deliver Laban into your hands."

When the angel had ceased speaking, he disappeared. As soon as he was gone, Laman and Lemuel began to complain again, saying that if they went back to Jerusalem Laban would kill them, for he had fifty servants to set upon them.

When Nephi spoke at last, his handsome face showed courage and his eyes glowed with faith. "Let us go up again to Jerusalem. Let us be faithful in keeping the commandments of the Lord; for he is mightier than all the earth, then why not mightier than Laban and his fifty, yea, or even than his tens of thousands? Let us go up; let us be strong like Moses, for he spoke to the waters of the Red Sea and they divided and our fathers came out of captivity on dry ground. The armies of Pharaoh followed and were drowned. You know that is true, and you also know that an angel has spoken to you, so how can you doubt? Let us go to Jerusalem, for the Lord is able to deliver us as he did our fathers, and to destroy Laban even as the Egyptians."

For a long time after Nephi had spoken, Laman and Lemuel sat silent and brooding, their hearts filled with anger. After a while they began complaining, saying that it would be madness to return to Jerusalem again. If they did they would surely be killed.

"I will go up to Jerusalem alone. All I ask of you is to wait for me here in this cave," said Nephi.

Laman turned and looked at Nephi and for a moment his eyes were filled with admiration, but then he turned and looked away without saying anything.

"I will go with you," said Sam simply.

Nephi was deeply touched by Sam's devotion and loyalty. What a wonderful brother he was—so true, so reassuring.

"There's no need for the two of you to go alone. Lemuel and I will go, too," said Laman. Lemuel nodded his consent.

What a strange combination of good and evil Laman was. Only a few minutes ago he had been boiling with hatred and resentment, and now he was full of understanding and even admiration. Nephi longed to understand him so that he might help him overcome his wicked ways. His mother was perhaps the only one who did understand him, and she always seemed to be able to bring out the best in him. At the thought of his mother, a wave of tenderness ran through Nephi. He wondered how she and his father were. He didn't like them to be alone in the wilderness.

By night, the four brothers crept up to Jerusalem. When they reached the city, they stopped in the shadow of the great wall and Nephi said, "You hide here in the shadows while I go to Laban's house."

"But you will be killed if you go alone," worried Sam.

"No, I will not be killed," said Nephi with conviction, "for the Lord has promised to deliver Laban into our hands and He will keep that promise."

Nephi stepped out of the shadows into the bright

moonlight and crept into the city. There was a strange, wonderful feeling about him. His feet moved as if by magic, taking him into a strange street without any effort on his part. He knew that he was being guided by the divine Spirit. As he came near to Laban's house he saw a man lying on the ground, drunken with wine. When he reached the body he discovered it was Laban lying there.

At that moment he saw Laban's sword and drew it out of its sheath. He stood looking at it for a long time. The hilt was pure gold and the workmanship on it was beautiful to see. The blade was of the most precious steel. Suddenly, the metal felt ice cold in his hand and he heard the voice of the Spirit saying, "You must kill Laban with his sword."

For a second Nephi was stunned by the words of the Spirit, and he stood staring down at the sword in his hand. He said in his heart, "I have never killed anyone in all my life and I would rather not now. Surely, there must be another way."

Then the voice of the Spirit spoke, saying, "The Lord has delivered Laban into your hands."

Nephi remembered that Laban had tried to kill him and that he had stolen all their silver and gold and precious things.

Again the voice spoke, saying, "The Lord has delivered Laban into your hands. It is better that one man should perish than that a whole nation dwindle and perish in unbelief."

When he heard these words, Nephi remembered what the Lord had said to him in the wilderness, that if he would keep His commandments, he would prosper in the promised land. He knew they could not keep the Lord's commandments according to the law of Moses unless they had the brass plates, for these records were engraved on the plates. He knew also that the Lord had delivered Laban into his hands so that he could obtain the plates according to the commandments of the Lord.

When Nephi had thought of all these things and had weighed each one carefully, he decided that he must obey the voice of the Spirit. He took the sword and cut off Laban's head, then dressed himself in Laban's clothing and strapped on the sword.

CHAPTER 6

Nephi felt uncomfortable in Laban's clothes. It was not that they didn't fit, because they did, almost perfectly. Perhaps it was because he was unaccustomed to wearing such fine, costly robes. He ran his fingers over the richly embroidered tunic and wished he were back in his own clothes. But he knew that it was an unwise wish, for if he were to get the plates, he would have to fool Laban's servants into thinking that he was their master. But how could he do that? He certainly didn't look like Laban. Then, suddenly, he was ashamed of his doubts. He would place himself in the hands of the Lord, to whom all things are possible.

With firm, quick steps Nephi set off for Laban's treasury. After he had gone a short distance, he met a servant with many keys fastened to his waist. He thought that perhaps some of them might be for the treasury.

"Come with me to the treasury," he commanded.

The sound of his voice startled him, for it was not his own voice he heard, but that of Laban. The servant, hearing Laban's voice and seeing Nephi dressed in his master's clothes, took him for Laban and obeyed without question.

As they walked along, the servant asked concerning

the elders of the Jews, knowing that Laban had been out among them tonight. Nephi answered carefully so as not to arouse the suspicion of the servant.

When they had the plates, Nephi said, "Come with me, for I must take these plates to my elder brothers who wait just outside the city wall."

The servant, thinking he referred to the brethren of the church, went along obediently. On the way, he asked more questions about the elders of the church and Nephi was fortunate in giving the right answers so that he didn't suspect that the man who walked with him was not his master.

At last, when they were outside the walls of the great city, Nephi breathed more easily. Where were his brothers? Had they gotten tired of waiting and gone back to the great cave? Were they safe or had something happened to them? Suddenly, he heard the noise of running feet and saw Laman, Lemuel, and Sam coming out of the shadows as fast as their legs would carry them.

He knew at once why they were running away. They had seen him coming, dressed in Laban's clothes, and took him to be Laban. They thought that Nephi had been killed and that now Laban was coming to kill them as well.

He couldn't help smiling as he called to them in his own voice, "Come back, it is I, Nephi! Come back!"

When Nephi's brothers heard him calling them, they stopped running and came back, but Laban's servant reacted quite differently. When he heard Nephi's voice and saw his brothers, he was very frightened and began trembling so violently that Nephi was afraid he would fall to the earth. When he had stopped trembling, he started to run back to Jerusalem, but Nephi quickly caught him and held him tightly. It was not a difficult thing for him to do, for he was larger than the servant and God had given him great strength. Nephi knew that if he went back to Jerusalem and told them all he knew, the Jews would follow them into the wilderness and destroy them all.

"As God lives and as we live, if you will listen no harm will come to you," said Nehpi. "God has commanded us to get the plates and take them to our father who dwells in the wilderness. If you will come you can dwell with and be a free man as we are."

"What is your name?" asked Laman.

"My name is Zoram," said the servant, "and I have been a slave all the days of my life. I used to dream that someday I would be free, but years ago I decided that that would never be true. If you will take me with you and let me dwell with you in the wilderness a free man, I promise to remain with you forever."

After he had given them his word, they started on their long trip back to their father and mother in the wilderness.

CHAPTER 7

L ate at night, in the full of the moon, the lone figure of
a woman slipped out of a tent. She made her way
slowly up a small hill, following a well-beaten trail. Her
face was thin and pale and her eyes were red and swollen
from long hours of weeping. She walked like a woman
twice her age. She shivered and drew her warm shawl
closer about her thin shoulders. From the top of the hill,
you could see for miles in every direction. When she
reached it, she stood staring out. As far as the eye could
reach, there was barren wilderness—a vast sea of loneliness. She looked all about her and then at last sat down.
Every day and night since her sons had gone, Sariah had
come to the hill to watch and wait for their return.

For the first few days after the boys had gone on
their journey, Sariah had waited patiently and cheerfully.
Finally, as the hours turned into days and the days into
weeks, she began to lose faith in ever seeing them again.
It seemed to her now, as she sat on the hill, that all she
had ever done was go up and down the hill and watch
and wait for the return of her sons. Scarcely eating or
sleeping, she had become a mere shadow of her former
self. She no longer thought of the good things in her past,
but remembered only the hardships of the present and
her great loss. Despair settled down on her like a heavy
blanket, smothering the very life out of her.

32

Lehi tried to comfort her but without success, for in her heart she blamed him for their present condition. Night after night, he would wake up to find her gone and follow her to the top of the hill. Most of the time she didn't know he watched and prayed for her from a distance. If only he could comfort her with his own faith, for he knew that God would bring the boys back to them safely. Never once had he doubted.

Soon after Sariah left the tent, Lehi awakened. Finding her gone, he quickly got up and dressed. He couldn't leave her out there all alone; it wasn't safe. Anything could happen. This was the desert, cruel and savage. He knew there were wild beasts, for only yesterday he had caught sight of a huge animal stealing away into the brush. Perhaps even now she was in danger. The very thought of it sent him racing out of the tent and up the hill. The thought of harm coming to her made him fully aware of how great his love was for her.

At the top of the hill, he discovered her in her usual place. Her small, dark form was huddled on the ground. The sight of her told him how deep her suffering was.

Sariah gave no sign of having seen Lehi come up the hill. She was so completely lost in her own grief that she didn't seem to see or hear anything. He fully intended to stay at a distance and watch and pray for her, but at that moment he heard a low moan and a sob. He hurried at once to her side and knelt down, putting his arm tenderly about her shoulders. She turned to him, sobbing out her anguish.

"Please don't cry like that. It breaks my heart to hear you."

After a while, she stopped sobbing and gently freed herself from his embrace. For a long time she sat staring out over the wilderness.

"Our sons are dead. We will never see them again," she said hopelessly.

"Don't say that. I am certain that they are alive and well. Any hour now, they will return and you will be happy once again."

"Our sons are dead," she repeated. "And you are to blame. If you hadn't had all those visions, we would still be in Jerusalem in our comfortable home, happy with our four sons. Now they are dead, and what is to become of us? Surely we will die here, too."

He reached out and took her small hand in his and said sympathetically, "I know how you have missed our sons, but believe me, they are alive and well and even now are on their way back to us. Won't you believe that and have faith for just a little longer?"

"I'll try," she sighed, resting her head on his shoulder.

"As for my visions, I would like you to know how proud and grateful I am to God for sending them to me. If I had not seen Jerusalem destroyed, we might have stayed and been destroyed with all the other Jews. But now when our sons return to us, and they will return, God will lead us to the promised land. What a wonderful land it will be, full of peace and plenty for all of us."

His words brought such comfort to Sariah's heart that she fell into a deep, untroubled sleep.

When the first signs of dawn began lighting the eastern sky, Lehi arose, lifted Sariah gently in his arms, and carried her to their tent. She slept on through the long day. Watching her as she lay so still and white, Lehi became alarmed, thinking that perhaps she had died in her sleep; but when he leaned over her, he saw that she was still breathing. When late afternoon came and she still slept, he became worried and wondered whether it would be good for her to sleep so many hours without eating. He was just debating whether or not to awaken her when he heard voices. Going out of the tent, he saw his four sons running toward him and shouting their greeting. Lehi hurried toward them.

"My sons! My sons! I thank God for your safe return."

"Yes, we have returned safely and have brought you the brass plates," said Nephi.

"But where is Mother? Why hasn't she come to greet us? Where is she?" Laman's voice was full of concern.

"She is asleep in our tent."

"Asleep? But Mother never sleeps in the daytime." Sam's tired face lost its smile.

"Is she sick?" the other boys demanded.

"No, she is only tired. She's been so worried about you boys that she has slept very little since you went away. Every day she went up to the little windswept hill to watch for you. She thought you were dead and grieved so deeply for you that she could neither eat nor sleep. Last night I asked her to have faith for just a little longer, and for the first time since you left, she found comfort in my words. And then she slept. She has slept ever since. I was just wondering if I should awaken her. Let us go to her. If you stand about her bed quietly, I think she will feel your presence and awaken."

They all tiptoed into the tent and stood looking down at Sariah. One glance at her told them how great had been her suffering. When they remembered that it was because of their absence that she had grieved, tears filled their eyes and rolled down their cheeks unchecked.

"She looks so thin and white. Oh, Father, is she still—" Laman broke off speaking. The thought was too painful to utter.

"Yes, she is still alive," said Lehi.

While he was talking, Nephi dropped to his knees beside his mother and tenderly kissed her on the cheek.

The motion aroused her and she stirred and looked at them through half-open eyes.

"Here we are, Mother; we're home again," said Sam.

Sariah lay a few minutes and then her eyes went wide in surprise. Still half-dazed by sleep, she said, "My sons! I must be dreaming."

"No, Mother, we're home safe and sound," said Lemuel. Then the four sons began recounting their adventures, telling how at last they had been able to get the brass plates from Laban.

Sariah lifted her eyes brimming with tears and said, "Now I know that God commanded my husband to flee into the wilderness. I know that He saved my sons and brought them safely to me. He delivered them out of the hands of Laban and gave them power to fulfill His commandments to get the plates."

Lehi and Sariah's hearts were so filled with joy that they praised God and offered up a sacrifice and burnt offerings.

As soon as it was daylight, Lehi began searching the records. He discovered that they contained the first five books of Moses, from the creation of the world down to and including the beginning of the reign of Zedekiah, king of Judah. They also contained a record of the Jews, the prophecies of the prophets, and the genealogy of Lehi's father.

When he searched the records further, he discovered he was a direct descendant of Joseph, the same Joseph that was sold into bondage and taken to Egypt. Furthermore, he found that Laban also was a descendant of Joseph, and that was the reason he had been keeping the brass plates. After Lehi learned all these things, he made a prophecy, saying: "These plates of brass shall go forth to all nations and people. These plates of brass shall never perish; neither shall they be dimmed by time."

CHAPTER 8

S pring came late to the little valley of Lemuel. It was
beautiful because even the desert blossoms in the
springtime. Sariah found great pleasure in gathering the
desert flowers. They were brighter and more delicately
shaped than any she had ever seen.

While Sariah's heart was filled with joy, Lehi was
thoughtful and quiet. He saw Laman and Lemuel grow
restless and more quarrelsome day by day. Soon they
would rebel openly. If only he knew how to strengthen
their faith and make them appreciate the many blessings
they enjoyed! Perhaps, if they were to start their journey
to the promised land, they would find life more interesting. He would pray to God for guidance. This thought
sent him out into the wilderness to be alone with God.

After a while God spoke to him, telling him that it
was not meant for him to take his family into the wilderness alone, but that his sons should marry first so that
they might raise families unto God in the promised land.
The Lord commanded him to send his sons back to Jerusalem to bring Ishmael and his family down to the wilderness, so that they might journey with them to the promised land.

After God had spoken to Lehi, he was troubled by

the thought of breaking the news to Sariah. He remembered how she had grieved when her sons had gone to Jerusalem before. But tell her he must, for he would keep the commandments God had given him. When he reached the tent, Sariah was inside, busily embroidering the fine linen Sam had brought her. When she saw him, she put it away quickly and waited for him to speak.

"Laman and Lemuel have worried me deeply of late," he said.

"Yes, I know."

"But how do you know? I have never spoken of it to anyone."

"When a person loves someone as much as I love you, there are many things she knows without being told."

"Yes, I believe that," he said, taking her tiny, worn hand in his.

"But you have something else to tell me."

Lehi's eyes went wide with surprise. "Yes, I do have something to tell you, something I am dreading very much. But please don't let it grieve you too much, for I know they will be safe."

"What is it?" asked Sariah, no longer smiling.

When he finished telling her what the Lord had said, he expected her to cry or grow very angry; he was completely unprepared for her reaction.

"Oh, Lehi, what wonderful news!"

"Wonderful? You're happy about it?" questioned Lehi with amazement.

"Yes, indeed. I have been troubled about it for a long time. I was afraid our sons would never have the opportunity to get married. I thought we would never see any grandchildren, and when our sons passed away, our family would be no more. But now we will prosper and have many grandchildren."

"God is wise and merciful."

"Will you tell our sons why they are making the trip?" asked Sariah.

"Yes, I think they should know, because Ishmael may think he is to come alone. Have you thought that Ishmael might try to harm our sons as Laban tried to do?"

"No, he will not harm them. We know Ishmael and his wife. They are good people, and besides, God will soften their hearts before our sons even reach Jerusalem."

"Oh, my dear," said Lehi. "Your faith is so strong now that it makes me very happy."

Ishmael, good-natured and smiling, sat talking to Lehi's sons. When they had knocked at his door earlier in the evening he had invited them in and asked them to sit and talk with him and have refreshments. As they talked, the brothers felt that they had gained favor in the sight of Ishmael.

"I know your father must have had a purpose in sending you to me. Did he send me a message?" questioned Ishmael.

The question came so suddenly that they were taken off guard, and sat looking at each other. Lemuel, Sam, and Nephi looked at Laman to reply, but Laman looked at Nephi and nodded to him to speak.

"Yes, my father did send you a message. The Lord commanded him to send it."

Now, Ishmael believed in the prophets of the Lord and said eagerly, "Come on, boy, don't keep me waiting. Give me the message your father sent me."

"The Lord commanded my father to send us up to Jerusalem to your house. We are to invite you to come down into the wilderness to my father's tent and go with us to the promised land," said Nephi.

"You and your household," amended Laman.

"My household? Would that include my five daughters?" asked Ishmael, with a twinkle in his eyes.

Nephi was plainly embarrassed; his face went a deep red and beads of perspiration stood out on his forehead, but he said with dignity, "Yes, the Lord told my Father that we should not go into the wilderness alone, but that we should marry and raise families to Him in the promised land."

"But there are only four of you, and I have five daughters," said Ishmael.

Laman told of Zoram.

"What kind of man is Zoram?" asked Ishmael.

"He is a fine man," said Laman, "and free."

"I favor the idea," said Ishmael, "but first of all, I must have a chance to talk to my family. I must tell my good wife, my two sons and their families, and my five daughters. Come back tomorrow night and I will give you my answer. Do you have a place to stay tonight?"

"Yes, we have camped just beyond the walls of the city," said Lemuel.

In the light of the setting sun, Ishmael and his good wife looked dusty and tired after their long journey. They had been cheerful traveling companions and Nephi thought that never before in all his life had he spent such a pleasant day as he had with Ishmael, his wife, and three daughters.

Ishmael turned and looked back every few minutes. All day long, Laman, Lemuel, the other two daughters of Ishmael, and the two sons of Ishmael and their families had traveled together, refusing to travel with Nephi and the others. They kept lagging so far behind that Ishmael was constantly worried about losing them.

"We have traveled a long way today," said Ishmael.

"Don't you think it would be wise to pitch our tents here for the night?"

"That suits me," said Sam.

"And me," said Nephi.

Nephi and Sam began preparations for pitching the tents while Ishmael stood shading his eyes with his hand and looking back toward Jerusalem. After a while, he called to one of his daughters, who hurried to his side. She was a beautiful young girl with lovely dark eyes and soft brown hair. Nephi had been impressed with the beauty of this youngest daughter of Ishmael as soon as he had seen her.

"Did you want me, Father?" she asked.

"Yes, my child, your eyes are younger than mine. Can you see anything of the others?" he asked in a worried voice.

After scanning the wilderness, she answered, "Yes, I see them. They are far behind, but still coming slowly."

"Are they all there?" he asked.

"Yes. Why do you ask?"

"Because I was afraid they would turn back as soon as we were out of sight. I think I will walk back to meet them."

"But you look so tired, Father."

"It's easier than waiting for them and wondering what they are planning. Tell your mother where I have gone," he said.

Nephi watched Ishmael go and his heart grew troubled. All day long he had been so happy. Not a single worry had crossed his mind. But now he remembered the worried look on Sam and Ishmael's faces as they watched the others continually lag behind. Laman and Lemuel were probably rebelling again. He hoped and prayed that they wouldn't start an ugly quarrel before Ishmael and his family.

When the tents were pitched and preparations had been made for the evening meal, Ishmael returned with Laman and his party. One look at Laman and Lemuel told Nephi that his worst fears were true.

"I have something to say to you, Nephi," said Laman sharply.

"Come eat your supper first," said a gentle but firm voice.

It was the voice of Ishmael's wife suggesting food at just the right time. Laman was hungry and he always enjoyed eating. Even if he hadn't been interested in food at the moment, he couldn't have resisted the patient, sad-eyed woman who confronted him. Her hand was light upon his arm; but in spite of her gentle touch, she guided him with determination toward the food.

"Very well, it can wait until we are through eating. But I promise you I'll not forget to say the things I have to say."

"Perhaps you will feel differently after you have eaten," she said hopefully.

But Laman was as good as his word, and as soon as they had finished eating, he said, "We have decided to go back to Jerusalem to live."

"But surely you don't mean to disobey God's commandments," said Nephi.

"How do we know they are God's commandments? Maybe they are nothing more than a bad dream. Anyway, we have decided that, in spite of everything, we are going back to Jerusalem to live."

Laman's words shocked and grieved Nephi.

"You are my elder brothers," said Nephi sadly, "but why are you so hard-hearted and so blind in your minds that you need me, your younger brother, to set an example for you?"

"Listen to the fool talk," said Lemuel.

"Why will you not listen to the word of the Lord? Have you forgotten that you have seen an angel or that we were delivered out of the hands of Laban and obtained the records? Have you forgotten that the Lord is able to do all things according to His will, for the children of men, if they exercise faith in Him? Let us be faithful to Him. If we are faithful we shall reach the promised land and know that all things the Lord has promised concerning the destruction of Jerusalem must be fulfilled. Now, if you go back to Jerusalem, you shall perish with them."

After Nephi had finished speaking, Laman and Lemuel went aside and talked in low tones. Then they confronted Nephi and said fiercely, "We have decided to do away with you. You have run our lives long enough."

Nephi faced his angry brothers with courage that sprang from his faith in God. He tried to reason with them, but they only grew more angry, until at last they bound him with strong cords. Looking up, he discovered the tearful eyes of Ishmael's youngest daughter upon him and he knew in his heart that he would never be lonely again as long as she was near him.

"Now," said Lemuel hatefully, "try and free yourself if you can."

"What are you going to do with me?" asked Nephi.

"We will leave you here and let the wild beasts devour you," said Laman.

Humbly, Nephi began to pray to the Lord, saying, "Oh, Lord God, according to the strength of my faith in Thee, look down and have mercy on me and free me from the cords that bind me."

When Nephi finished his prayer, suddenly the cords fell away from his hands and feet. Sam and Ishmael and his family marveled at the miracle they had seen. But Laman and Lemuel were unimpressed by it and were about to lay hands on Nephi again. Just then Ishmael's wife stepped between them and Nephi, saying, "Don't do this thing. Think of your mother. If Sam is the only one who returns to her, she will surely die of a broken heart."

When Ishmael's wife was through speaking, one of her daughters and a son came forward and pleaded Nephi's cause. Finally, Laman and Lemuel listened to their pleading and their anger passed away. There was nothing left in its place but regret for their cruel treatment of their brother. Their remorse was so great that they fell on their knees before Nephi and begged his forgiveness. He forgave them freely and asked them to pray to the Lord for forgiveness. After they had prayed, they set out on their journey.

After three days of travel, they came to Lehi's tent. There was great rejoicing and they thanked God and offered a sacrifice and burnt offerings.

CHAPTER 9

The members of Lehi and Ishmael's families set to work gathering seeds of every kind. They stored them away carefully to keep them safe until they reached the promised land.

Early one morning, Lehi called his family to him and said, "I have dreamed a dream, and because of what I have seen, I am overjoyed with Sam and Nephi, for they will be saved and many of their seed also. But oh, Laman and Lemuel, I am fearful because of you. I thought I was lost in a dark, dreary wilderness when suddenly there came and stood before me a man all dressed in white who asked me to go with him. After a while, it grew so dark that I lost my way and could see nothing. Then I prayed to God to be merciful unto me. He heard my prayer and soon after, I beheld a very large field. I saw a tree and I knew at once that I must eat some of its fruit to be happy. When I tasted it I found it was the sweetest fruit I had ever eaten and it was white—the whitest white I had ever seen in all my life. After I had eaten of the fruit, I was so filled with joy that I looked about to see if I could find my family so that they might partake of the fruit, too. I saw a river running by the tree and looking up I saw, at its head, your mother, Sam, and Nephi. I beckoned to them to come to me and they did. When they had partaken of the fruit, they too were very happy. I looked around again to see if I could find Laman and Lemuel. Then I saw a rod of iron running along beside the river, and beside the rod was a straight and narrow path that led to the tree. The rod and path started at the head of the river and there stood Laman and Lemuel. I called to them to join us and partake of the fruit of the tree, but they refused and turned away. Then I saw a great crowd of people. Some of them started along the straight and narrow path, but after a while a mist arose and it grew so dark that they lost their way. But some held to the rod and finally found their way to the tree, where they ate of the fruit and were filled with joy."

Lehi talked on and on about his dream, and when he finished, he predicted many great and wonderful things that were to be fulfilled in the future. Nephi was so deeply impressed by all that his father had seen and heard that he went out and humbled himself before the Lord and prayed that he, too, might be permitted to see all the things that had been shown to this father. God heard his prayer and he saw many marvelous things, even the coming of the Lamb of God and the bringing forth of the Book of Mormon.

Sariah lay staring into the blackness of her tent. She was far too excited to sleep. Tomorrow was the great day—the day she had waited for for so many years. Tomorrow, her four sons and Zoram were to be married. Five marriages in one day! She had always dreamed of a great celebration for each of her sons. Now it would be a humble affair, but nevertheless favored in the sight of God. For days, she and Ishmael's wife and daughters had been preparing the food for the feast. The men had killed many kinds of wild game, so all was in readiness for the morrow. In the days and weeks that had passed since Ishmael and his family had joined them, Sariah had grown to love them and she was proud that her sons were going to marry such fine girls.

"Sariah, are you awake?" asked Lehi.

"Yes."

"Try to get some rest. Tomorrow will be such a hard day for you."

"My head is too full of preparations to sleep."

"Is that all, or is something else troubling you?" asked Lehi.

Sariah hesitated before she answered, and then she said slowly, "Yes, the thought of losing all my sons at once bothers me. Of course, I would have it no other way. But in spite of that fact, after tomorrow someone else will have first claim on their loyalty."

"Yes, I know," said Lehi, "but you'll see it will be the best thing that ever happened to them."

It was a comfort to Sariah to know that Lehi understood. She could always depend on him. Perhaps it was his wisdom and depth of understanding that set him apart and above other men. He was both a great and a good man.

When Sariah didn't speak, Lehi said, "Marriage will bring our sons new responsibilities that, in turn, will make their lives fuller and more complete. We must only rejoice in their happiness."

"I do! I do!" protested Sariah.

"Yes, I know."

"Of all the boys, Nephi seems the happiest," she said.

"Why shouldn't he? He is marrying the youngest and prettiest of Ishmael's daughters."

"The other four girls are nice looking too," said Sariah.

"But not as pretty as she is. When you were her age, you looked very much like her, only you were far more beautiful."

"Thank you, Lehi," said Sariah, smiling into the darkness.

At daybreak one morning, several days after the five marriages, Lehi leaned over Sariah and shook her gently, calling her name. Slowly, she opened her eyes and looked at him.

"Surely it isn't morning already?" she said.

"It is still very early. I hated to wake you, but I have important news."

She lay back on her pillow, still half-asleep, and then suddenly the word *news* caught at her mind and brought her wide awake. Lehi's news was never ordinary. Once it had changed the very course of their lives. Once it had sent her sons into danger and once it had sent them to bring back wives, and now he had news again. She braced herself for the shock.

"Tell me at once, Lehi."

"Last night the Lord spoke to me and commanded that on this very day, we start to the promised land."

Sariah heaved a great sigh and Lehi looked at her and said, "I thought you would be pleased. Our sons have been so anxious to start that they have questioned me every day about the time of our leaving."

Sariah lifted her dark eyes to his and said reproachfully, "I'm not as young as our sons; neither am I as fond of adventure, nor as able to endure the hardships of a long journey."

Lehi stood looking at her, a surprised expression on his face. It had never occurred to him that she would take this attitude.

"But you know we can't build a home in the wilderness. The Lord has promised us a rich, fertile land for our home. Don't you want to go?"

She was quick to sense his disappointment in her.

"I'm sorry. Of course I want to go; but even so, I dread the long, hard journey across the desert."

Lehi came to her and tenderly embraced her.

"You have suffered a great deal, but just you wait and see how richly you will be repaid when we reach the promised land. You will soon forget your suffering and know only happiness."

He arose and walked swiftly to the tent door and was gone. Sariah lay still while she planned for the journey.

What was that? She thought she heard voices. Yes, she did and they were excited—all talking at once. What had happened? Her mind rushed off in a dozen directions. Had Lehi been hurt, or had something happened to some of the rest of them? Maybe Laman and Lemuel had deserted. She raced through her dressing and quickly ran out of the tent. Standing a little distance from her were five or six men gathered around Lehi. Immediately, she was frightened. She couldn't bear it if anything had happened to him. She ran to the group and pushed herself forward to Lehi. He was all right.

"What is it?" she asked.

"See what was outside of our tent," said Lehi.

Lehi held a small round ball of gleaming brass. On its surface was curious workmanship.

"Look inside it, Sariah," he said.

She saw two spindles. "What are they for?" she asked.

"They are to point the direction we are to take on our journey," said Lehi.

"But," said Sariah, "the spindle points to the river Laman. Does that mean that we are to cross the river?"

"Yes," said Lehi. "I suppose there will be many rivers

and streams for us to cross before we reach the promised land."

Sariah stood looking at the river and then said doubtfully, "Where will we cross? It looks so deep."

"Look at the spindle, Mother," said Nephi, pushing his way through the group until he stood beside her. "See, it points to an exact spot on the river. If we cross there we will be safe, for the Lord is directing us by means of this compass."

"But the spindle points south," said Laman, frowning, "and we know that the great desert is south of us. I have heard that neither man nor beast can stand to live in it for very long."

"If we are faithful in keeping the Lord's commandments, the spindle will point to the fertile part of the wilderness where we can find food and travel in safety. But we must be faithful," said Nephi, his handsome face full of concern.

CHAPTER 10

It was cool beneath the big tree where Nephi lay, looking up through its lacy branches. He had been hunting since dawn along the borders of the Red Sea. Here the land was fertile, with rich, dense vegetation. From where he lay, he could hear the waves splashing and slapping against the rocky shore. The cool shade and the noise of the water were very soothing to tired muscles and worn nerves. In fact, it was so restful that he was afraid he would fall asleep and be overtaken by nightfall. Night was full of dangers in the wilderness.

Where were his brothers? They were to have met him here about midday, but Nephi knew by the lengthening shadows that it was late afternoon. He had such a good day hunting that he needed their help. He had killed enough meat for everyone and had found great clusters of the sweetest grapes he had ever eaten. Best of all, he had found a hollow tree filled with delicious honey. He smiled when he thought how they would enjoy such a treat after their hard journey. It had been four days since they had left the valley of Lemuel. They had traveled in a south by southeast direction. If his brothers didn't come soon, he would have to leave part of the food behind. He would have to travel fast while he

51

had the sun to guide him. His young wife was probably worried already.

The thought of his lovely wife brought a soft light to his eyes and drove away all his weariness. She was an amazing girl. Beautiful, yet completely unspoiled; full of the joy of living, yet highly sensitive to the pain and suffering of others. He remembered, as he lay in the cool shade of the tree, how every morning of the four days' journey from the valley of Lemuel he had taken special care to see that the load she carried was light; but constantly he would come back to find her loaded down with the burden of someone else. How often she divided a portion of her food among those who thought they needed it more than she. She was capable of deep love and great understanding. In each other they found all their hearts desired. Nephi had never known such happiness existed. Every day he thanked God for bringing them together.

"Nephi."

It was Sam's voice calling. He quickly jumped up and answered him. After a few minutes, Sam pushed his way, empty-handed, through the dense underbrush into the clearing where Nephi waited for him.

"Are you alone?" asked Nephi.

"Yes."

"Where are the others?"

"They have gone back to Shazer."

Now, Shazer was the name Lehi had given to the place where they had camped after their four days' journey from the little valley of Lemuel.

"But why have they gone back to Shazer? They promised to meet us here," remarked Nephi.

"It was getting late and since they had gathered little food, they suggested that they carry mine while I came on here to help you."

"I'm sure I don't know how we will carry all the food

I've gathered, but we can try. What kind of luck did you have today, Sam?"

"Fine," said Sam. Then, noticing for the first the great stack of food Nephi had, he gave a low whistle. "Well, now that I've seen your food, I didn't do fine at all. You have gathered more food than all of us put together. How do you do it?"

There was great admiration in Sam's voice, coupled with a slight touch of envy in his eyes.

"Oh, I have a much better bow than any of you," said Nephi agreeably.

"These grapes are good," said Sam, stuffing great handfuls of them into his mouth. Nephi smiled to himself as he thought that if Sam didn't soon stop eating them, perhaps the load wouldn't be too heavy to carry.

After a long rest at Shazer, they started on their journey again, following the direction of the spindles in the brass ball. They pointed to the most fertile spots in the wilderness where they found plenty of food each day for their families. They traveled for many days without stopping. Then one evening, Lehi told them to pitch their tents and rest for a space of time.

As Nephi walked toward his tent, he saw his wife sitting beside the door. It struck him as being very odd, for usually at this time of day she was busily preparing the evening meal before darkness set in. But now she was just sitting with head bowed. She was so completely lost in thought that she didn't notice his coming. He saw how the sun, wind, and rain had burned and darkened her skin. It had faded her hair along with her clothing. In spite of the effect of the weather, she was still very beautiful.

"What is troubling you, my dear?" he asked kindly.

She jumped and looked up. When she saw who it was, she smiled her greeting.

"It's Father. I'm worried about him, Nephi."

"Is he ill?"

"Yes. I'm afraid he is, but he says he is just tired."

"My father has ordered a long rest. Ishmael will have plenty of time to get well before we start on the journey again. I promise you, my dear, that I will do everything in my power to bring him comfort," said Nephi kindly.

"Thank you. I blame myself for not insisting that he remain in Jerusalem. He is far too old and weak to make such a long journey."

"Your father is a man of great faith," said Nephi sternly, "and when he learned that God had chosen him as one to go the promised land, nothing on earth could have stopped him. He believes in God and no one could make him disobey His commandments."

"I'm sorry, Nephi. It must seem to you that I lack faith, but I really don't. You see, I am so worried about you that I say foolish things." There was repentance in her voice.

"About me? But why?"

"If Father should die, Laman, Lemuel, and my brothers would break out in open rebellion against you and your father. There is no telling what they would do to you."

"Don't worry about that," said Nephi. "We will meet that problem when it comes. As for your father, if he should die, his passing would be mourned by all of us, because his gentle, loving kindness has endeared him to everyone. But we must remember that he is an old man, and through God's mercy and goodness he has lived longer than the allotted time of most men. You must remember, too, that the great faith of your father makes it possible for him to meet death with peace of mind. He knows that it is not the end but the beginning of a richer, fuller life. It opens the door to the greatest adventure of all."

At daybreak, Nephi and his brothers set out to hunt.

They took their bows, arrows, slings, and stones. They planned to hunt during the early morning hours because their families were low on food and needed a fresh supply for the noonday meal.

Little did they know that bad luck awaited them. By noon they hadn't shot a single wild beast or obtained any other kind of food. Then a great misfortune happened—Nephi broke his bow. It was of fine steel, the best bow of any in camp, and as though that wasn't enough trouble for one day, his brothers discovered that their bows had lost their spring. Weary and sick at heart, they returned to their families empty-handed. That night, everyone went to bed hungry.

Days passed and still they found no food. Real and terrible suffering set in. They all wore the gaunt, gray expression of starvation. As the discomfort of Laman and Lemuel increased, so did their hatred for their brother. They complained bitterly against him, saying, first of all, that he must have been careless in order to have broken his bow. When that did not arouse Nephi, they said he had broken it on purpose and that he had food stored away which he ate in secret. Even Lehi began to complain. He said many bitter things against the Lord.

At last, Nephi rebuked them and pleaded with them to soften their hearts and humble themselves before God; otherwise He might let them starve. He said many things in the energy of his soul.

Nephi carved a bow from wood and made an arrow from a straight stick. Taking them to his father, he said, "Father, I have made a bow and arrow. Will you ask God where I can hunt to find meat?"

God spoke to Lehi and he was bowed down in sorrow for his unfaithfulness.

"Look at the spindles," said Sam. "There is writing on them telling you where to hunt."

When Lehi saw the things which were written upon

the ball, he was frightened and trembled violently, as did everyone in the camp. Nephi saw immediately that the pointers which were in the ball worked according to the faith they gave to them. The new writing could be read plainly. It was changed from time to time according to the faith they gave it. Thus it was by small means that the Lord brought about great things.

Nephi climbed to the top of the mountain to the exact spot where the writing on the brass ball directed him to go. He had wonderful success hunting and in just a few hours he had killed enough wild beasts to supply everyone in camp. When he returned from his hunting and they saw all the meat he had brought—enough for everyone—their hearts were filled with joy and they thanked God for His goodness and mercy.

CHAPTER 11

L ehi and his followers set out on their journey once
again. They followed the same direction they had
from the beginning. After they had traveled many days,
they pitched their tents at a place they called Nahom, to
rest for a time.

Here it was that Ishmael died and was buried. His
loss was felt by all of them, but his five daughters were
bowed down into the depths of sorrow. As time passed
and their grief became less intense, they began pitying
themselves and recounting all their hardships. At last,
they turned on Lehi and blamed him for bringing them
into the wilderness, where they had suffered so much,
when they could have stayed in Jerusalem where they
had known so much happiness.

"Our father is dead," they said, "and we, too, will
perish in this terrible land. Will we never stop our wan-
derings? Here we have known unbelievable suffering. We
have been cold, hot, hungry, thirsty, and weary. Let us be
done with all this and turn our faces toward Jerusalem
and home."

Zoram, Sam, and Nephi spoke to their wives gently,
convincing them that it was God's will and that they must
be faithful in keeping His commandments. But Laman

and Lemuel joined with their wives and added to their anger against their father and Nephi.

Laman turned to Lemuel and said, "Let us destroy our father and Nephi so that we might rid ourselves of these hardships."

Lemuel looked at his brother in shocked surprise, but Laman met his gaze with the coldness of steel and Lemuel weakly submitted, saying, "If they were put to death, we could return to Jerusalem in peace and once again know the comforts of home."

"Look at Nephi," said Laman. "He has taken it upon himself to be our ruler and our teacher. Has he forgotten that we are his elder brothers? He says the Lord has talked to him and angels have ministered to him. We know that he lies. He tells us these things and works his cunning art so that he can deceive our eyes, thinking, perhaps, that he can lead us away to some strange wilderness. When he has succeeded in doing that, he plans to make himself our king and rule over us according to his will and pleasure."

The threatening sound of Laman's voice alarmed Nephi's wife. She felt her hands grow cold with fear. She knew by the angry, cruel look on his face that his threats were not idle, but capable of becoming dangerous to Nephi and his father. She would be lost without Nephi. Life would have no purpose. The thought of his danger made her so weak and ill she could scarcely stand.

She looked about for Nephi and saw him standing with his father, a little apart from the others. How tall and handsome he was! He stood head and shoulders above his own brothers and hers. He was a born leader. His fine intelligence, resourcefulness, and human kindness made him capable of leading his people in the ways of God.

Half-listening, she heard Laman going on and on,

stirring the others to angry hatred against Nephi, making them believe he wanted to rob them of their freedom. His words went home, for they were all frightened of losing their personal rights.

Suddenly, with great courage, Nephi's wife faced Laman with blazing anger in her eyes, coupled with fear for her beloved husband, and said, "How can you say these things about your brother? Don't you remember that when you were ill, he nursed you and restored you to health? When you were thirsty, he gave you water to drink. When you were tired, he carried your burden, and when all of us were starving, he fashioned a bow from wood and an arrow from a straight stick and with these he brought us wild beasts from the forest. Can't you see that he loves you and does all these things out of the goodness of his heart?"

"If he is so great," said Lemuel, "why doesn't he do something now? We are all starving again. All he does is lie to us and trick us with his cunning."

"You know in your heart," said Nephi's wife, "that he is honest and loyal to you all. He is a man of God and it is your wickedness that has angered the Lord and brought us to this low condition. If you would seek God in faithfulness, He would hear you and guide you to a fuller and better life, as well as to food and water."

Just then, a marvelous thing happened. They heard a wonderful sound. It was the voice of the Lord speaking to them. He rebuked the brothers for their cruel treatment of their father and Nephi. They began to tremble violently. Their hearts were softened and they bowed down in all humbleness before the Lord and asked His forgiveness. He heard their sorrowful voices and granted their prayer, making it possible for them to find food and water.

CHAPTER 12

After leaving Nahom, Lehi and the others traveled almost due east. Late one afternoon as they climbed a low hill, Nephi walked beside his wife with strong, firm steps.

"Why are you smiling?" asked Nephi.

"Oh, I don't know. I suppose it is because we are climbing a hill. I'm always happy then. Hills hide such great surprises. You never know what you'll see on the other side."

"I agree with you," said Nephi. "It is far more interesting to be kept in suspense than to be able to see for miles and miles, especially when everything looks the same."

"I have a feeling," she said, "that this hill will be different. Just think how it would seem if when we reached the top we discovered a fertile valley filled with good things to eat."

"You paint a wonderful picture, my dear. Sam and Zoram must have the same idea. See how they are going on ahead of everybody. They must be very anxious to be the first to discover your bountiful land. Are you tired?"

"No," she answered happily.

"Do you remember, dear," he asked, "how tired you

60

became the first day after we left the little valley of Lemuel? I thought then you would never be able to stand the long, hard journey; but as the days and weeks and months have passed, God has made you strong and sturdy enough to endure the hardships and suffering that have been ours to bear."

"Think of it, Nephi, eight long years have passed since we commenced our journey. We have waded and wandered through the wilderness, sometimes almost dead from hunger and thirst and even fatigue."

"Many things have happened to us during these eight years," said Nephi thoughtfully. "Children have been born and God has blessed them with fine, strong bodies."

Just at that moment, they heard a shout from the hilltop. Looking up, they saw Sam and Zoram shouting for joy and waving their hands wildly. Without a single word, Nephi caught hold of his wife's hand and began running up the hill, pulling her after him.

When they reached the top of the hill, Sam called to them excitedly, "Come over here and look down."

They did as he directed, and when they looked down, they stood speechless with amazement. There below them was the most beautiful valley they had ever seen, and beyond the valley lay a great sea of water, stretching eastward as far as the eye could see. It sparkled like diamonds in the sunshine. They waited for all the others to join them and then they eagerly went down the hill to explore the valley. They found fruit of every kind and wild honey in abundance. When they had feasted and thanked God for His goodness, they pitched their tents beside the sea. Because the land was rich and bore much fruit, they called it Bountiful; they called the sea Irreantum, which means many waters.

Many days passed in peace and happiness. Then one

night, God spoke to Nephi and said, "Arise and go up into the mountain."

Nephi did as he was commanded, and when he reached the top of the mountain, he cried out to the Lord.

The Lord spoke again, saying, "Build a ship after the manner I show thee, that I may carry your people across these waters."

Nephi said, "Lord, where shall I go that I may find ore to melt to make tools to build the ship?"

The Lord told Nephi where to go. Nephi made a bellows from skins of beasts to blow the fire; then he struck two stones together to make fire.

Laman and Lemuel saw Nephi at work and were very curious to know what he was making. They wondered and wondered. First they thought he was building a metal trap to catch wild beasts. Later they decided that he was making tools to use in building himself a house. At last, they asked him to tell them what he was doing.

"I am making tools with which to build a ship," answered Nephi.

"A ship," said Lemuel, astonished.

"Are you crazy?" asked Laman. "You don't know how to build a ship, do you?"

"No," said Nephi, "but the Lord our God knows all things, and he has promised to guide me in building a seaworthy vessel."

"Where do you propose to sail it?" asked Laman, growing more angry every minute.

"The Lord has commanded us to sail across Irreantum," said Nephi quietly.

"You mean you expect us to sail across this great sea in a ship you build? No, my brother, we are not as foolish as you think we are," snapped Laman.

By this time, a crowd had gathered and stood listening. Lemuel turned and said to them, "Our brother is a fool, for he plans to build a ship and carry us off across the sea."

"Only a crazy man would think that he could cross these great waters," said Laman.

Nephi was bowed down in sorrow because of the hardness of his brothers' hearts. When they saw the worried look on his face, they rejoiced.

"We knew you could not build a ship," they said. "You are lacking in judgment and could never accomplish such a great work. You are like our father: led by your foolish imagination. He led us out of Jerusalem, and so great has been our suffering that it would have been better to have died first. We know the people of Jerusalem were good people, for they kept the commandments of the Lord, and our father has judged them wrongfully."

Out of the goodness of his heart, Nephi spoke to them, saying, "You are swift to do wrong but slow to remember the Lord your God. You have seen an angel and he spoke to you. You have heard God's voice from time to time and He has spoken unto you in a still, small voice; but you would not listen. Then He spoke to you like a voice of thunder that caused the earth to shake as if it were being torn apart. He can cause the earth to pass away, and you know that by His word He can cause the rough places to be made smooth and the smooth places to be broken up. Oh, then, why is it that you can be so hard in your hearts? My soul is torn with anguish because of you, and my heart is pained. I fear that you shall be cast off forever. Behold, I am so full of the Spirit of God that my body has no strength."

Now, Laman and Lemuel grew very angry at Nephi for pointing out their faults, especially before the others.

"Our brother says hard things to us, Lemuel," said Laman in a loud, angry voice.

"And he is only our younger brother," shouted Lemuel.

"He thinks that by this manner of speaking, he will frighten us and force us to do labor on his ship," said Laman.

"And when we have built this ship, he expects us to sail on it. If we do we will surely go down to a watery grave," argued Lemuel.

"Since he likes water so well, let us throw him into the sea." Laman's face looked ugly and cruel as he said this.

Nephi had listened to all they had to say in silence, but now he stepped forward and said in a voice charged with the Spirit of the Lord, "In the name of Almighty God, do not touch me, because if you do you will wither and dry up and you shall be as nothing before the power of God. You must say no more against our father from this time forward. You must work on the ship that God has commanded us to build."

Nephi waited for Laman and Lemuel to speak. When they were silent, he said, "If God had commanded me to do all these things, I could do them. If he commanded me to say to the waters, change to earth, it would be done. Now, if the Lord has such great power, how is it that he cannot teach me to build a ship?"

As Laman and Lemuel listened to all Nephi had to say, their faces grew pale and their hands cold with fear. They knew in their hearts that he spoke the truth. They stopped their quarreling and stood speechless before their younger brother. When they opened their mouths to speak, no words came. This so frightened them that they began to tremble, and beads of cold perspiration rolled down their cheeks. They moved back away from Nephi, for they were afraid of touching him. No longer did they dare to lay hands upon him or touch him with a single finger, for fear that they would wither and die. They sensed the powerful Spirit of God upon him.

For the space of many days, Laman and Lemuel were afraid of coming near Nephi for fear of touching him. Then one day, the Lord said to Nephi, "Stretch out your hand to your brothers, for they will no longer wither and die; but when you stretch out your hand I will shock them, so that they might know that I am the Lord their God."

Nephi called to his brothers and they said, "We dare not come to you because if we do we might touch you and then we would surely die."

"I give you my word," said Nephi, "if I touch you, you will not die, but the Lord will give you a sign that he is all-powerful."

Laman and Lemuel were eager for a sign, so they came to Nephi. Suddenly Nephi stretched forth his hand to his brothers. They did not wither, but the Lord shook them so hard that they almost fell to the ground.

They said with trembling voices, "We know that surely the Lord is with you, for we know that it is the power of the Lord that has shaken us."

So saying, they fell down on the ground and were about to worship Nephi, but he would not let them.

"I am your brother," he said. "Yes, even your younger brother. Worship the Lord your God and honor your father and your mother that your days may be long in the land which the Lord your God shall give you."

CHAPTER 13

Sariah sat in the shade of the tent, resting. Her hands, unaccustomed to idleness, lay still in her lap. Her eyes, once keen and bright, were so dimmed by time that she could no longer work miracles upon a piece of cloth with needle and thread. She was old and weary and now she found resting pleasant. Her hair had turned to silver, but still she smiled as warmly as ever. On the ground beside her lay two small boys.

"Mother, where is Jerusalem?" asked Jacob, the elder of the two children.

"It is a long way from here, my son. We traveled eight years to get here," she replied.

"Father told Joseph and me," said Jacob, looking at his younger brother, "that because we were unfaithful at times, the compass would not work and we lost our way and wandered for days in the wrong direction. And that if we had been faithful we could have reached here sooner."

"That is true," answered Sariah. "But there was one among us who was always faithful and never doubted."

"Oh, I know who that was," said Joseph. "It was Nephi."

"Yes, my son, it was Nephi, and had we all been as faithful as he, our journey would have taken only a few months instead of the eight years we spent wandering about."

"Mother, Joseph thinks I was born in Jerusalem."

"No," said Sariah. "That is not so. You were both born in the wilderness."

The very thought of it made Sariah sigh heavily. The children heard her and looked up. When she saw their eyes upon her, she smiled to reassure them and was rewarded by their look of loving devotion.

In a small clearing beside the sea, Sariah and the children could see the men at work building the ship. They had worked on it for the space of many days and still it was not completed. They would be busy for several weeks longer. How happy they seemed, laughing and singing as they worked. Even Laman and Lemuel seemed more content and interested in what they were doing than they had ever been before. Ever since Nephi had stretched his hand toward them and God had shaken them, they had been humble and had worshiped God in all earnestness. A great cloak of peace had settled down over the whole camp.

"Why aren't you helping your brothers?" Sariah asked the children.

"We asked Laman what we could do and he told us to go away and not bother him," answered Jacob.

Sariah knew, well enough, that neither Laman nor Lemuel had any time for the children; but with Nephi it was different. He always had time to find a task for them to do, making them feel that they had a part in building the ship.

"Why didn't you ask your brother Nephi for a job to do?" inquired Sariah.

"Nephi has gone to the mountain," said Joseph.

"He goes every day," said Jacob. "He prays to the Lord. Mother, do you know why he does that?"

"Nephi has never built a ship before, and neither have any of the rest of them. God promised Nephi that he would guide him. So each day, Nephi prays to the Lord to instruct him in building a new part of the ship."

"Nephi must be a very good man for God to make him a teacher over his brothers," said Jacob.

"Yes, indeed," said Sariah, smiling to herself.

Several weeks later, heavy, dark clouds had hung low over the land of Bountiful all day long; but when late afternoon came, the clouds parted and the sun flooded everything with its warmth. At the very moment when the sun first showed its face, there was a loud shout. It was the shout of rejoicing men. The ship was finished at last. Even the elements seemed to rejoice over its completion by wearing a bright face.

As Lehi stood looking at the ship, Nephi came up behind him and put his hand on the older man's arm.

"She is a fine-looking ship, my boy," said Lehi.

"Yes, she is, and just as sturdy as she is good-looking," said Nephi proudly.

"I've seen many a ship in my day, but never one like this." The old man rubbed his chin with satisfaction.

"She is different," answered Nephi, "because God fashioned her after his own pattern. There isn't another ship like her."

"Let us always remember she was built under divine inspiration, and when we sail on her, let us conduct ourselves as the children of God."

They held a great feast and thanked the Lord.

Lehi gathered them around him and said, "The Lord has commanded me to load the ship and set sail across the sea with you, my people. Each person will take along provisions according to his own needs."

Sariah looked up at her husband and a feeling of deep peace settled on her. She was grateful to God for honoring Lehi with the leadership of his people, even though he was now an old man.

The next day they gathered much meat, fruit, and honey from the wilderness. They loaded the ship with provisions according to the Lord's commandments, including seeds of every kind. After the ship was loaded, they went down into it and sailed away.

From the deck of the ship, Nephi and his small brother Jacob looked out on a bright, blue sky and sea. The wind was cool and fresh—just strong enough to drive the ship steadily before it.

Jacob lifted his eyes to the huge sails of the ship. To a young boy, the experience was more than a little frightening. The sails looked to him like great white mountains towering high above his head. His eyes went wide with amazement as he watched the wind catch in the sails and drive the ship far out to sea. Then he saw something that brought a worried expression to his face. One of the sails had a great tear in its side and went flapping and humming in the wind. If the wind had already torn the sail, how long would it be before they would all be destroyed? He moved closer to his big brother and, reaching up, grasped Nephi's hand.

"Your hands are like ice," said Nephi, looking down at Jacob. "Perhaps you had better go below where you can get warm."

"Oh, no," pleaded Jacob, "I want to stay on deck with you. Nephi, did the wind tear the sail?"

"Oh, so that's it. I knew something was worrying you. Well you don't need to worry about that any longer, because the wind didn't tear it. We did that before we left the land of Bountiful and it can easily be mended."

Just then, Jacob caught sight of a flock of birds flying overhead, their huge wings pounding against the wind. He watched them until they were gone: lost in the mist, their voices unheard above the greater voice of the sea. His eyes searched for the land they had left behind. It was only a dim speck, far to the west of them. He watched it until it was gone and now there was no land, only the restless, unfriendly sea. With lonely heart he looked up at Nephi and the sight of him brought peace and courage.

CHAPTER 14

For the space of many days they sailed toward the promised land, driven by the wind. Sailing was a new experience for most of them and the great joy it brought was plainly seen on their faces and in their actions. They went about their duties aboard ship cheerfully and eagerly. Not one of them suffered seasickness.

Nephi was overjoyed at the success of the voyage thus far, but deep in his heart he was concerned over Laman and Lemuel. Rebellion on land was one thing; to have mutiny at sea would be quite another. Here it might bring misery and even death to all of them. He watched their faces for signs of anger and discontent, but each time, they met his gaze with smiling, happy faces. As the days passed and their contentment continued to last, Nephi put aside his worries.

One evening Nephi and his wife stood on deck, watching the full moon slowly rise above the water.

"See, my dear," said Nephi, "how the moon makes a silver pathway straight across the water to our ship."

"Yes, isn't it beautiful," she answered, "and so peaceful."

Scarcely had she spoken the last words when the peace she spoke of was destroyed by loud shouting and shrill laughter.

71

"That's Laman and Lemuel." Nephi was alarmed. "I'll go and see what they are doing."

"No, wait," she said. "They are coming up here."

Just at that moment, Laman and Lemuel, the two sons of Ishmael, and their wives came on deck, shouting and making merry. They danced and sang and raised their voices in rude talk. Nephi watched them with troubled heart. Laman called several times to Nephi's wife to join them. Frightened by his advances, she moved closer to Nephi and linked her arm through his.

"Don't be frightened," he said. "You are safe with me."

How well she knew that; but what of Nephi himself? How long would he be safe? Fear clutched at her heart as she saw Laman approaching them.

"Why do you pull such a long face?" asked Laman disagreeably. "Why won't you join in the fun with us?"

"Have you forgotten that this is a holy ship, given us by the Lord to carry us to the promised land?" asked Nephi.

"So you say," said Laman in an unbelieving voice. "We have only your word for it. How do we know you are telling us the truth?"

"If you listen to the still, small voice inside you, the Lord will convince you of my truthfulness. You will also know that it is wicked for you to act with such rudeness. I am worried that the Lord will become so displeased that he will let the sea swallow us up. I beg of you, repent before it is too late."

By this time, the others had gathered around them and were saying all manner of evil things.

"Is this our younger brother speaking?" Lemuel cried out.

"To hear him talk, you would think he was the elder brother and our ruler. I, for one, am sick and tired of having him place himself above us. I think it is time we put him where he cannot bother us anymore." Laman's dark face had an evil, tense look and his hands kept opening and closing as though he already had them about Nephi's throat.

"What shall we do with him?" asked Lemuel.

"We will tie him up," answered Laman, "and throw him below deck."

When Nephi's wife saw that their threats had meaning, she threw herself between them and her beloved husband; but neither her fine courage nor her pleadings could soften their hearts. They put her roughly aside and seized Nephi. He struggled to free himself, but when he saw how hopelessly he was outnumbered he gave in to them. With cruel hands they bound his legs and arms, rejoicing in any signs of his suffering. Nephi was determined not to give them this pleasure. In order not to think of his pain he kept his mind on God, remembering all the great and marvelous things he had heard and seen. He knew that the Lord let his brothers do these cruel things to him so that later on He could prove to them His great power over wickedness.

As soon as they had bound Nephi and thrown him below deck, they discovered that the compass had stopped working and they didn't know in what direction to steer the ship. A great black cloud rolled up and hid the face of the moon. Thick blackness descended upon them. The next morning, the storm broke. The great sails creaked and swayed crazily in the wind. For three days the ship went plunging through heavy seas, only to be driven back upon the waters. But in spite of all this, Laman and Lemuel refused to release Nephi.

To people unaccustomed to the sea, the storm was terrifying. Sariah's two children, white-faced and shaken, held to her skirts for comfort and reassurance.

Above the watery confusion, one of the men cried out, "Lower the yard, furl the sail."

Lehi, old and bowed down with grief over the wickedness of his two elder sons, said many things to them and to the sons of Ishmael. But his words did not soften their hearts, and they grew angry and threatened him with death. It so disturbed both Lehi and Sariah that they fell ill and were confined to their beds.

Jacob and Joseph stood hand in hand beside their mother's bed. They had been so frightened by the storm, and now added to this was the terrible dread of losing their mother. There was no one to whom they could turn for comfort. Their father was ill and Nephi was tied and hidden away in some dark corner of the ship. Everyone was too busy with his own cares to be interested in them. Jacob had often tried to imagine what it would be like to lose his mother, but the thought was so chilling that he would put it out of his mind at once.

At that moment, the ship rolled and lunged, throwing them both sprawling on the floor. They got to their feet quickly and looked at their mother. They didn't mind their own bruises, but their mother was so sick. Being tossed about only added to her pain. This time she didn't seem to notice it, for she lay still with eyes closed. As they watched her, a great lump arose in Jacob's throat. It felt as if it would surely choke him. Tears filled his eyes and rolled unheeded down his sunburned cheeks. If only the terrible storm would stop, maybe their mother would get well; she was so old and weak she wouldn't be able to stand much more.

While Jacob stood silently praying, Sariah opened her eyes and said in a weak voice, "Jacob and Joseph, you must not cry. Promise me you will be brave and comfort your father."

"Oh, Mother," sobbed Jacob, "we can't live without you."

"There, there, my son." Sariah's voice was soothing. "Don't cry. If you both continue to pray, I am sure the Lord will hear your prayers and spare my life."

The ship lunged again, this time almost throwing them onto their mother's bed. When they had regained their footing, they saw that her eyes were closed again and her cheeks were wet with tears. Seeing her cry, they cried, too. It was then that Jacob thought of Nephi with his hands and feet tied. He would have no way to protect himself from the angry sea. The little boy's heart was filled with sympathy for his brother.

Sariah was thinking of Nephi, too. She was deeply concerned over his safety. It had been three days since he had been tied up. By now, his wrists and ankles would be swollen and sore. Unable to protect himself, he would be battered and bruised from the rolling ship. She wondered if he had food and water. She added her prayers to the many others that were said in his behalf. Although she worried about his comfort, there was no doubt in her mind that his life would be spared, for God watched out for his faithful ones. And Nephi had always been firm and true in keeping the Lord's commandments.

Her thoughts drifted to Laman and Lemuel. Would God destroy them or give them another chance? She prayed for His mercy. Laman and Lemuel needed her prayers. All their lives, they had been wayward, but as the years passed, they grew more hardened in their wickedness. For this last evil thing they were doing to their brother, perhaps God would send them all to a watery grave. Always before they had listened to her pleadings. Perhaps they would again—especially when they saw how sick she was. She would send Jacob to bring Laman to her.

Jacob set out in search of Laman at once. He moved slowly with feet wide apart in order to balance himself against the rolling, rocking ship. He searched everywhere but could not find him. Then suddenly and without warning, the ship gave a great lunge forward. It took him entirely off guard, tossing him in the air like a stick of kindling wood and then sending him sprawling face downward on the floor of the ship. Quickly he threw out his hands just in time to protect his face.

He scarcely had time to know what had happened to him before he heard a roar of loud laughter. Raising his head, he discovered Laman in a dark corner, stretched out on a pile of tents. With great effort, Jacob got to his feet; as he did so, he saw that his knees and hands were skinned and bleeding. He shut his teeth down on his lower lip to keep from crying.

"What a poor sailor you are, little brother," said Laman, still laughing.

It had taken all the courage the child had to keep from crying when he had seen the blood on his hands and knees. When Laman laughed at him, that was too much, and he burst into tears. To Laman, who enjoyed the power to hurt others, the sight was a pleasant one.

"Are you a little girl to cry over falling?" shouted Laman, having a delightful time.

"No, I'm not!" cried Jacob.

The little boy was flushed with anger. He wanted to run away, just any place to get out of Laman's sight. But then he remembered that his mother had sent him with a message for Laman. He would tell him quickly and run back to her.

"Our mother is ill," he said.

"Ill?" asked Laman.

At that moment, Jacob had a glimpse of the old Laman, the Laman that loved his mother dearly.

"Yes, she is very ill," explained Jacob. "So ill that she may even die."

Suddenly, Laman fixed Jacob with an evil eye and asked suspiciously, "What does our mother want with me?"

"I don't know. She didn't tell me what she wants. Please hurry," urged Jacob.

Laman started to get up and then changed his mind. Running his tongue over his lips, he said, "Tell her I won't come. It's just a trick to get me to free Nephi!"

"A trick?" asked Jacob.

"You know full well your mother wouldn't trick you."

Jacob turned quickly to see who had spoken. It was Nephi's wife, pale and tired from long hours of worry and fear for her husband. Upon seeing her, Laman pulled himself to a sitting position and hurriedly stroked his unkempt beard. He had always secretly admired Nephi's beautiful wife.

"I have just come from your mother and she is very ill. So ill, in fact, that she may go to a watery grave," she continued.

"So might we all," said Laman, growing angry. "Who am I that you should blame me? Am I able to stop the storm?"

"You know well enough that if you would free Nephi and humble yourself before the Lord, the storm would pass by and we would all be saved."

But in spite of her pleading and the pleading of the others, there was nothing, except the power of God which threatened them with destruction, that could soften Laman and Lemuel's hearts. Even though they began to be frightened that they would be drowned in the sea, they would not set Nephi free.

On the fourth day, the storm lashed out in all its fury. The waves dashed and pounded themselves into white foam all around them. The ship rolled and was half-lifted out of the water, where it shuddered and seemed to pause before being plunged deep into the waves. At last, Laman and Lemuel began to see that the judgment of God was upon them and they must die if they did not repent, so they went to Nephi and untied him.

Without a single word of complaint about his suffering, Nephi arose and thanked God for His goodness and mercy. Suddenly, the storm died out and the sea became calm. With the aid of the compass, which was now working, Nephi guided the ship toward the promised land.

CHAPTER 15

It was high noon at sea. The skies were clear and bright, the water calm; there was just the right amount of breeze to keep the ship going steadily. For the space of many days, they had sailed toward the promised land under perfect weather conditions. As a matter of fact, ever since Laman and Lemuel had repented and set Nephi free, it had been ideal weather for sailing. The great calm of the sea had seemed to enter all their hearts and bring them peace. Sariah and Lehi were well again and very happy. Nephi's wife and children were so delighted at being with Nephi again that they found joy in every waking hour. For the first few days after the storm Laman and Lemuel kept to themselves, ashamed to show their faces. But as the days passed, they forgot their guilt and began to go about the ship as boldly as ever.

Today Lehi stood on deck, old and wrinkled and white-haired, with hands clasped behind his back. Nephi knew he had stood in the same place, without moving, for over an hour. Was something wrong? His father was so quick to sense difficulty of any kind that Nephi began wondering what had happened. From where he stood, he saw his father gently clasp and unclasp his hands. The movement seemed calm enough; nevertheless, he decided to clear up the mystery and hurried to his father's side.

"Father, may I join you?" he asked.

Too late, he discovered that his father was praying silently. He started at the sound of his son's voice.

"I didn't mean to disturb your prayers," said Nephi, humbly.

"I have finished my prayers. I was thanking God for sparing your mother's and my life so that we might see the promised land," he said, smiling as one who had been granted a rare gift.

"I have thanked God, too, for sparing your lives. Your wisdom and guidance will be needed by all of us when we reach the new land." Nephi's voice was filled with respect and great admiration.

"I shall continue to guide and teach my people while life shall last, and when I have passed on to my Maker, I shall rest in peace, knowing that you, Nephi, will take over the leadership. I know that you will lead our people in the ways of God. This will not be an easy task, for Laman and Lemuel are apt to become more rebellious than ever, but if you continue to deal with them justly and patiently, without hatred, you will be blessed of the Lord. Are you listening to me, Nephi?" the old man asked.

Nephi had turned his face away to hide the sorrow he felt upon hearing his father's words. How strange it would seem to be unable to take his problems to his father or share with him some newfound happiness.

"I am listening to you, Father," he answered, forcing a smile.

"Laman and Lemuel walk in darkness. They like the shadows better than the light. The older they grow, the more wicked they will become, until at last God will forsake them. Then, my son, beware, for they will seek to destroy you and all others who are faithful in keeping the commandments of God. Watch out for Jacob and Joseph. I leave both children in your care. Teach them well, my son."

"Father, Father!"

Both men turned to see Jacob running toward them at breakneck speed.

"Don't run so fast, boy. You will fall and hurt yourself," said the old man.

"Look," said Jacob, excitedly pointing a finger toward the east.

"Where?" asked Lehi. "I see nothing."

"There," said Jacob, still pointing. "It's land."

When Lehi heard Jacob's announcement, a thrill of excitement ran through him. For the moment, he felt young again, eager for adventure in the new land. But then, shading his eyes, he stared out to sea and discovered that he was no longer young, for his eyesight was greatly dimmed by time.

Turning sadly to Nephi, he said, "I can see nothing but the water. Can you make out any signs of land?"

"Why yes, I do see a dark blur on the water," answered Nephi, alive with excitement.

"Do you think it could be land you see?" asked Lehi.

"We are too far away to be sure. It is possible that it is," he answered.

"Wait, Jacob." Lehi caught the small boy by his tunic and held him fast. "Where are you going?"

"I am going to tell my mother and Joseph and all the others that I have discovered land. Please let go of me, Father," said Jacob, tugging to free himself.

"Wait, my son. You must not tell them yet. We do not want to excite them before we are sure," said Lehi, sternly.

"But I want them to know that I was the one who saw land first," said the little boy in a hurt voice.

"If it is really land," said Nephi pleasantly, "we will give you the credit. Laman and Lemuel are growing tired of sailing, and if we tell them we can see land and then it turns out to be only a dark spot on the water, they will be so disappointed they are apt to rebel again. So don't you think our father is right in wanting to wait until we can see it plainly?"

"Yes, Nephi," answered Jacob, happy again. "But I want to be the one to tell them."

A flood of memories ran through Lehi's mind as he stared out to sea. The good man had no doubt in his mind that what his son saw was the promised land. They had come at last to their journey's end. It had been about eleven years since they had left Jerusalem, and during all that time he had waited, planned, struggled to reach this day—and now it was here. He felt humble in the sight of God. During the years that had passed in the journey through the wilderness, great and terrible had been their suffering. They had walked across the burning sands of the desert. They had been hungry, thirsty, hot, weary, and sick. They had endured sandstorms that had torn at their flesh, and storms at sea that had terrified them and made them ill. And now, at last, their journey was over.

Aside from their suffering, they had found joy in the beauties of God's creation. They had seen the desert sunset, flaming forth in all its crimson glory. They had watched the matchless beauty of a desert rainbow, bridging earth and sky, and underneath its glowing colors they had walked with God. They had known the fresh, clean smell of rain on the parched desert sand. They had heard the mysterious voice of the wind as it went sighing through the great trees of the forest. They had known the joy of diving headfirst into a clear, sparkling pool of water and they had slept out under the stars and watched the moon climb over the highest mountain peak. They had seen it rise above the sea, making a shining pathway of silvery light.

Rich and varied had been their experiences. Their joys and suffering had taught Lehi and most of his people of the mercy and goodness of the living God. During the years of their journey, they had grown quiet and thoughtful with understanding and a gentle devotion for all those around them. But a few of them, including Laman and Lemuel, had grown more embittered. They saw in each new experience fresh cause for complaint against Nephi and their father.

Lehi remembered his life in Jerusalem. What an easy, comfortable life it had been! But he had no regrets about leaving it far behind. He was certain that, if he had it all to do over, he would hasten to keep the Lord's commandments just as he had done years before. He was proud and grateful that the Lord had chosen him, a humble man, to lead Ishmael's and his own family to the land of promise.

In the days that had passed, he had learned the goodness and mercy of God. There had been times when the Lord had tested their faithfulness. Suddenly, Lehi brought his hand to his face as if to ward off a blow. The thought was painful, for he was remembering the time in the desert when they were starving that he, Lehi, chosen of the Lord, had complained and even doubted God. Ever since that day he had implored God's forgiveness.

"Father," questioned Nephi, "will you know the promised land when you see it?"

"Yes," answered Lehi. "God permitted me to see it in a dream."

"Tell us Father," said Jacob eagerly, "what it will be like."

"It will be the most wonderful land you can imagine," said Lehi, earnestly. "The land will be rich and fertile. As a matter of fact, the soil will be so good that our seeds will grow into the finest plants we have ever seen. There will be great forests filled with animals of every kind, provided by the Lord for our use. I saw great mountains containing silver and gold and other kinds of precious metals."

"I heard Laman and Lemuel talking and they said that food would be everywhere and all we would have to do would be to pick it and eat it. They said we would never have to work again and we could spend all our time just enjoying ourselves." Jacob's voice glowed with excitement.

"No, Jacob, that is not God's way." Lehi sounded tired and discouraged.

Jacob looked up at his father, puzzled at his words. At times it was very hard to understand what grown-up people meant.

"What does that mean, Father?" he asked after a while.

"God has commanded that we earn our bread by the sweat of our brow. In other words, we work if we want to eat, and what a wonderful blessing it is to be able to work! It is, perhaps, one of God's greatest gifts. When you are older, my son, you will know the joy and deep satisfaction that come from creating something out of your own imagination and with your own hands. The right amount of work brings health to your body and peace to your soul. Idle hands and minds place men in Satan's grasp. Yes, Jacob, God in his wisdom knew that work was good for man and it will be no different in the promised land."

They waited for what seemed to Jacob an endless length of time before his father spoke again.

"At last, I see land," he said, "and it is the promised land. Run, my boy, and tell the others."

Jacob was off like the wind and Nephi exchanged a smile with his father. In a few moments, everyone aboard ship crowded onto the deck, filling the air with their rejoicing. The men slapped each other on the back. Women laughed with tears streaming down their faces. The children danced and sang. When the first wave of excitement passed away, Lehi spoke to them, asking them to humble themselves and praise God for bringing them all safely to their journey's end. Even Laman and Lemuel prayed earnestly.

Upon reaching the land, they left the ship and pitched their tents beside the sea. The first thing Lehi did was to pick up a handful of earth and let it trickle through his fingers. He was delighted at the rich fertility of the land.

The promised land was a land of matchless beauty. There was a narrow strip of land lying between the ocean on the west and a great mountain range on the east, whose lofty peaks were snowcapped. These mountains stretched north and south for hundreds of miles. Down their sides came great waterfalls, rushing and roaring into the green valleys below. In the deep, dark forests were to be found the cow and ox, the horse and the ass, the goat and the wild goat, and all kinds of wild animals for their use. In the mountains they found gold, silver, and copper ore.

Immediately they set to work, tilling the soil and planting the seeds they had brought with them from Jerusalem, and God blessed them with an abundant harvest.

PART 2

The Precious Land of Promise

CHAPTER 16

The sun was going down and the wind sang softly through the sleepy leaves. Lehi, white-haired and bent by the weight of many years, sat with his back against the trunk of a mighty tree. The good man, and that was exactly what he was, liked the peace and quiet he found here. It was his habit to spend one or two hours here each day reliving in his memory the days of his past, solving problems of the present, or projecting himself into the mysteries of the future. Above all, he came here because he felt the nearness of God. His children and grandchildren never disturbed him here, for they knew of his desire to be alone.

The last rays of the sun reached his face and touched it with a golden light, showing a noble forehead and a courageous chin. The deep lines about his mouth and eyes told of the joy and the sorrow, the pleasure and the pain, that had been his to bear. With the setting of the sun came the hour of prayer, when the family met and prayed together and Nephi, his beloved son, read from the brass plates the history of his forefathers and prophecies of Isaiah and many others chosen by God to carry His commandments to the people. With humility, he remembered that he and Nephi were chosen of the Lord to teach His word.

It was time now for the evening prayer, but Lehi had
lost all sense of time. He was thinking of Jerusalem where
he had lived many years ago and of the day he had gone
into the hills to pray to God for his people. On that day, a
great and marvelous thing had happened. Before his very
eyes, a pillar of fire had come and dwelt upon a rock and
then he had seen and heard many things that caused him
to tremble and grow weak. When the vision ended, he
had gone home and lain upon his bed and had beheld
another vision. He saw the heavens open up and God
sitting on His throne. All about him were angels singing
and praising God. As he watched, one of them began
descending to earth. Twelve other angels followed the
first and they came down and stood upon the earth. The
first one stood before him and gave him an open book to
read. He read of the wickedness of his people. He saw
Jerusalem destroyed and many of his people killed and
many others carried away into Babylon. He remembered,
too, how God had commanded him to go among the
people and tell them what he had seen and heard. He had
kept the commandments of the Lord, but when he had
pleaded with them to repent, they had grown very angry
and had sought to take his life. God came to him again in
a dream and commanded him to leave Jerusalem. He remembered, too, how Sariah, his lovely wife, had given up
her comfortable home, her friends, and her own family
to go with him and her four sons, Laman, Lemuel, Nephi,
and Sam, into the wilderness. What great faith she had
had in the Lord, and how dearly she loved him to have
given up so much!

"Sariah, my dear, how I miss you." Lehi spoke aloud
to himself, and as he spoke, a sad and tender light filled
his eyes.

Sariah had been dead for a long time, but Lehi's
memory of her was as bright and fresh as though he had

just seen her. How much she had endured! During the long, hard years while they journeyed to the promised land, she had borne him two sons, Jacob and Joseph, and daughters as well. In spite of all her suffering, she had seldom complained. She had lived only a short time after they reached the promised land—but long enough to know that all God had promised was fulfilled. She had helped in planting the seeds they had brought from Jerusalem and had seen how rich and abundantly they had grown. She had discovered the fruits of the forest, the streams of pure sparkling water, the great variety of animals, all meant for their use, and in the great lofty mountains rich deposits of gold, silver, and copper ore. Lehi thanked God for allowing Sariah to live long enough to enjoy some of the rich blessings of their new and wonderful land.

Sariah's last words were of Laman and Lemuel. She was deeply concerned about them. She was afraid they would anger the Lord by their wickedness and be cut off from His presence. She pleaded with Lehi to be patient and untiring in his efforts to guide them in doing the will of God. Lehi sighed heavily, wondering to himself how well he had carried out her request. He had certainly tried. They were indeed wayward sons. Night after night, he had lain awake worrying about them. He thought, almost bitterly, that they had given him more cause for worry than all the rest of his children combined.

"Oh, here you are, Father Lehi. I've looked everywhere for you." It was the warm, pleasant voice of Nephi's wife.

She went quickly to him and laid her slender hand gently on his shoulder. He was so lost in his memories that for a second or two he thought it was the voice of Sariah coming to him in a vision. But then immediately he knew who it was. He raised his head and looked at her. Once again, he noticed how closely she resembled his dead wife. Perhaps this was the reason that such a close bond existed between them.

She spoke again. "Are you all right? We were so worried about you."

"Worried?" he asked, puzzled. "Why should you be worried over me?"

"In all the years I have known you, I can't remember a single time that you have missed or were late for family prayers," she answered.

Quickly, he took his eyes from her face and lifted them to the towering mountains. The crimson of the setting sun was gone now and the lofty peaks were already becoming obscured in the gathering gloom of approaching night. He was startled to learn that he had completely lost all sense of time. Sighing deeply, he thought this was only further evidence of his old age.

"Are you all right, Father?" she asked him once again.

He liked her concern for him. It gave him a sense of security—a feeling of being loved and wanted still.

"Yes, I am all right—just getting too old to remember that time waits for no man. I am very sorry I missed the evening prayer. Is Nephi reading from the brass plates?"

"Yes," she answered, simply.

"That was wise." His voice sounded troubled and sad. "Laman and Lemuel grow restless so quickly."

Lehi and his daughter-in-law knew how difficult it was to catch their interest and hold it, especially when dealing with spiritual matters. Nevertheless, Nephi continued to teach and read from the records engraved on the brass plates. In spite of his untiring efforts in their behalf, they rewarded him with insults and abuse. A number of times, in the very middle of Nephi's reading, they had stood up and walked away. There had been times when they had laughed at the prophecies of the chosen men of God. At such times Lehi would become so agitated that he would rebuke them in angry tones, while his eyes became clouded with a hopeless expression.

"Perhaps," she said, "if we hurry we shall be able to hear part of the reading."

"Yes, yes, my dear."

He struggled to his feet with great difficulty. Her heart ached for him. She longed to help him, to spare him pain, but instead she waited quietly. She knew from past experience that he would only refuse her help. He was a proud, independent man who seldom admitted, even to himself, that he was in need of help. Old age was a burden to him, but he carried his years with dignity.

Nephi's wife walked beside him on the path, adjusting her stride to suit his slower one. When they reached the meeting place, Lehi stood for a few minutes, unnoticed among the shadows. As his eyes searched the group, an aching loneliness settled down on him because he realized that among all the group, he was the only one left of his generation. The others had passed on to their Maker. It seemed to him only yesterday that he had been young and that most of the people around him had been older than he. There were so many things he had planned to do and now there wouldn't be time, for he knew his days were numbered. In spite of the hardships he had suffered, he had loved life. A feeling of peace settled on him when he remembered that he would soon be with Sariah and his friends.

His searching eyes came to rest on Sam's face. Here was a son that any father would be proud of. He had been faithful and loyal to God and his fellowmen. Now he was listening intently to the warm, rich voice of Nephi as he read to them from the brass plates.

Seated beside Sam were Jacob and Joseph, his two

youngest sons. What fine, handsome men they had grown to be, and how closely they followed in the footsteps of Nephi and Sam.

Laman and Lemuel sat apart from the group, their faces dark and sullen as they listened without interest to Nephi's reading. They had taken their hunting knives from their belts and sat whittling impatiently.

At that moment, Jacob caught sight of his father and immediately gave him his place. Nephi was reading the prophecies concerning the coming of the Savior, his crucifixion, and resurrection. When he had finished reading, he put the plates aside and said:

"And now I have finished reading to you, for I dare not speak as yet concerning further happenings. I wish you would consider that the things written on the plates of brass are true, and they testify that a man must be obedient to the commandments of God. And I say to you, my brethren, do not suppose that my father and I are the only ones that have testified concerning the truthfulness of these things. If you will be obedient to the commandments and endure to the end, you shall be saved at the last day. Amen."

CHAPTER 17

Jacob and Joseph had taken the day to explore in the mountains which rose in stony folds up and up thousands of feet above the village. From the lofty snow-capped peaks, a stream ran swiftly down the canyon and out across the little valley and then lost itself in the great sea. The village might be ever so hot, but the canyon was always cool.

The two men made their way up the stony side of the mountain, dodging in and out among the sharp rocks, always keeping watch for a snake or a crouching animal. As they climbed higher and higher, the red, stony walls of the canyon became so narrow that they were no more than a hundred feet apart. When at last they reached the mouth of the canyon, they saw that it was barred by high rocks with only a tiny opening where the water came tumbling through. Without hesitation, they skillfully climbed these rocks and for a moment sat down to look.

"I think this is the most beautiful place in all the world," said Jacob.

In front of them lay the narrow canyon where the stream flowed from rocky pool to rocky pool.

"It's breathtaking, isn't it? But just turn around and you will see a far greater sight," said Joseph.

Far below them, nestled at the foot of the great mountain range, lay the little village made up of brightly colored tents. On either side the farms spread out like a bright blanket in matchless shades of green. Beyond the valley the restless sea sparkled in the sun.

"Do you remember when we were boys, how we used to like to play in these rocky pools?" asked Joseph.

"Yes, indeed I do," answered Jacob. "And I remember how often we came here with Nephi to help him gather ore for the plates he made."

"Do you know what he writes on the plates?" asked Joseph.

"Yes," replied Jacob.

"Is the record secret?" asked Joseph, in a thoughtful voice.

"No, he would show it to you if you asked him," said Jacob, smiling at his brother. "He has engraven a record of our forefathers and of our father. He has written of our long, difficult journey through the wilderness and our voyage across the great sea. Perhaps the most important part of his record is the account of our father's prophecies and of his own."

"Did Father ask him to make this record?" A note of humility came into Joseph's voice.

"No, God commanded him to make it. It is to be handed down to the next chosen prophet of the Lord."

"It seems to me, after reading the brass plates and knowing Father and Nephi, that God chooses the very best men to carry His word to the people. I like to think of them as being in tune with the Lord so that when he sends a message, they understand without actually talking to him." Joseph sat with his chin cupped in the palms of his hands, looking down into the valley below.

"I think you are right, Joseph. Our chosen leaders have all been great men—great in the sight of God—

humble, and yet with the courage to express their opinions regardless of personal safety. They are all men of great faith with the strength of character to carry out God's commandments to the letter. Ah, Joseph, how I should like to be chosen to carry forth this great work."

"I believe you will. You are very much like Father and Nephi. As for me, I shall be content to be a follower. The more I look at this beautiful land, the more I realize how blessed we are," said Joseph.

"Father saw this land in a vision as clearly as we see it today. God promised that this should be our land and the land of our children so long as we are righteous and keep His commandments."

"If we are to reach the upper canyon and get home by dark, we will have to start climbing," said Joseph to his brother.

Now, Jacob and Joseph had never been to the upper canyon, but they had been to the opening a number of times. Nephi always left them by the rock pools while he went alone to pray to God. The opening was not hard to find, but it was hard to enter. A small stream of water slid over a cliff and went dashing down the rocks, beating itself into foam and sending up tiny clouds of mist until it lost itself in the main stream.

The two men were good climbers, but the ten-foot cliff presented a real problem. They soon discovered that they could not climb it directly; they had to start about a hundred yards off to the side and wind their way up to the top. By the time they had reached the rocky floor of the canyon above, they were out of breath and bleeding a little where the sharp rocks had cut their hands.

Joseph gave a low whistle. "Well, did you ever see anything like this before?"

"It's like a great, giant bowl. See how the sides rise up and up hundreds of feet."

It was indeed breathtaking. In the center of the bowl was a pool of crystal-clear water whose glassy surface mirrored the lofty, snowcapped mountains. When they stood on its banks, it was like a fairyland. The bottom was covered with bright colored stones—yellow, red, and green. Jacob, seeing a glittering pebble by his foot, stooped to pick it up.

"Why, it's gold! Laman and Lemuel are forever talking about gold and telling of all the things they could buy in Jerusalem with it."

"The water seems to be washing it down from the mountain. It is beautiful. Let's take a few pieces back with us," suggested Joseph.

"Say, that's a curious thing." Jacob appeared puzzled.

"What do you mean?"

"Can't you feel that current of air?" asked Jacob.

"Listen! Someone is moaning."

The two men stood still, listening intently. Suddenly, there came a low moaning sound that made them shudder and draw close together. It was such a lonely place and so silent except for the moan that came again and again.

Suddenly, Jacob's face brightened and he said: "It's the wind that makes the noise. It has something to do with the shape of the rocks and the way the wind whistles through them."

"It sounds odd, but you are right, it is the wind."

For two hours or more, Jacob and Joseph explored some of the caves in the canyon walls. When the purple shadows began to gather, they turned toward home. Upon reaching the mouth of the lower canyon, they sat down to rest and enjoy the view. They were silent for a long time until at last Jacob spoke:

"Looking at this beautiful land, I keep remembering what our father said, that this is 'a land of promise, a land which is choice above all other lands; a land which the Lord God has given to me and my children and also to those who are led out of other countries by the hand of the Lord. And if they will serve Him and keep His commandments it shall be a land of liberty; but if they sin, they shall be cursed.'"

"Father is worried. He grieves over the behavior of Laman and Lemuel. He would like to give Laman the first blessing since he is the eldest son, yet he knows he is unworthy. So unworthy that God may even cut him off from His presence," said Joseph.

A note of sadness came into Jacob's voice. "Father won't be with us much longer. If only he could go to his grave with a joyful heart."

The words his brother spoke were a shock to Joseph. True, he had noticed that his father was growing weaker day by day, but he had never admitted, even to himself, that Lehi would soon pass away.

"I can't bear to think of his passing. It will be a great loss—no one can ever take his place." Joseph's voice betrayed his emotion.

"It was only last night that Father said, 'A few more days and I go the way of all the earth. You must soon lay me down in the cold and silent grave, from where no traveler can return,'" said Jacob.

Joseph was too filled with despair to make any comment. He only stared out at the restless sea. At last Jacob spoke again:

"Father would not like to see you grieve. Try to think how happy he will be when he meets Mother. He has been lonely without her. Remember, too, that he is going to a better place where he will be richly rewarded for his faithfulness. He is no longer young, but old and tired. His soul cries out for peace and rest. He will never die so long as you and I keep him alive in our hearts. Many a man has become a greater influence for good after death than he was in life."

It was dusk when Jacob and Joseph reached the village. A full moon had risen over the mountains, shedding a soft, mellow light on everything it touched, making it almost as light as day.

"Good evening, brothers." It was Nephi who spoke from where he sat beside the path, half-hidden in the bushes. He was mending his fishnets in the dim light.

"Good evening," answered the brothers.

"We missed you in the fields today. You two do more than any of the rest of us. I hope you had a pleasant day. Did you explore new territory?"

Nephi stood up as he spoke and came to them where they stood on the path. Jacob and Joseph were very fond of their brother Nephi. They both respected and admired him and it was with smiling faces that they greeted him now.

"New territory for us, but old for you," answered Jacob. "We went to the upper canyon today. When we were younger, you always took us with you on your exploring adventures, but you always left us in the lower canyon to play in the rocky pools while you went alone to the upper canyon."

"I had a good reason for not taking you, and besides, it is a difficult climb—too difficult for me now."

His last words were somewhat of a shock to the brothers. They had always thought of Nephi as being young and strong, but when he spoke, they were made to realize that he was middle-aged.

"Don't look so worried, Joseph," Nephi continued. "I am really as strong as ever. Nevertheless, I am not anxious to make that climb again. But come, tell me about your adventure today. Did you discover anything new?"

"Hold out your hand, Nephi, and I'll show you what we found," said Joseph eagerly.

Nephi did as he was asked and Joseph placed two gold nuggets in his hand. Jacob and Joseph stepped closer to enjoy their brother's pleasure, but they were disappointed; the sight of the gold saddened their brother's eyes.

"What is wrong?" asked Jacob.

"A few minutes ago, I told you that I had good reason for not taking you with me to the upper canyon. Well, this was my reason. I didn't want anyone to know about the gold. Of course, I talked it over with Father, and he advised me to keep it a secret."

Nephi was worried.

"But why?" asked the two brothers at once.

"Well, you never lived in Jerusalem; if you had, you would know how gold can turn the heads of men. When it is used wisely it is a blessing, but when it falls into the hands of wicked men, it can be a source of evil. Laman and Lemuel had a great lust for gold and often they bought wicked pleasures. Our father and mother worried so much over them that they grew old before their time."

"But surely it couldn't harm them here," said Joseph.

"Father thought that, remembering all the things they could buy in Jerusalem, they might decide to carry a load of it back with them," said Nephi.

At that moment, from out of the gathering shadows, came a hand with long, dark fingers. Instantly, the hand snatched up the gold and was gone, leaving nothing but the ringing sound of evil laughter.

"Laman," said Nephi angrily. "Our father was right. There is no telling what they will do."

CHAPTER 18

Lehi, knowing that he had but a few more days left on this earth, sent for his sons, Ishmael's sons, and Zoram. He had something to say to each of them, but he wanted to say it before all of them so that when he was gone there would be no misunderstanding.

As they gathered about him, the thought came to him that, perhaps, this would be the last time he would see them all together. The idea gripped him in an agony of pain. He looked at them a long time with searching eyes, hoping to imprint their dear faces upon his very soul.

He spoke first to Laman and Lemuel, telling them of the goodness of God in bringing them to this precious land of promise. He reminded them of their rebellion at sea and how God had shown mercy and spared their lives.

"Behold!" said Lehi, "I have seen a vision in which I know that Jerusalem is destroyed, and had we remained in Jerusalem we should also have perished."

"That's just another of your bad dreams," said Laman disagreeably.

Lehi saw the flush that dyed Nephi's face a deep red. He saw him clench his fists, but before anything could be said to start an angry quarrel, the old man began talking in a stern, clear voice:

"Oh, my sons, awake and listen to the words of a trembling parent. My heart has been weighed down with sorrow, for I have been afraid that the hardness of your hearts would make the Lord angry, and that He would cut you off from His presence or curse you for many generations. If only you would repent, you might be a choice and favored people of the Lord. Oh, how I wish you would bring me joy so that I could leave this world with gladness because of you. I beg of you not to weigh me down with grief and sorrow to the grave."

"Nephi is righteous. Have pleasure in him," snapped Lemuel.

A troubled frown furrowed Lehi's brow and his voice trembled as he answered:

"Rebel no more against your brother Nephi. His views are glorious. He has kept the commandments of the Lord from the time we left Jerusalem, and he has been an instrument for God in bringing us to the land of promise. If it were not for him, we might have perished with hunger in the wilderness; nevertheless, you have sought to take away his life. He has suffered much because of you. I am afraid that you will make him suffer again. You blame him for wanting power over you and it is not so. All he wants is your eternal welfare."

Lehi sighed heavily. He felt old and very weary. His sons saw how ill and weak he was and their hearts ached for him. Even Laman's heart was touched and, in a moment of regret, he tried to say something that would lessen his father's sorrow—but his words were ill chosen.

"We are not entirely to blame," he said. "From time to time, Nephi has spoken very plainly. He has said many sharp and angry things to us."

"No, my son," said Lehi. "He has spoken plain, harsh,

and angry words when you have been wicked, but he is not to blame, for he could not help himself. It was the Spirit of the Lord in him and He used him for an instrument to speak to you. And now my sons, Laman, Lemuel, and Sam, and the sons of Ishmael, behold, if you will listen to the voice of Nephi you shall not perish. If you listen to him, I will leave you a blessing, even my first blessing. But if you will not listen, I will take away my first blessing and give it to him. And now, Zoram, I speak to you. You were the servant of Laban; nevertheless, you were brought out of the land of Jerusalem, and I know that you have been a true friend to Nephi. Because of your faithfulness, your children shall be blessed with his children and they will prosper long upon the face of this land and nothing except their wickedness shall harm or disturb their prosperity. If you will keep the commandments of the Lord, you and your children will be secure in this great new land."

Nephi came forward and stood, regarding his father anxiously: "Father, you look so tired. Hadn't you better rest awhile?"

"No, Nephi, there are many things left for me to say and there is so little time to say them. My strength is slowly ebbing away and my voice grows weaker. I wish to speak to Jacob. Will you ask him to come forward so that I might study his face while I give him my blessing?"

"Here I am, Father," said Jacob.

"Jacob, my faithful son. What joy you have brought me! You were my firstborn in the wilderness. Your suffering has been great and much of it was due to your brothers Laman and Lemuel. You know the greatness of God, and He shall reward you for your faithfulness. You shall dwell safely with your brother Nephi, and your days shall be spent in the service of God. You have beheld, in your youth, His glory. Wherefore, you are blessed even as those who shall see the Savior in the flesh, for the Spirit is the same yesterday, today, and forever. I know there is a God and that on the judgment day, we will stand before Him and be judged according to our works. We are free to choose liberty and eternal life or to choose captivity and death, according to the power of the devil; for he wants all men to be miserable like himself. Obey God's commandments and be faithful to His words, and choose eternal life, according to the will of His holy spirit. My object in speaking to you is for the welfare of your soul. A glorious life awaits those who are faithful and salvation is free to those who wish it."

Lehi placed his hand on Jacob's head and said "Amen."

"Thank you, Father." Jacob's voice was filled with tender emotion. "I shall always remember your blessing and I will keep the commandments of the Lord."

As Jacob moved away from his father, Lehi called Joseph to him. Joseph was a handsome youth, with large, serious eyes. He reminded his father of Sariah. Lehi closed his eyes for a moment. Suddenly, he felt as though he were drifting toward Sariah and away from his sons. He must arouse himself, for he wanted to bless all his children. With that thought, he felt strength coming back to him.

"Joseph," he said, "you are my youngest son. You were born in the wilderness during the days of my greatest sorrow. May the Lord bless you so that you, too, may inherit this most precious land. If you are faithful in keeping the commandments, you will be secure here forever. Your descendants will never be entirely destroyed. Now, Joseph, you are my son and I am a descendant of Joseph of old, the Joseph who was taken captive and sold into Egypt. He was a great prophet and he foretold many things about our day that we know are true. He told of our breaking away from Jerusalem and starting a new branch of the house of Israel. Now, Joseph, after we are gone many generations shall pass away and another Joseph will be brought forth whose father's name will be Joseph, too. And the Lord, through him, shall bring my people salvation. Joseph, you are blessed. You are young, so listen to the words of your brother Nephi, and all the promises I have made you will come true. Remember the words of a dying father. Amen."

When Lehi finished giving Joseph his blessing, he was so tired that he had to rest a few minutes. Then he called Laman and Lemuel's sons and daughters to him and said:

"You are the sons and daughters of my two eldest sons and you are my grandchildren. I have a blessing for you—a very special blessing. God has said that if you keep His commandments, you shall prosper in this land; but if you will not keep His commandments, you shall be cut off from His presence. However, I cannot go down to my grave without first leaving you with a blessing; I know that if you are brought up in the way you should go, you will not depart from it. If it happens that you are cursed, I leave my blessing upon you, that the cursing may be taken from you and be answered upon the heads of your parents. Now, because of my blessing, the Lord thy God will not let you perish. He will be merciful to you and to your descendants forever. You will never be entirely destroyed, but in the end, your descendants will be blessed."

They were to remember this blessing for generations to come, and to find in it encouragement and comfort.

When Lehi had finished speaking to them, he spoke to the sons of Ishmael and to all his household. Sam had waited patiently, hoping that he, too, would be given a blessing. Unable to wait any longer, for he saw how weak his father was growing, he moved closer to him. Suddenly, Lehi's face lit up as he caught sight of his son and motioned him to come to his side, saying:

"Blessed are you and all those who come after you, for you shall inherit this land like your brother Nephi. And your children shall be numbered with his children, and you shall be like your brother, and your children like his children; you shall be blessed in all your days."

Lehi asked to be left alone with Nephi.

"Nephi, my son, I leave you to guide my people. Make a record of my prophecies so that they will help guide you."

"Yes, Father, I will record them. There are not many greater."

A gentle light fell upon Lehi's face. He closed his eyes slowly and relaxed into a peaceful sleep from which he never awakened. With loving hands, they laid him to rest beside Sariah, in the rich soil of his inheritance.

CHAPTER 19

A hush had fallen over the little village, for it was mid-morning and all the able-bodied men, women, and children had gone to the fields to work. All, that is, except Laman and Lemuel, who were resting beside Laman's tent. As a matter of fact, they had been resting every day for two weeks, since their father's death. Nephi had urged them each day to join them in the fields and do their share of the work; each day they invented new excuses to stay at home. Finally, growing impatient, he asked them to go fishing or hunting and at least supply the village with fresh meat. It worried Nephi to see them spend so much time in idleness, but the more he urged them, the more determined they became to do nothing. Nephi knew that the less they did, the more time they would spend in plotting against him. He saw their hatred in their eyes and heard it in their voices. He longed to live in peace with all the village, but he was at a loss to know how to achieve it.

The sun was hot today and as it moved higher in the heavens, the shadows grew shorter, leaving the two brothers lying in the sun. After a while, they were forced to find a shady spot.

"Nephi spoke sharply to us today," said Lemuel, watching Laman carefully.

"Uh-hmmm," replied Laman, without a single flick of an eyelid to show how he felt about Nephi.

"Did you hear him say that those who didn't work wouldn't eat?"

If Lemuel had hoped to arouse Laman's anger he was disappointed, because Laman's face remained expressionless. Lemuel simply couldn't understand his brother. He knew Laman hated Nephi and would like nothing better than to harm him. Always before, Laman had been the first to anger.

"You are the firstborn, and it is your right to be our leader now that Father is dead. You should be giving the orders, not taking them. By what right does Nephi order us to do his bidding?" With the last word, Lemuel drove his hunting knife viciously into the ground.

At last, Laman smiled slyly at his brother and said, "What would you think, Lemuel, if you and I were to go deep-sea fishing! I think it would be nice to take our brother Nephi with us."

"Take Nephi with us? Have you gone crazy? I, for one, don't want to spend the entire day with him," said Lemuel, angrily.

"You're a stupid fellow, Lemuel. What would you say if I were to tell you that on this fishing trip, we will meet with a great disaster, in which our brother Nephi will be lost at sea. We will be bowed down with grief, just at a time when we had come to love our brother." Laman's voice was filled with cunning.

"Are you serious?" Lemuel was scornful.

"Why, yes, I am. Is there anything wrong?" asked Laman, watching his brother narrowly.

"You called me stupid. You're being worse than stupid. All the people in the village love Nephi—that is, with a few exceptions. They look upon him as their leader. His word is law. The one who destroys him will forfeit his own life."

"But Lemuel, it would be an accident at sea. No one could prove otherwise," said Laman.

"But they wouldn't believe you even if it were true. They would immediately be suspicious and, for that reason alone, they would never consent to your rule."

"Yes, I think you are right." Laman was impressed with his brother's cunning.

"It must be a plan so clever that no one will suspect either of us. Neither of us must be near when death comes."

Laman began to speculate. His evil mind found pleasure in his wicked plans. He thought of poison or a trap wherein the victim could fall to his death.

"Our plans will have to be made carefully so there will be no mistakes. And you, Laman, must begin now to make friends with all our people, so that when they learn of Nephi's death, you can step in and take over as ruler without any serious objections. Once they have accepted that fact, we will give the orders while they do our bidding. We will live on the fat of the land without having to work another day." The very thought of it sent Lemuel into a fit of laughter.

All day long Nephi, who was usually so calm and even tempered, was nervous and jumpy, on several occasions he spoke sharply to those working with him. His wife watched him anxiously. She wondered if he were ill. He had always had such excellent health, but of late, he had been sleeping poorly. He would get up in the night, dress, and walk through the village. Perhaps he was grieving over the loss of his father. However, she didn't believe that was the reason for his nervousness and ill temper. For the first time in their lives together, he had been annoyed with her. It made her sad to realize that they had grown apart during the last two weeks. As her eyes followed him, she saw that he kept stopping in his work to listen. It was as though he were waiting for something to happen—something that he was trying to prepare himself for. To his wife, whose whole world revolved about him, it was unbearable to watch his peace of mind being destroyed. She wanted to help him but, first of all, she must find out what was troubling him. When the work was finished in the field, she detained him until the others had started for the village, so that they might be alone.

"Nephi, you are disturbed about something. I wish you would tell me what is troubling you," she said.

A look of surprise flashed across his face. He thought he had kept his true feelings hidden. He should have known he couldn't fool her. She had such a rare gift of understanding—especially where he was concerned. Sometimes she knew what he was thinking and feeling even before he told her. Through the years, he had come to value her opinion.

"Yes, something is troubling me, but I didn't want to weight you down with my problems," he answered.

"Nephi, I want to share your problems as well as your joys. Besides, I worry far more when you don't discuss them with me, because then I imagine all sorts of things. Tell me if you can. I may be able to help you some way," she said.

"There are a number of things that are troubling me. It began with Father's death." Nephi's voice was filled with emotion.

"Your father wouldn't want you to grieve for him," she said gently.

"I know that," he replied. "He had lived a long, full life and he has gone to a rich reward. Of course, I miss him even as you do, but I know he is far happier now than he was with us. With Father's passing, I felt that all his responsibilities were passed on to me."

"But Nephi, even when your father was alive, you assumed a great share of the leadership of our people."

"But I always had him to turn to. Anytime, night or day, I could go to him and discuss my problems. With his passing, Laman, Lemuel, and the sons of Ishmael unloosed all their hatred on me. While father lived, he kept it in check. They think that I want to rule over them and by right of birth, they feel that they should rule." He turned his troubled eyes toward her.

"We all know that whatever you have said to them is for their own welfare. You would never rob them of their freedom. You have had far more patience with them than anyone else would have had. It is the evil in them that makes them reject you."

The gentle warmth of her voice comforted him and gave him a sense of peace that he hadn't known since his father's death. He took her tenderly in his arms and kissed her.

"Thank you, my dear," he said. "I must confess that I have not been entirely blameless."

"What do you mean?" she questioned him.

"I have not always been as patient as you may think. That is what troubles me. Since Father died, my anger at them has grown day by day. I know it is displeasing in the sight of God. It's a weakness I must overcome. Father begged me to be patient with them, knowing that through patience and constant teaching, they may yet mend their wicked ways. Father's dying hope was that they would repent and be saved. Otherwise, God would cut them off from His presence and curse them in some way that would affect them the rest of their lives. I have failed to reach them—perhaps because of the anger in my heart."

"God has been angry with them, too," she said so quietly he could scarcely hear. "You must try again when your heart is free from anger."

"There is something else I haven't told you," he said. "They are plotting to kill me. I have been expecting it any day. I see it in their eyes and hear it in their voices. They may plan a surprise attack if they can get enough followers to be sure of overcoming us. They already see themselves as rulers. Woe unto this people if they come into power, for they will enslave us all."

"God will never forsake us." Conviction sounded clearly in her voice. "Think of the times, Nephi, when He saved you from your enemies. Once He loosed the cords that bound you, and once He stilled the angry waves that were about to swallow us all up; there have been other times as well. No, Nephi, He will not desert us now—not as long as we are faithful to His teachings. Tomorrow, go into the mountains and pray for guidance. If we put our faith in the Lord, He will protect us no matter how great the danger that faces us."

Nephi looked at his wife tenderly. How wise she was, and how great her faith in God! Immediately, he felt that he could face the future with courage and a knowledge of the victory of good over evil.

CHAPTER 20

In the still darkness of the night, Nephi walked noiselessly through the village streets. It was the hour before midnight. It was a beautiful night— not a cloud in the sky, and a million stars twinkled as Nephi lifted his eyes to the heavens. It was a night of nights—a night of high adventure and one they would remember all the days of their lives. Although everyone appeared to be fast asleep, yet the air he breathed seemed to be charged with excitement and mystery. At midnight the moon would rise. Already the eastern sky was growing light above the lofty mountain peaks. He knew, as he passed each tent door, someone watched and waited within.

A few days before, God had warned Nephi that he should flee into the wilderness and take all those who would go with him. Quietly, he went among his people, talking to them and telling them of God's will. Nephi knew how attached they were to their homes. Here they had lived in peace and happiness. Many of them remembered the suffering they had endured while they wandered in the wilderness, and now to be asked to go forth into the unknown was a great sacrifice. Nephi knew these things, and expected that some of them would decide to stay and take their chances with Laman and Lemuel and the sons of Ishmael. How great was his surprise when, without a single word of protest, all those who had been faithful to God wanted to follow him! With great caution, they began getting their things ready. Each one was to carry his own load. All their preparations had to be made secretly. Their very lives depended upon it. They would need to take their tents and what other things were possible, but the tents would have to be the last things to be packed so as not to arouse the suspicion of their enemies.

This was the night they had chosen, and God had made it perfect in every respect. They were to slip away just as the moon came up: within the safety of their tents were Nephi's family, Zoram and his family, Sam and his family, and Nephi's sisters, waiting for the signal. Jacob and Joseph were going, too, but at this very moment, they were keeping watch beside the tents of their enemies. Shortly, they would meet Nephi at an appointed spot to report to him.

Nephi thought of his father as he walked along through the darkness. It seemed to him that Lehi was very close tonight. He remembered that night, so long ago in Jerusalem, when they had fled from their home. He had been little more than a boy then, and the excitement of the adventure had appealed to him, but now he knew how his father must have felt. How great was the responsibility of taking so many from their homes into the unknown wilderness.

He thought of his wife. How dear she was! When he told her of the Lord's warning, she had agreed to go willingly—almost eagerly. But he knew it took a great deal of courage to leave the home that had brought so much happiness. Her hands betrayed her. She had a way of curling her fingers around her thumbs and gripping until the knuckles turned white. He had glanced at her hands and she had quickly hidden them behind her back, and he had said nothing. He thought of all the others and sighed heavily under the burden of his responsibilities. But then, quick as a flash, he remembered that they had not put their faith in a mere man; it was God's warning and His revelation that they were obeying. He knew that their faith in God equaled his own. This thought was comforting.

"Nephi!"

Nephi was startled by the sound of his name. Quickly his eyes searched the shadows of the night and he saw Joseph stepping onto the path.

"Come, we can't talk here," whispered Nephi.

The two men walked along in silence until they reached the great tree. It was the place their father had loved dearly. Nephi had expected to see Jacob waiting for them, but he was not there. It was growing lighter every minute. Nephi wondered if he had planned to leave too late. The moon would be up in less than an hour. He had thought that they could leave the village in the darkness and reach the mountains when the moon had risen to mark their way; he hadn't thought of its growing so light even before it had risen.

"What have you to report regarding Ishmael's sons and their families?" asked Nephi.

"They went to bed early and are sleeping soundly," answered Joseph.

"That's good." Nephi's voice was low and guarded. "I wonder what is keeping Jacob."

"I wish I knew," replied Joseph.

"Since there is no need for us both to wait here, I am going to ask you to do me a favor. I'd like to entrust my family into your keeping. Watch out for them until we have made our escape."

Suddenly, Joseph felt light-hearted—almost merry. All his life, he had respected and admired Nephi and had longed to look good in his eyes. And now, at last, to be entrusted with his family—it made him feel very proud. Nephi was waiting for Joseph's answer, so he said immediately, "I shall be more than glad to watch out for them and I can assure you, your trust in me will be justified."

Nephi smiled at his eager young brother and said, "Wait until you hear the signal before starting."

"What if trouble has befallen Jacob?" asked Joseph.

"Then there will be no signal. If anything has happened to Jacob, we'll just have to postpone the starting time. Go now, Joseph, and God be with you."

As Joseph disappeared into the darkness, Nephi thought again of his wife's fingers curled about her thumbs, with knuckles white. It seemed to keep coming back to him and left a little nagging worry. He was glad he had thought of sending Joseph to help them. He was such a fine young man: so eager to please. Nephi raised his eyes to the towering mountains. They looked impassable from this distance. He thought of the mysteries that lay beyond them. From this point, they seemed to rise straight up—so steep as to be insurmountable. But he knew from experience that once you started to climb, they seemed to flatten out and it was possible to climb them quite easily. Most problems were like mountains. Once you started working on them, they didn't seem as difficult to solve as when viewed from a distance.

What was that? Something was moving in the nearby bushes. It wouldn't be Jacob. Instantly his hand went to his hunting knife, while his eyes tried to pierce the darkness. Then suddenly he almost laughed aloud, as a tiny black creature came dashing toward him. He discovered it was just a cat.

Five—ten—twenty minutes went by and still Jacob didn't come. Nephi began to grow uneasy. Was Jacob in danger? Had he fallen into the hands of his wicked brothers? He thought of all sorts of things. Why had he sent Jacob? Why hadn't he gone himself? As the minutes sped by, his regrets grew. He was so lost in his thoughts that he failed to see the man who slipped from shadow to shadow until he was within a few feet of him. As soon as he saw who it was, he spoke to him.

"Jacob?"

"Yes."

"Are you all right?"

"Yes."

"I've been worried about you. What happened?" asked Nephi.

"When I arrived at Laman's tent, I found Laman and Lemuel sitting outside. They have been talking until just a few minutes ago."

"Strange they should have stayed up so late. Do you know what they were talking about?" asked Nephi anxiously.

"I couldn't get close enough to hear very much of what was said, but I did hear them say your name several times. It was some devilish plot, with you as their victim. It pleased them very much, for several times their evil laughter rang out. Oh, yes, they kept mentioning something about slaves," said Jacob.

"How wicked they are! But I am determined to carry out God's commandments with as little anger as possible," Nephi said earnestly.

"I think they are asleep now. I stayed for a few minutes after they had gone inside. Shall we give the signal?"

"I will give the signal, Jacob. I want you to go to the tent of our sisters. Help them and guard them against danger. You are to lead the group. I am taking Laban's sword, the brass plates, and the compass God gave our father, Lehi. Don't worry about me. I plan to stay until you have all gone. I don't want anyone left behind. Go now, Jacob, and ask God's guidance, for without His help, we shall all perish." As Nephi spoke, he laid his hand affectionately on Jacob's arm.

When Jacob had disappeared down the village street, Nephi humbled himself before God and knelt down and asked for continued guidance and protection. When he had finished praying, he stood erect and gave the signal. Suddenly, as if by magic, the tents came down, and in less than half an hour all his people were fleeing from the village. The moon had risen, flooding everything with a white light.

Nephi walked back through the deserted part of the village, looking carefully about him. When he had made sure that no one had been left behind, he turned his face toward the tents of Ishmael's sons and those of Laman and Lemuel. There was no anger in his heart now—just regret, terrible regret that caught in his throat. Why, oh why, did it have to be? He remembered the great love he had felt for his elder brothers as a boy, but all they had ever given him in return was hatred and great suffering. If only they had kept the commandments of the Lord, there would be no need for parting. Perhaps he would never see them again. He felt as though his heart were breaking and, out of the goodness of his soul, he prayed:

"Oh, God in heaven, be merciful to these, my brothers."

With the prayer still on his lips and love in his heart, he turned away and followed the others into the unknown.

They traveled for the space of many days, until at last they pitched their tents and planted seeds. They called the place Nephi and they called themselves the people of Nephi. The Lord blessed them and made them prosper.

CHAPTER 21

When the sun came up next morning, it looked down on a very strange sight. Fully two-thirds of the village had disappeared. The marks where the tents had been and a number of household articles too heavy to move were all that remained to tell that anyone had lived there. The other third of the village lay fast asleep. All the animals were fast asleep, too, and even the birds in the trees were sleeping. This was most unusual, because they had been in the habit of rising early. At daybreak each morning, Nephi would blow a horn to awaken them. Then they would prepare their breakfast and, as soon as that was over, they would hurry off to the fields to work. Normally, even before the sound of the horn the birds began to chatter and sing. This morning there had been no horn, and every living creature slept a deep, heavy sleep. The sun rose higher and higher. The morning passed and noon came, but still they slept on.

At last Laman awoke. He had slept so heavily that his head was aching. He lifted his hand and drew it across his forehead. It came back dripping wet with sweat. The tent was very hot; that seemed strange to him because other mornings when he awakened it was cool—sometimes even cold. Never had the tent been hot like this. Then he remembered there had been no sound of Nephi's horn. It was strangely silent. Could it be that everyone had gone to work in the field? He drew himself to a sitting position and slowly began dressing. This was the day he and Lemuel would rid themselves of Nephi and take their place as rulers of their people.

When he was dressed, he stepped outside. The first thing he noticed was the sleeping birds; next he saw the animals all asleep, too. Quickly, he lifted his face to the sun and discovered that it was midday. Someone had played a trick on him. He ran toward Lemuel's tent, calling to him as he went.

"Lemuel! Lemuel, get up!" He beat his fists on Lemuel's tent door as he kept calling.

In a few minutes Lemuel came out, stretching and red-faced.

"What's up, brother?"

"Have you any idea of the time of day?" asked Laman, grimly.

Lemuel looked up, still half-dazed by heavy sleep. When he saw the position of the sun, he was so astonished that his mouth dropped open.

"You can shut your mouth now, brother," suggested Laman rudely.

"What is this, some trick?" demanded Lemuel.

"Trick? I never thought of it, but that's exactly what it is."

"Laman! Laman!"

The two men turned to see Laman's wife running toward them, carrying a pitcher of water that splashed as she ran and went dripping down her dress.

"Well, woman, what do you want? Can't you see we're busy?" Laman spoke angrily. He didn't like to be disturbed at the very moment when he was getting an answer to the problem.

"Something strange has happened!" she said, setting the pitcher of water on the ground.

"We know that," replied Laman in disgust.

"You do? How could you possibly know?"

"Because, wife, we have eyes in our heads just as you have." Laman spoke sharply.

Now, Lemuel liked his brother's wife, and when he saw how frightened she was at the sight of Laman's anger, he spoke softly to her:

"Laman just awakened me to tell me that the sun stands at midday. I think it is some sort of trick."

"Oh, that isn't what I had to tell you. You don't know after all," she said happily, thinking to impress Laman.

"Whatever it is, tell us and be gone," said Laman.

"When I reached the spring a little while ago, I thought I was dreaming. They have all gone," she said excitedly.

"Gone? Who has gone?" demanded Laman, disgusted at the way his wife told a story. She never could tell a thing straight out. She always had to go the long way around.

"Even their tents are gone!" She was so excited she paid no attention to her husband's rising anger.

Laman reached out, took her by the shoulders, and shook her roughly.

"Laman, you're hurting my shoulders," she said.

"I'll let you go when you tell me what you mean," Laman shouted.

"Nephi and all his people have taken their tents and disappeared," she told him.

Laman turned about quickly and ran through the open space between the tents. When he reached the bushes that screened their tents from the other part of the village, he fought his way through them angrily. As soon as he reached Nephi's street he saw, at once, that what his wife had told him was only too true. He stood speechless with rage; when at last he found his voice he began shouting curses and talking wildly, like a madman. His anger was so frightening that all the women and children went back to their own tents for safety.

"Dogs! The sneaking dogs!" he yelled. "I'll kill every one of them for this. Where are Ishmael's sons?"

"Here we are; what do you want with us?" they answered quickly, hoping all the time not to displease him, for they were really afraid of his terrible anger.

"I want you to find where they have gone. There are sure to be fresh tracks," said Laman.

Evil plans started to race through his mind. He comforted himself by thinking of all the things he would do to them when he found them. Lemuel reminded him that Nephi and his people outnumbered them two to one, but Laman wouldn't listen.

"I wouldn't care if there were ten to one; I have a few fancy tricks of my own. I'll—" Laman stopped and his eyes went wide as he stared at his brother.

"Why do you stare at me, brother?"

"Your face has changed color and your hands, too."

Lemuel looked at his hands and out of the agony of his soul, he cried out: "It's the curse! Father and Nephi both told us that someday God would be so angry with us that he would cut us off from His presence and curse us in some terrible way. Woe unto us!" He threw himself on the ground and moaned in agony.

For a few minutes, Laman stood stunned by what he saw and heard. Then, slowly, he lifted his own hands and found them dark—yes, even darker than Lemuel's. He, who had such white, delightsome skin, was now cursed. Suddenly, he ran to the spring and dropped to his knees. When he beheld his face mirrored in the water, he groaned aloud. Covering his face with his hands, he gave way to grief and remorse.

Laman, Lemuel, and the sons of Ishmael and all their families were cursed with dark skins. Lehi had foreseen this tragic event, but on his deathbed he had made a promise to the children of Laman, Lemuel, and the sons of Ishmael. He had told them God would be merciful to them and they would not be destroyed if they would listen to the word of God and keep His commandments. After a while they remembered their grandfather's words and found comfort in them.

CHAPTER 22

N ephi and all his people were faithful to the commandments of the Lord, according to the law of
Moses. The Lord God was pleased with them and blessed
them with abundance. They sowed seeds and reaped a
rich harvest. They began to have flocks and herds of many
different animals. In every way, they prospered and
multiplied in the land.

Nephi taught them to be industrious and to work
with their hands. He taught them to build buildings and
to work in all kinds of wood and iron, copper, brass,
steel, silver, gold, and precious ores, which were in great
abundance.

He built a temple and constructed it like the temple
of Solomon, except that it was not built of so many precious things. The construction of the temple was very
fine.

The people were happy, and because of their happiness, they asked Nephi to be their king. But Nephi said
there should be no king, however, he did everything in
his power for them.

Nephi took the sword of Laban and began to make
many like it. One day, while he was busy at work, his wife
came to him.

"What are you making?" she asked him.

"I am making swords after the pattern of Laban's."

"But why do you make them?"

"So that every able-bodied man and boy will have one."

"But surely we have no need for swords in this land of peace and happiness," she said.

"Have you forgotten the Lamanites?" he asked her.

"They could not harm us. They don't know were we are."

"I'm afraid they do—at least, we can't be sure, and in case they do come to destroy us, we will be prepared. I know their hatred toward me and my children and those who are called my people. Some time ago, I sent Jacob and Joseph on a scouting trip to see if the Lamanites were making plans to come upon us, and also to determine if they were in want. Even though they are my enemies, I don't want them to suffer while we live in happiness and have plenty to share with them."

"You are a good man, Nephi," she said. "Did Jacob and Joseph find the Lamanites?"

"Yes."

"If you would rather not tell me about it, I'll understand."

"No, I want to tell you, but I just kept putting it off, hoping to spare you," he said.

"Then it is bad news?" she asked. "Are they suffering?"

"Yes, it is bad news, but they are not suffering for want of food. They have become a lazy, sly people, preying upon the wild beasts of the wilderness. They are making plans to come against us in battle, and the swords I make are for our protection."

"Oh, of course. There is no other way."

Her words were brave enough, but Nephi knew

without seeing, that her fingers were curled tightly about her thumbs. He reached out and put his arm around her thin shoulders.

"Don't be frightened, my dear. There is something else I must tell you. You remember how often God warned Laman and Lemuel to give up their evil ways or He would become angry and cut them off from His presence and curse them. They would not listen and their hearts became hard as flint. Well, God has cut them off from His presence and cursed them with a dark skin."

"Oh, how terrible." Tears filled her eyes as she spoke. "They were so proud of their fair white skin. My heart aches for them."

"You must remember, dear," he said, "that God was very patient with them and long-suffering. He gave them every opportunity to repent, but they wouldn't. They have only themselves to blame."

Thirty years had passed away since the time they had left Jerusalem. The Nephites had been faithful to the commandments of God and He had blessed them with great happiness. Now, Nephi had faithfully recorded the history of his people on the plates of ore which he made, but the Lord said to him, "Make other plates and engrave many things upon them, which are good in my sight, for the profit of your people."

Nephi was obedient to the commandments of the Lord and went and made the plates.

As the years passed, the Lamanites' hatred for the Nephites grew and deepened until it became a fearful thing to see. Their dark skin was a constant reminder to them, not of their unfaithfulness to God, but of their betrayal by their brother Nephi. As time went by, they blamed themselves less and less and Nephi more and more. Their hatred for all the Nephites made them unhappy and discontented. Their laziness increased until almost all they did was fish and hunt. Nephi regarded them as dangerous enemies to be pitied rather than hated, and he would have been glad to help them if they would only soften their hearts toward God. Forty years passed and, already, there had been wars between them. The swords Nephi had made helped them to gain victory over the Lamanites.

One afternoon, in late springtime, Jacob stopped for a moment to catch his breath. He was climbing to where the weeping willow tree grew high on the foothills of the great mountain range. He raised his eyes to the mountaintops. It was an inspiring sight. The dazzling white of the snowcapped peaks rose up and up until they were lost from view in the heavens beyond. He planned some day, to climb the highest peak and see how his precious land of promise looked from that great height.

When at last he reached the willow tree, he turned about, facing east, and sat down beside it. A swarm of wild bees were busily humming as they gathered honey from the many colored flowers that raised their heads above the tall, waving grass. They paid no attention to him whatsoever. Their humming made such a soothing sound to his ears that he felt as if he could easily fall asleep.

Suddenly, his attention was drawn to a pair of angry swallows that began cutting swift circles about his head. Once, they came so close they touched his cheek. He guessed that they were building a nest nearby and were alarmed that he would bring danger to their new little home. He knew that if he sat very still, they would soon get used to his presence and stop darting at him. Perhaps they were building their nest in the shallow cave back of the willow tree. He hoped not, for he had made the long climb for the purpose of bathing in the warm mineral spring just inside the cave. The warm, sea-green water came bubbling up and was held in a deep basin of rocks.

It was crystal clear and just pleasantly warm. He could hear it now as it spilled over and trickled down the mountain slope, where it had cut a deep gulley. When it reached the valley below, it disappeared from sight.

Jacob looked out across the valley to another giant mountain range, which formed its eastern border. The mountains ran north and south, parallel to the western range, leaving a broad valley between. From where he sat, he could see one of the many foaming waterfalls as it rushed down the mountain slopes to the lush, green valley below. At this time of year the valley floor, where the crops were grown, and the foothills, where grew the pasture grasses, all wore a carpet of rich green. There were dozens of different shades of green, blended so skillfully together that even an artist would find difficulty in telling where one shade ended and another began.

The willow tree beside which Jacob sat was in the southern part of the valley. Far to the north was a beautiful little cold-water lake. Jacob knew that on the foothills herds of horses and cattle were grazing. However, the distance was too great for him to see the lake or the grazing herds. In the center of the valley stood the village—a village no longer of tents, but of sturdy houses built of wood, stone, and precious metals. On a small hill overlooking the village stood the temple Nephi had built, patterned after the Temple of Solomon. In the southern part of the valley, a number of flocks of sheep were tended by shepherd boys. They had named their new home Nephi. This was part of the precious land of promise. One had only to see this valley to know how rich was their inheritance. Jacob's heart was full of thanksgiving to God for blessing them so abundantly.

Jacob lay back on the grass and closed his eyes. He could hear the faint tinkling of the sheep bells. It was a pleasant and peaceful sound. The people of Nephi were a happy people and Jacob intended to do all in his power to help them keep their happiness.

His thoughts turned to a day, not so long ago, when Nephi had called Joseph and him to his house and ordained them priests and teachers over the people of the land. Since that day, Jacob had gone among the people advising them in the ways of the Lord and urging them to keep His commandments faithfully. Furthermore, he read to them from the brass plates—especially Isaiah's prophecies, because he spoke of all the house of Israel and Nephi's people were of the house of Israel.

Jacob loved his people, and he taught them the words of his father and spoke to them of all things that were written, from the creation of the world. He told them of the great prophecies regarding the birth of Christ, son of the living God, who would come to earth and be rejected, crucified, and resurrected.

Jacob remembered he had said to his people, "How great is God's goodness and mercy to us. He loves the world so much that He plans to give His only Son, and because of His death and resurrection we will know everlasting life. When we die, we'll be called to the judgment seat of God, and in that moment we will remember all the good and the evil deeds we have done. God will know them, too, and will judge us accordingly. On resurrection morning, if we have been faithful, we will come forth out of our graves. Our bodies will be made whole and will be united with our spirits. Those who have been unfaithful to God's commandments and do not repent will be deprived of everlasting life. And now my beloved brethren, out of the anxiety of my heart, I give you these words of warning: Woe to the learned that think they are wise, and will not listen to the counsel of God, for they shall perish. Learning is good if coupled with the counsel of God. Woe to the rich who are only rich in the things of this world. For behold, their wealth shall die with them.

Woe to the deaf that will not hear, for they shall perish. Woe to the blind that will not see, for they shall perish, also."

Suddenly, Jacob's train of thought was broken by the sound of someone climbing up the mountain. He raised himself quickly on one elbow and looked down the slope. He saw that it was a shepherd boy, carrying a lamb and talking to it as he climbed. It was his brother Sam's boy.

"Hello, lad," called Jacob.

The shepherd boy was so startled that he came very close to dropping the lamb.

"Oh, hello, Uncle Jacob. I didn't see you there. How are you, sir?"

"Fine, thank you," said Jacob. "And how are you this nice spring day?"

"My health is good," said the shepherd boy, "but this little lamb has a bad leg and, if you will look into his eyes, you can tell how it pains him. He is so patient in his suffering."

"A little lamb can teach us a great lesson in how to accept the misfortunes that come to us. Just see with what gentle dignity he bears his pain. Where are you taking him, Nephew?"

"I'm carrying him to the spring to bathe his wound in mineral water. They say it's very healing," answered the shepherd boy.

Here was a boy that a man could be proud to call his son. Jacob knew that his nephew had a good example to follow in his father, for Sam was ever faithful to the commandments of God and he trained his boys to love Him and all His creatures.

"I think you're right about the mineral spring healing the lamb. I will help you. We will build a tiny pool so the little lamb won't be frightened," said Jacob.

And they did.

Chapter 23

There was a gentle knock at Nephi's door. Without lifting his eyes from the record he was engraving, he called, "Come in."

His wife came in and closed the door softly. She watched Nephi anxiously.

"Do you know how late it is?" she asked.

"Mhm," he answered, and kept right on with his work.

"It's midnight and you started working at sundown. There isn't any great hurry, is there?"

"Perhaps not, but—" his voice trailed off without finishing the sentence.

Suddenly, she discovered that her beloved husband was growing old. There had been a great change in him during the last months and now, even in soft candlelight, she could see new lines about his eyes, and his forehead, too, was more deeply furrowed. Her thoughts drew her to him and she went and stood behind his chair, looking over his shoulder at the work he was doing. She was not an expert; as a matter of fact, she knew very little about engraving, yet she knew that the work he was doing was skillfully done. Her interest was drawn to his hands. They were the hands of an artist. Yet, in spite of their artistic molding, they possessed great strength—almost super-human strength. He could do so many things with his hands.

She leaned over and pressed her lips to the nape of his neck, saying, "Please go to bed now. You know this light is bad for your eyes."

"Thank you, my dear." He reached up and patted the hand that rested on his shoulder.

"Why do you thank me, my husband?"

"For your concern over my welfare. You are always looking out for me. I don't know what I would do without you."

A rosy warmth spread over her face and she smiled happily.

"What have you been writing?" she asked.

"I have just finished the words of Jacob to my people and what he read to them from the brass plates. It is not all he said or read to them, but it is enough. When I am gone, Jacob will keep the records; then, perhaps, he will write more concerning his teachings."

"I hope that won't be for many years to come. What will you record next?" she asked him.

"I shall write more of Isaiah's words, for his teaching brings great joy to my soul. I shall write the things that can be likened to my people. You know, my dear, he has seen our Redeemer, even as I have seen him and as Jacob has seen him, also." Nephi smiled as he mentioned Christ, for it brought him great happiness just to think of His coming.

"Isn't it recorded somewhere that God will prove his words by three witnesses?" she asked.

"Yes, indeed it is. Not only we three can bear witness to the coming of the Christ, but many others as well. I am delighted in proving to my people that only through the coming of Christ can all men be saved. For, if there is no

Christ, there is no God, and if there is no God, we do not exist and there was no creation. But there is a God, and He is Christ, and He will come in the fullness of His own time." Nephi spoke earnestly.

Nephi went among the people, teaching them his prophecies and those of his father and Jacob. Furthermore, he read to them Isaiah's prophecies, as recorded on the brass plates. Now, the people loved Nephi and enjoyed learning about God through him. When Nephi saw how prosperous they were, he rejoiced at their good fortune, but, at the same time, he was disturbed for fear they would begin to love their riches more than God. He went about warning them to be humble and to remember the source of their blessings.

One day, he told them a great and marvelous thing. He told them that long after the birth of Christ, God would bring forth another great prophet in the latter days, and that he would be called Joseph.

"And in that day," he predicted, "the Lord God will bring forth a book and the book will be sealed. In the book will be a revelation from God, from the beginning of time to the end of the world. This great book will be delivered to a man and it shall be hidden from the eyes of the world and no one shall see it except three witnesses, besides the one to whom the book shall be delivered. They shall testify to the truth of the book and also to the things that are written in it. And the man who receives the book shall be unlearned and shall say, 'I am not learned.' Then the Lord God shall say to him: 'The learned shall not read the plates, for they have rejected them. I am able to do my own work; therefore, you shall read the words which I will give you. Do not touch the things that are sealed, for I will reveal them at some future time. Therefore, when you have read the words which I have commanded you and obtained the witnesses, then you shall seal up the book again and hide it for me, until I see it is wisdom to reveal all things to the children of men.'

"In the last days," Nephi continued, "when the book has been brought forth, many Gentiles will say: 'A Bible! A Bible! We already have a Bible and there can be but one.' And then God will say to them: 'Oh, you fools, don't you know that there are more nations than one? Don't you know that I, the Lord your God, have created all men, and that I remember those who are upon the isles of the sea, and that I rule in the heavens above and in the earth beneath, and that I bring forth my word to the children of men, yes, even to all the nations of the earth? For behold, I speak to the Jews and they shall write it; and I shall also speak to the Nephites and they shall write it; and I shall also speak to the other tribes of Israel, which I have led away, and they shall write it; and I shall speak to all the nations of the earth and they shall write it.'

"And now I, Nephi, wish to prophesy more about the Jews and the Gentiles. After the book comes forth in the latter days and shall be written to the Gentiles, it will be sealed up to the Lord. In that day, many will believe the words which are written. They will carry the words to the last of our descendants, the Lamanites. In that day, the last of our descendants will know how we came out of Jerusalem, and that they are the descendants of the Jews. The gospel of Jesus Christ shall be brought to them and they will know in that day, that after Christ had been resurrected, he appeared to their forefathers upon this, the promised land. They will rejoice, knowing that it is a blessing to them from the hand of God. Then their scales of darkness shall begin to fall from their eyes; and after that, not so many generations will pass away until they shall be a pure and delightsome people again."

CHAPTER 24

Nephi stepped out into the warm summer sunshine and closed the temple door behind him. He stood still a few minutes and looked down upon the city of Nephi. It was a beautiful city, and in it lived his people. How prosperous they were! With this thought came a feeling of uneasiness, for of late, it seemed to him that many of the Nephites were growing more and more fond of worldly riches and cared less and less about the things of the Spirit. It seemed to him that the richer they became, the less happy they were. Only a short time before this day, the temple would be crowded with worshipers; now there were not more than a dozen who had taken time to honor God.

Suddenly, he reached back and grasped hold of the door latch to steady himself. At that moment, in spite of the warmth of the sun, a chill raced through his body and shook him so that he had to cling to the door latch to keep from falling. It passed in a few seconds, but it seemed to him that the icy hand of death had reached out and touched him. He knew it was God's way of warning him that his days on earth would be but few.

Nephi walked slowly to the stairway that led to the temple and seated himself on the top step.

He must think of himself. His was an unselfish nature, and this, combined with the fact that he had always had excellent health, made thinking of himself a pastime he had seldom indulged in. Now, however, he found it impossible not to think of himself, because a terrifying weakness had settled upon him, like a heavy cloak whose weight was almost too heavy to bear. He looked at his hands and saw that they trembled violently. He clasped them tightly together, but still they shook. Never before had he known such a feeling of helpless insecurity. He buried his head in his hands and cried out in his agony, asking God to make him whole again. God heard his prayer and took away the cloak of weakness and the tremor from his hands. He praised God for His goodness and mercy.

"Good morning, Nephi."

It was Sam coming up the steps. Nephi greeted him warmly. A flood of memories raced through him. He and Sam had always been very close to each other. No matter what Nephi did or said, he always knew he could depend on Sam to back him up. What a good man he was—loyal, faithful, true to any trust, and completely unselfish. Nephi knew few men who could sincerely rejoice in the good fortunes of others, but Sam was such a man. He was always on hand to cheer Nephi in time of trouble or to rejoice with him in his happiness. Nephi remembered too, that he had never known him to ask for reward. Now, as he watched him coming up the steps, he thought that in spite of Sam's snow-white hair, the quick, easy way he moved made one think of a far younger man than he actually was.

"Are you ill?" For the first time, Sam realized that Nephi was old. There was a grayness about his face that sent a pang to his heart.

"What made you ask that?" questioned Nephi.

"You look pale, brother."

"Well, Sam, God has just sent me a warning that my days are numbered," he answered sadly.

Sam stood speechless, shocked at his brother's words. Now that he looked closely at Nephi, he could see that he was ill. He couldn't bear to think of life without Nephi.

Nephi waited for Sam to speak, but when he was silent, Nephi spoke again: "Don't grieve over me, for I am about to have a new adventure which will be far greater than I have ever had in life. I have often thought of the hereafter and, at those times, a feeling of peace and unspeakable joy has settled upon me, because I know that God is the same yesterday, today, and forever. When I come before His judgment seat, he will see my life unfold before Him and I shall be judged by my deeds."

There were tears in Sam's eyes as he spoke. "Your passing will be a great loss to us all. Our people love you as much as they did Father. You have been the means of sparing their lives time after time. Through you, they have found a God of mercy and a God of love. You have taught them how to keep the commandments of the Lord and, through righteous living, they have found true happiness and great prosperity. You ask me not to grieve. I, who have walked side by side with you all through the years and shared with you joy and sorrow, can no more stop grieving than you can stop the sun from shining."

"I praise God for giving me a brother like you. Grieve if you must, but remember, with your grieving, that we two will meet soon in the spirit world," said Nephi.

"I do not doubt your word, my brother, because I know God reveals many things to you," replied Sam.

"Yes, that's true," said Nephi, "and not so long ago, God revealed a wonderful thing to me. I saw Jesus being baptized with water, and after he was baptized, I saw the Holy Ghost in the form of a dove come and sit upon his shoulder."

"But he is the Holy One. He has no sins, for He is the Son of God," said Sam.

"Yes, but even the Son of God must enter the kingdom of heaven by the right gate. Christ will humble Himself before the Father and be baptized and receive the Holy Ghost. God in His great mercy has revealed these things to me, in order that my people might find eternal life."

"Often, my brother, have I heard you say 'repent and be baptized'; I have never known the true meaning of it until now." Sam spoke earnestly.

"Once you have entered in at the gate, you must walk the straight and narrow path in order to gain eternal life," said Nephi.

"How do you follow the straight and narrow path?" asked Sam.

"By keeping the commandments of God," said Nephi. "I am very happy that you have lived such a good life, for you will surely find eternal salvation."

For a long time the two men sat silent, looking out over the city, but neither of them saw it, for they were busy with their memories. At last, Sam spoke:

"It's fifty-five years since we fled from Jerusalem. Do you remember our life there?"

"Strange that you should speak of Jerusalem," Nephi said. "I was just thinking of it, too. What a happy childhood we had."

"The reason our home was so happy was because Father and Mother loved and respected each other and we felt secure in their love," Sam said.

"They set us a good example," said Nephi thoughtfully. "I was thinking, too, of our elder brothers, Laman and Lemuel. How far we have drifted apart! As a boy, I loved them very much. As a matter of fact, I still do. There isn't a day goes by that I do not pray for them, and in my prayers I plead with God to be merciful to them."

"Have you forgiven them for all the pain and suffering they caused you?" asked Sam in amazement.

"Yes, my brother," said Nephi.

"It's moments like these that make me realize what a great and good man you are."

The two men looked at each other affectionately.

"I shall miss this precious land of promise. It would be difficult to imagine a more beautiful place. Here we have known peace and happiness. Our children and their children's children can go right on, generation after generation, living here in peace and contentment if they will but remember one thing. God will save this land for them if they will only keep His commandments. It's so little to ask for so great a gift. When I am gone, Sam, you and Joseph and Jacob must remind them constantly to be faithful to God."

For the next few days, Nephi stayed at home, working all day long and far into the night, engraving the records upon the plates. At last, one morning, he made an end to his writings and sent for Jacob. When he came, he was shocked at the great change that had taken place in Nephi and he knew instantly that Sam had been right when he had told him that Nephi was a dying man.

"You are ill, Nephi. Wouldn't it be better if I came back some other time, when you have rested?"

"No, Jacob. My time is very short and I have much to say to you, for you are to follow me in being a teacher and a prophet to my people. Furthermore, you will keep these small plates."

"The small plates are the ones you made last, aren't they?" asked Jacob.

"Yes, that is correct. Consider well the things you write. Choose just the most precious things and only touch lightly the history of this people. The history of my people is to be engraven upon my other plates. Take care of these plates, for they are to be handed down from generation to generation."

"Tell me, brother, am I to record just the prophecies?" asked Jacob, in a troubled voice. He wanted to do the work in a pleasing manner, but he was not sure he understood what was required.

Nephi smiled at his brother and hastened to reassure him, feeling happy that he had chosen Jacob. He was a man you could depend on.

"If there is preaching that is sacred, or revelation that is great, or prophecy, record it on these plates, and touch upon it as much as possible, for Christ's sake, and for the sake of our people."

"You may rest assured that I shall fulfill the commandments you have given me," said Jacob.

When Nephi had finished his instructions to Jacob, he lay back on his couch and felt at peace with himself. Now his work was nearly finished. When he had rested, he anointed a man to be king and ruler over his people, according to the reigns of the kings.

Now, the people loved Nephi very much and they remembered what a great leader he had been, protecting them in every way possible, even to using the sword of Laban in their defense. They remembered how, all through his life, he had labored for their welfare. Therefore, the people were anxious to remember his name, and for that reason they called the new king second Nephi, and all the kings thereafter were named third Nephi, fourth Nephi, and so on, according to their reign, no matter what their real name was.

A few days later Nephi died, happy in the knowledge

that he had left his people in good hands. He knew, too, that many years after the coming of Christ, his voice would rise from the dust by means of a latter-day prophet who would bring forth his plates.

CHAPTER 25

Jacob's wife sat sewing by the open doorway. The light was better there than any place in the room. A few years ago, it hadn't bothered her to sew in a shaded room. But now, time had so dimmed her sight that, in spite of the good light, she had to rest her eyes every few minutes. She put her sewing down, leaned her head against the back of her chair, and looked about her. It was a large room, made beautiful by her skillful hands. Every place she looked, she saw her needlework. It adorned the furniture, the walls, and the floor. Her mother-in-law, Sariah, had taught her to use her hands skillfully. The very thought of Sariah made her happy because the memories of the older woman were so pleasant. She had taught her many things. But perhaps the most important was the art of gracious living. Through Sariah, she had come to know Jacob and to love him.

At the far side of the room sat a young man at the table, poring over the brass plates that Nephi had brought to the new land from Jerusalem. She observed his broad shoulders and fine head and thought how handsome he was. A gentle smile touched her lips and eyes as she looked at her son, Enos, and remembered that once she had said to Jacob: "Enos, our son, is a very handsome man."

Jacob had smiled at her and said, "No, my dear, he is not handsome. As a matter of fact, he is very plain; but he is a good man. Sometimes, when he is reading from the brass plates, I think he has the face of an angel."

Jacob's wife had said no more, but still, in her secret heart, she considered her son handsome. She knew, too, that many girls and women were attracted by his good looks. He was a good man. Never, in all his life, had he given them a moment's worry. As a small boy, he knew he would be chosen to take his father's place, and this knowledge made him serious and thoughtful. He was determined to be worthy of the calling by making thorough preparations. He searched the records to find guidance for the problems that daily confronted the people.

At that moment, the sound of voices drifted into the room. Enos arose immediately and walked to the door.

"Mother, will you please excuse me?" he asked politely. "I see Father and Uncle Joseph talking at the garden gate. I have something I want to ask my uncle."

"Very well, my son, but invite your uncle to share our noonday meal."

She arose and went to stand in the doorway, looking after her son as he hurried down the path to where the two men stood talking. When he reached them, Jacob turned and started toward the house. He seemed tired and more than a little discouraged. She knew he was deeply troubled over his people, for under the rule of the new king, Nephi the second, many of the people had hardened their hearts and grown proud of their worldly riches. He felt so deeply his personal responsibilities for the welfare of their souls that he worked night and day in their behalf. He and Joseph had been out since dawn, going among the people and teaching them the word of God.

Jacob was so lost in thought that he hadn't noticed his wife standing in the doorway. If only she could help him in some way. Now he had stopped and bent down to look at a small flower. She knew, without seeing it, that it was a field lily. The week before, he had brought it home with him and planted it in the garden. It was so like him, to find joy and beauty in the simple things of life. To his wife, as she stood watching him, he seemed the wisest and greatest man she had ever known. He gave of his time and worldly possessions freely, never counting the cost. He spent hours each day listening to the woes of those who suffered, and never turned them away without giving them help or an encouraging word.

He stood up and, seeing his wife for the first time, replaced the troubled look with a warm smile of greeting.

"I told Enos to invite Joseph to dine with us," she said.

"He said to thank you for your kindness, but to tell you that he must return home before he joins me at the temple this afternoon. Oh, my wife, it grieves me to think of the things I must say to the people regarding their wickedness. I know my plain speech will offend the delicate ears of the women and children, but alas, the Lord has commanded me to speak plainly and I must obey Him."

"God will give you the right words to use, so do not worry, my husband. Can you tell me what troubles you so deeply?"

"Yes, I am free to talk about these things to you. Besides, it will help to put my thoughts into words. At least, we can talk until Enos comes. Come and sit beside me."

"You talk and I will listen, my husband."

"Many of our people seem to be forgetting the commandments of God in their search for riches. They spend most of their time hunting for gold and silver and other precious metals. They wear costly clothes and stiffen their necks and hold their heads high. They hate those less fortunate and feel themselves too good to even touch the poor. They have forgotten that God provided this beautiful land of promise for all of us. The poor, as well as the rich, are His children. I wonder if they think God justifies them in their greediness? But I know He does not. If they persist in these things, His judgments will surely come upon them. I have pleaded with my brethren to think of their neighbors as themselves and to be free with their wealth, so that all can enjoy the good things of life. Before we seek for riches, we must seek for the kingdom of God. And after we have obtained a hope in Christ, we shall obtain riches if we seek them. When we obtain them, it should be for the wish of doing good—to clothe the naked, to feed the hungry, to set free the captives, and to give relief to the sick. Oh, if they would only soften their proud hearts and know that all human beings are precious in his sight!"

Jacob stopped speaking and sat silent, his eyes clouded with his troubled thoughts.

"You are sad today, Jacob," she said. "Your sadness makes me unhappy."

"If this were all I had to speak to the people about, I would not be sad; but I must tell them of a greater crime. They try to excuse themselves because of the things which were written concerning David and his son Solomon. Now, David and Solomon had many wives, which was hateful in the sight of the Lord. God has commanded that man have but one wife, and the people must keep God's commandments or the land will be cursed. God knows that many of our brethren have taken more than one wife, and great is the sorrow and the mourning of their wives and children. These commandments were given to our father, Lehi. Therefore, they have known them before. They have done a greater wrong than the Lamanites, our brethren. They have broken the hearts of their tender wives and lost the confidence of their children. The sorrow of their hearts ascends up to God against them. It grieves my soul that I must use such bold speech concerning my brethren, before their wives and children. They will come up to the temple for consolation and all I can do is make their wounds greater."

When Jacob, Joseph, and their wives reached the temple, it was as Jacob said it would be, for many of the women and children had red, swollen eyes from long hours of weeping. When they saw Jacob and Joseph, they implored them to give them the good word—the word that would heal their troubled souls. The men were bold and declared that they were following the example of David and Solomon.

When Jacob began to speak, God inspired him with a mighty tongue and he denounced them for their pride and for their great sins. When he had finished speaking, they were humble.

CHAPTER 26

M any years passed away and Jacob and Joseph continued to go among the people, teaching and
prophesying. Enos was married now and had a family of
his own. However, he came to talk to Jacob and listen to
his advice almost every day. Jacob had returned home
early today and Enos found him resting in the garden.

"Good afternoon, Father," said Enos.

Jacob greeted his son and saw at once that, in spite of
his studied calm, there was great excitement in his
manner.

"You are disturbed, my son," Jacob said wisely. "What
is it that troubles you?"

"I met a man today, by the name of Sherem. Have
you heard of him, Father?"

"Now that you mention it, I have heard that name
spoken in hushed voices and whispered behind my back,
as though they were afraid of letting me hear what was
being said."

"And well they might, Father, for it is a name that
could bring us all disaster," said Enos gravely.

"You make me very curious. Has God sent us a new
prophet?"

"No, God has not sent anyone. It's more likely that

this man was sent by the devil." As Enos talked, his excitement grew, flooding his face with bright color.

"What manner of man is he?" asked Jacob.

"He is a handsome man, Father, with unusual intelligence. His language is perfect, filled with smooth flattery. Some refer to him as the man with the silver tongue. People are drawn to him, because he says the things that feed their vanity."

"But Enos, my son, beautiful language and a handsome face are not evil things, but quite the opposite."

"I know that, Father. I'm not making myself clear. You see, it's the wicked things he teaches. He says them so convincingly and puts them into such beautiful words that the people listen in spite of themselves. Some of them have begun to believe in his words." The very thought of the harm this man was bringing the Nephites made Enos's eyes blaze with righteous anger.

"As yet, you haven't told me what it is he says to the people," said Jacob, a bit impatiently.

"He denies the Christ, Father. He says there never has been a Christ and there never will be."

"Do you know that he says these things, or is it just talk in the marketplace?" asked Jacob, sternly.

"Not more than an hour ago, he stopped me as I was coming out of the temple and told me that I was quite wrong in believing in Christ."

"Good afternoon, brethren."

The sound of a third voice startled both Enos and Jacob. Jacob looked up to see a tall, handsome man smiling his greeting. He knew him at once. It was Sherem. Jacob studied him. He was well dressed and soft-spoken, just as Enos had said, but Jacob saw that his eyes were hard and cruel. He immediately said to himself that here was a man you could not trust. Before Jacob or Enos had time to answer his greeting, he spoke again:

"I see I have startled you. I beg of you to forgive me for coming into your garden uninvited. Such a beautiful garden is quite a temptation for any man—especially for one who loves temptation."

Jacob instantly disliked the stranger, as Enos had done. But in spite of his dislike, Jacob was a gentleman, and so now he hastened to make the stranger welcome.

"Good afternoon, Sherem. You are welcome to enjoy the garden with us."

"You know my name, I see. Perhaps your son has told you about our meeting near the temple. I have been trying to meet you, Jacob. I have asked a number of people where I might find you. However, your friends thought you should be spared the things I have to say to you." In spite of Sherem's friendly smile, his eyes betrayed his hatred for Jacob—a man he had never seen before. He seemed to know instinctively that Jacob would be his enemy.

Without waiting for Jacob to answer, he continued, "I have heard that you go among the people, preaching the doctrine of Christ. You have led away many of this people, and turned them away from the law of Moses, which is the right way. Instead of doing the will of God, they worship a being you say will come hundreds of years from now, and I, Sherem, declare that you lie. No man knows such things. You cannot tell about the future any more than I can."

Jacob stood like a man stricken, half believing that he was actually listening to the vile words Sherem spoke. In that moment he offered a silent prayer to God, asking Him to bless him with wisdom and power to reveal this man as a false teacher. Suddenly, a small hand clasped his large one, and he was surprised to see his grandson, Jarom, standing beside him and looking up with wide, frightened eyes. Jacob had been too deeply stirred by the stranger to notice his coming.

"I am right beside you, Grandfather, and I'll help you if you need me."

There was such trust and faith in the child's eyes that Jacob felt God had given him a powerful ally.

"God bless you, my grandson," he said, patting the child on the head. With blazing eyes he turned to Sherem, saying, "You dare deny the Christ who is to come?"

"If there should be a Christ, I would not deny Him; but I know there is no Christ and there never will be," said Sherem.

"Do you believe the scriptures?" asked Jacob.

"Yes," he replied.

"Then you do not understand them, for they truly testify of Christ. All the prophets tell of His coming, and furthermore, I have had a vision revealing His manner of coming."

Sherem laughed an evil laugh and said, "Show me a sign by the power of the Holy Ghost if you know so much."

Then Jacob said, "What am I, that I should tempt God to show you a sign about the thing that you know is true? Of course, you will deny it because you are of the devil. Nevertheless, not my will be done, but if God will smite you, let that be a sign unto you that He has power both in heaven and in earth—and also, that Christ shall come."

As soon as Jacob had finished speaking, the power of the Lord came upon Sherem and he fell to the earth. He was taken to his dwelling place and had to be cared for for many days.

When the people heard what had happened, they gathered around his house and were afraid that they, too, had displeased God.

One day, Sherem said to them, "Gather here tomorrow, for I shall die: and I have something to say to you."

The people went forth and told everyone in the land.

When the next day came, a great multitude gathered outside the house where Sherem lay dying. When he appeared to speak to them, a great stillness fell upon the crowd.

Sherem spoke plainly: "I have been deceived by the devil. I want to tell you that I know there will be a Christ, that there is a Holy Ghost, and that there are ministering angels. I have lied to you and I am afraid that I have committed the unpardonable sin—for I lied to God. I know my punishment will be an awful one. I confess my sins."

With these words, he gave up the ghost and died. When the people heard his words and saw him die, they were greatly astonished. Suddenly, the power of God came upon them and they fell to the earth. After this, love and peace were restored to the Nephites. They searched the scriptures and were faithful to the commandments of the Lord.

Jacob, Joseph, and Enos tried all manner of means to reach the hearts of the Lamanites so that they, too, might know the great truths concerning God and receive His blessings. But all their efforts were in vain. The Lamanites hated the Nephites with a deep and terrible hatred. They came upon them in battle, bringing them all suffering. The people of Nephi built forts to protect themselves against the Lamanite armies. They trusted in God and He rewarded them with victory.

Now, Jacob grew to be an old man. One day as he sat in the sun, his whole life began passing before him as if in a dream. He had tried to keep the records according to Nephi's commands. He saw his people as a lonesome and sober people, wanderers, cast out from Jerusalem. He, Jacob, had been born in the wilderness during a time of great suffering. Now he was about to die and his face grew sad as he thought of the hatred of the Lamanites. He wondered if, after his death, they would continue to make war upon his people.

Jacob knew that he must soon go down to his grave, so he called his son, Enos, to him and said: "Take these plates and write the things that Nephi commanded should be written."

Enos promised obedience to the commands and Jacob made an end of his writings, saying: "I make an end of my writing upon these plates, which writing has been small; and to the reader, I bid farewell, hoping that many of my brethren may read my words. Brethren, adieu."

A few days later Jacob died, and with his passing, they buried the last of Lehi and Sariah's sons.

CHAPTER 27

O ne crisp autumn day, Enos went into the forest to hunt wild animals. He was a clever hunter. He could walk through the woods as noiselessly as an animal. He could look at a trail and tell you whether anything had passed that way, what it was, which way it was going, and whether it was running or walking. Jarom, his son, was very proud of his father's skill as a hunter. One day, Enos overheard him telling some of his friends that his father could trail a bear for a whole week, night and day, and never even get tired. Later, he pointed out to Jarom that part of his story was false. He had often tracked an animal for several days, but he did sleep at night. The thought of his son's pride in him brought a smile to his serious face.

Enos's long legs carried him far into the deep, dark forest. Since he was following a new trail, he took time to leave his mark at the crossings. Being lost in the forest was an unpleasant experience he had had years ago.

At midday, he came upon a small clearing beside a babbling brook. Here he rested and built a small fire. Then, washing his hands in the brook, he lay face downward and drank lustily of the clear, cold water. While he was drinking, he caught sight of a shoal of fish. In a few minutes, he had snared three large ones. Taking his hunting knife from his belt, he quickly cleaned them and cooked them to a golden brown over his campfire. He ate them with relish, then feasted on honey cakes that his wife had baked. Still hungry, he looked about him and was rewarded by the sight of a grapevine, loaded with huge clusters of purple grapes.

After eating, he lay down beside a great pine tree. He listened, carefully, to the mysterious voices of the forest. The wind went sighing and whispering through the giant pines and the mournful, haunting sound of a dove came drifting to him from far or near. It was a curious thing about a dove. In spite of all his experiences as a hunter, he could never quite judge whether it was on a limb above his head or a hundred yards away.

As he lay there, he thought of his father, Jacob. He had taught him to read and write—and far greater than this, he had taught Enos to know God and how to gain eternal life. His father had been a just and good man, whose life had been spent teaching his people the ways of God. He thanked the Lord for such a father.

After Jacob's death, Enos became the keeper of the records and the spiritual leader of the Nephites. Remembering his father's true greatness, he felt unsure of himself. He wondered if he would be equal to so great a trust. Suddenly, he felt ashamed of himself. He was not alone. All he had to do was to ask God for help.

His soul hungered for guidance. He knelt down before his Maker and cried out to Him in mighty prayer for his own soul. He prayed all the day long, and when the night came, he still raised his voice until it reached the heavens.

At last there came a voice, saying: "Enos, your sins are forgiven and you shall be blessed."

Enos knew that his guilt was swept away.

"Lord, how is it done?" asked Enos.

God answered: "Because of your faith in Christ, whom you have never seen or heard, go your way. Your faith has made you whole."

Now, when Enos heard these words, he began to feel a desire for the welfare of his brethren, the Nephites, and he prayed again for them. While he prayed, the voice of the Lord came into his mind again, saying, "I will visit your brethren according to their faithfulness in keeping my commandments. I have given them this land. It is a holy land, and I shall not curse it unless they become wicked."

After Enos heard these words, his faith grew strong. He prayed again for the Lamanites. He asked God to preserve the plates for them, in case the Nephites should fall into sin and be destroyed, so that the Lamanites might be brought to salvation. Enos knew that their hearts were so hard that they would destroy the records and the Nephites, if they had the opportunity. Therefore, knowing that the Lord was able to preserve the records, Enos cried to him continually, believing that whatsoever you ask in faith, believing that you shall receive it in the name of Christ, you shall receive it.

God answered him, saying: "I will grant your desire because of your faith. Thy fathers have also asked that I preserve these plates. Their faith was like yours."

At last Enos stood up and walked to the center of the clearing. Lifting his face to the sun, he saw that it stood at midday. He remembered that he had begun to pray at this time yesterday and that he had prayed continually ever since. He had had no sleep, yet, strangely enough, he felt rested. However, he did feel hungry, so he built a small fire and caught more fish. While he cooked his midday meal, he thought of all the wonderful things he had seen and heard. Never before had he felt so much at peace with himself and the world. A great joy filled his soul. Jacob had taught him to pray as a small boy, but never had he known the great power of prayer until today.

He was no longer in the mood to hunt for wild animals, so, after he had eaten, he carefully put out his campfire and turned his footsteps homeward.

From that day forth, Enos was like a new man. He spent his time going among the people, prophesying of things to come and testifying of all the things he had seen and heard.

The people of the Lord learned to love Enos as much as his father before him. As a matter of fact, they often called him Jacob, forgetting for the moment that it was the son to whom they were speaking.

CHAPTER 28

Jarom, son of Enos, had now reached manhood and it had been 179 years since Lehi and his family had left Jerusalem. Life in the great city had almost been forgotten. In the beginning memories and stories about Jerusalem had been told often to the younger generation, but as the years passed by, they were told less frequently, until at last they were almost lost in the dim, dead past. Almost, but not quite, for all those who could read and had the desire could learn about Jerusalem from the records God had commanded Nephi to make.

As Jarom climbed upward toward the mountain pass, he began worrying again. He had tried to push the nagging thoughts from his mind, but they kept coming back in spite of his good intentions. He was worried about his father, Enos. He had been gone from his home for six days, and he had said before leaving that he would be back in two or three days, at most. Jarom kept telling himself that his father was safe, that no harm had come to him, that he had friends wherever he went and that they would protect him. He told himself all these things and more, yet he couldn't quite convince himself that they were true. He knew that his father had gone to labor among the Lamanites, and this only served to make him more uneasy. It was not his first visit, for God had commanded him long ago to carry His word to them so that they, too, could find eternal life. In spite of his efforts and the efforts of many other Nephites, they hardened their hearts against them and would not listen.

At any time, he expected to see his father coming down the path toward him. They had never harmed him before; why should they now? Still, he did not trust them, and that was his reason for climbing to the mountain pass to search for Enos.

Jarom remembered how, many years ago, his grandfather, Jacob, would take him on his knee and tell him about the Lamanites. Being a small boy at the time, he found it difficult to understand that Laman and Lemuel, the first of the Lamanites, were his grandfather's brothers and his great-uncles. Jacob took great care to point out to him that they were not entirely bad, that they had many good qualities as well. He often told Jarom what a really great and good man his brother Nephi was, and how Laman and Lemuel had sinned against him. Their hatred for him was deep and abiding. Often they sought to take his life, but each time, the Lord God protected Nephi.

Jarom liked best of all to hear about the time when God commanded Nephi to take all those who believed in Him and kept His commandments and flee into the wilderness. He thought it very exciting, the way they fooled the Lamanites and escaped in the middle of the night. His grandfather told him that there had been peace for a long time after that, because the Lamanites couldn't find them. However, he felt very sad when he heard his grandfather tell how God had cursed the Lamanites with a dark skin. It made his grandfather sad, too. He would sit for a long time and think about it and wonder how he could bring them to repentance, so that they could receive eternal life. His father, Enos, believed as his grandfather did, that it was their duty to teach the Lamanites the word of God, and he constantly labored with them.

The thoughts of Enos brought his worries back again. Never had he stayed with the Lamanites for so long a time. They were usually unfriendly, boasting that someday and in some way, they would get the records he had in his keeping and destroy them. Furthermore, they boasted that they intended to destroy all of the Nephites as well. His thoughts disturbed him and he hurried his steps.

The trail grew steep and stony and went winding in and out among the jagged rocks. Suddenly, rounding a turn in the path, he came upon a young shepherd boy. He was sitting on a rock by the side of the path, his elbows on his knees and his face buried in his hands.

"Good morning, boy," said Jarom, surprised.

There was no answer. However, the boy raised his head a little and looked out at him from between dirty fingers.

"Are you ill?" asked Jarom, in a friendly tone.

Still the boy did not answer; instead, he began rocking himself from side to side and moaning bitterly.

Jarom tried again, saying, "Come now, whatever your trouble, it can't be as bad as all that. Can't you tell me what it is?"

"Woe! Woe is me," he wailed.

"Whatever has happened to you? Are you in pain?" asked Jarom, growing impatient.

"I'm all right. It's my goats," said the shepherd boy, without taking his hands from his face.

At the mention of his goats, he gave way to a fresh outburst. His moans became louder and his tears found their way through his fingers and went running down the backs of his hands, washing clean little tracks where they ran.

"If you'll stop that wailing and tell me what has happened to your goats, perhaps I can help you." Jarom spoke firmly.

Something about the tone of Jarom's voice and the hope in his words made the boy sit up and remove his hands from his tear-stained face.

"Well now, that's better. Have you lost your goats?"

"Woe, woe is me! If they were only lost, perhaps I could find them again. All ten of them are gone and they were the finest and best goats in the land of Nephi. He took every one of them. It was all the goats I had." He began sobbing and moaning again.

At that moment, Jarom recognized who the lad was. He and his sister lived alone. They had taken care of themselves since their parents' death, a year ago. The sister was a few years older—about fifteen. When Jarom discovered who the little shepherd boy was, his heart filled with pity, for he knew how great had been their struggle and how brave they had been in caring for themselves. The loss of ten goats would, perhaps, mean the difference between plenty and starvation.

"You say he took your goats. Who was it and where did he take them?" questioned Jarom.

"It was a great big man; a Lamanite."

"Are you sure?" asked Jarom, surprised.

"Yes, sir! I saw him with my own eyes," answered the boy, resenting the question.

"What did he look like?" questioned Jarom, still wondering whether the boy was not mistaken.

"He was a big, dark man. His head was shaven and he had a third eye painted in the middle of his forehead. He wore a short skin girdle about his loins," answered the boy, angry that his word had been questioned.

"There's no doubt about his being a Lamanite. But tell me the whole story. Where were the goats feeding at the time?"

"Well, you see, sir, my goats are not just ordinary

goats. They like very special things to eat. The grass on the foothills doesn't tempt them at all. They like the kind of grass and leaves that grow here, among the rocks. Daisy Bell was on lead this morning and she took them higher and higher up the mountain. It was too steep for me to climb so I stayed below and just kept an eye on them, and the first thing I knew, just out of nowhere, came this big Lamanite and started driving them up toward the pass. I ran as fast as I could go, yelling at him to stop. Daisy Bell thought I was playing a game, because she started running as fast as she could go, right over the pass and on down the other side into the land of the Lamanites. All the other goats ran after her and the big Lamanite turned around and laughed at me. Before I knew what was happening, he began shooting arrows at me. I think it was just to frighten me, because they all went far above my head. Oh, my poor goats! They need me so badly. You see, sir, I'm the only one who knows how to take care of them." This thought brought a fresh outburst of tears and moans.

"I have a flock of goats and you can pick out ten of the very best," said Jarom, soothingly.

"I don't want your goats—I want my own. He won't know how to feed them. You see, I raised them from little kids and they don't know anyone but me. I heard a man say the Lamanites kill animals and eat the meat raw. Do you think they will kill my goats?"

He didn't wait for Jarom's reply. The thought was so dreadful that he threw himself on the ground face downward and sobbed bitterly. Jarom was at a loss to know how to lessen his grief. He had hoped to make things right by giving him some of his own goats, but that only seemed to make matters worse. He felt sure that there would be no way of getting the boy's goats back from the

Lamanites. It had happened many times before. As a matter of fact, they were constantly stealing from the Nephites.

"There, there, don't cry." Jarom was deeply disturbed by the boy's constant wailing. "I'm on my way to look for my father in the land of the Lamanites, and I shall look for your goats while I'm there."

The shepherd boy stopped crying and sat up, rubbing his swollen eyes.

"I'll go along with you. I'm very brave," said the boy.

Jarom smiled at him and said, "No, you must stay here. It's too dangerous."

"But you won't know my goats."

"You can describe them to me."

"If you won't let me go with you, at least let me walk to the top of the pass," said the boy stubbornly.

In a few minutes they had reached the top and could look down into the land of the Lamanites. From where they stood, they could see a beautiful lake shimmering in the sunlight. At the north end of the lake were many brightly colored tents. The Lamanites were always shifting from one place to another, looking for fresh hunting and fishing grounds.

Bidding the boy good-bye, Jarom started down the mountain toward the village. At once, he began feeling that he was trespassing upon enemy land. He had a feeling he was being watched by hostile eyes, and he knew he would have to move cautiously or he would find an arrow in his back. This thought made him so uncomfortable that his back actually began to ache. The foolishness of it all appealed to his sense of humor and brought a smile to his lips. Nevertheless, he avoided open spaces and kept to the cover of the trees. Then, somewhere behind him, a twig snapped. He had been right. Someone was following him. He walked on a short distance, pretending he hadn't heard the sound, then, quick as a flash, he wheeled around just in time to see someone slip behind a tree.

"Come out from behind that tree. You are very disobedient," said Jarom sternly.

The shepherd boy came from his hiding place with bowed head.

"I didn't mean to disobey you, but from the summit, I saw a man start up the mountain, driving several goats. If they're my goats, I know how to keep them from running away, so I decided that you would be glad of my help." The shepherd boy pleaded his case well.

Just then, the sound of a bleating goat came to their ears and Jarom smiled his consent.

In less than half an hour, they came face to face with the driver of the goats. It was Enos. Jarom was so delighted at seeing his father alive and safe that he failed to see the shepherd boy's joy at finding his beloved goats. At last, the boy ventured to ask how Enos got the goats from the Lamanites.

"Well," said Enos, "when I came to their village, I found the king of the Lamanites so ill that they expected him to die. I asked to be allowed to see him. Through God's help, he is now on the way to recovery. The young Lamanite who stole your goats is the king's son. When I told the king what had happened, he ordered that the goats be sent back to you."

Great was the rejoicing in the land of Nephi at the safe return of Enos, their beloved prophet.

CHAPTER 29

After the death of Enos, his son Jarom became keeper of the records. Since these plates were small and Jarom's prophecies were the same as those of his fathers before him, he didn't record them. However, he did record other things about his people.

During Jarom's time there were many among the Nephites with hard hearts and stiff necks, but many others who kept the commandments of God and received revelations. The Lord God was merciful to the wicked and did not destroy them. Two hundred years had passed away since Lehi had left Jerusalem, and the people of Nephi had become very strong in the land. They kept the laws of Moses; they did not profane and they kept the Sabbath day holy. The Nephites were scattered far and wide over the precious land of promise, but, although they were numerous, the Lamanites outnumbered them. The Lamanites were a wicked people, living on the raw meat of wild beasts. They made war many times on the Nephites, but the kings and leaders were mighty men in the faith of the Lord and the Lamanites were swept out of the land. After a while, the Nephites became very rich in gold, silver, and precious things. They were skilled in the workmanship of wood and they built many buildings, machinery, and all manner of tools to till the soil. Much of their time was spent in making weapons of war and in preparation for war. They were so well prepared to meet the Lamanites that they won many victories. The promise the Lord made to the Nephites was fulfilled: "As long as you will keep my commandments, you shall prosper in the land."

The prophets, the priests, and the teachers labored earnestly, persuading the people to look forward to the Messiah and believe in Him as though He had already come. By their faithful teaching, they kept the people from being destroyed.

One day, after 238 years had passed away, Jarom sat down and wrote his final message to his people:

"And I, Jarom, do not write more, for the plates are small. But, my brethren, you can go to the other plates of Nephi; for the records of our wars are written upon them, according to the writings of the kings. And now I deliver these plates into the hands of my son Omni, that they may be kept according to the commandments of my fathers."

The records were handed down from father to son for many generations. About 200 B.C., or about four hundred years after Lehi and his family left Jerusalem, Amaleki became the keeper of the records. He wrote many things concerning a man named Mosiah. There had been years of long, bitter wars between the Nephites and the Lamanites, as well as years of peace and plenty. However, in spite of the wars, the Nephites became very numerous and spread out over the land.

Mosiah was a fine-looking man, whose chief charm was in his goodness of soul. It was a joy to be in his company, because he spread such warmth and understanding. Wherever he went, the people gathered about him. He was loved by rich and poor alike. They welcomed him to their homes because he always brought happiness and good cheer. He was strong in the faith of his fathers and kept God's commandments faithfully. Much of his time was spent in teaching the people the way to eternal life.

Now, Mosiah loved the precious land of promise, and he knew that if his people grew wicked the Lord would destroy them, for He would not permit the unfaithful to dwell in this new land. God had been merciful and very patient for many generations, but Mosiah knew that He would not continue to overlook their sins forever.

At the northern end of the valley of Nephi rose a small hill. That is, it seemed small when compared to the lofty mountain ranges that bordered the valley on the east and west. Mosiah came here often. It was such a quiet place and, when troubled, he came to pray. Today he sat atop the hill, gazing out over the valley below with unseeing eyes. He was deeply troubled, for God had commanded him to leave the valley and seek a new home in the wilderness. There was no question in his mind as to whether or not he would obey the commandment. He would carry it out to the letter. Nevertheless, it caused him great suffering to think of leaving the home he loved so dearly. That was not his only worry. God had commanded him to take the faithful with him. He wondered just how he would convince them that they should leave their homes and go into the unknown. He thought of Nephi, who hundreds of years ago, had faced the same problem. Suddenly there was a ray of hope. He would go to Amaleki and ask him to let him read from the plates Nephi's own account of their flight from the Lamanites.

A cold breeze swept down and made Mosiah draw his cloak more closely about him. The ever-lengthening shadows of late afternoon went unnoticed. Already the sun had left the valley, but the little lake at the foot of the mountain caught up the flaming crimson of the sky and mirrored it on the calm surface of its waters. It looked like a gleaming jewel set among purple shadows. When at last the sun had gone and the gloom of night was falling fast, the lonely man still sat on the hill, while punishing thoughts blotted out all sense of time or place. He knew he must keep the commandment God had given him, but just the thought of never seeing the land of Nephi again was sheer torture to his soul. He knew that the wilderness into which he must go was rugged and difficult to travel. It must be said, to his credit, that it was not his own suffering that tried him so sorely, but that of his wife, his children, and his faithful friends. It was asking so much of them; yet to stay here meant destruction. Again, his thoughts turned to Nephi. He would go to Amaleki and read the records. Perhaps, through them, he could solve his problems.

Suddenly, he was aroused by the howl of a wolf. The sound made him shudder and brought him to his feet. It had grown so dark that it was difficult to find his way down through the trees.

At the home of Amaleki, Mosiah had his faith renewed and strengthened. All his doubts and fears left his mind. He went among the people, presenting God's message so convincingly that a great many of the faithful followed him into the wilderness. Their journey was a difficult one. Much of the way was rough and mountainous. However, they were continually led by the power of God's arm and by the preaching and prophesying of the anointed. It was their custom to travel for several days and then to rest for a few days. While they rested, Mosiah would leave the camp and scout the surrounding country. In this manner, he was able to spare them needless suffering and many steps by choosing a course that would take the least effort.

Late one afternoon, they chose a resting place. To the delight of Benjamin, Mosiah's young son, his father told him that he would take him with him on the morrow.

They would see what was on the other side of the mountain by the base of which they were camped. Early next morning, father and son sat down to rest just before they reached the top of the mountain. After a few minutes, Benjamin asked if he might go on alone and wait for his father at the summit. Mosiah couldn't refuse his son and soon Benjamin was out of sight. In less than half an hour, the boy returned, red-faced with excitement and effort.

"Father, come quickly! I have just discovered a band of Lamanites."

"But that's impossible," said Mosiah. "We are far from the land of the Lamanites."

"If it isn't Lamanites, it's someone else, for there is a big city of them, right in the middle of a green valley."

Mosiah was astonished, for he believed they were far away from both the Lamanites and the Nephites. He hurried up the mountain so fast that Benjamin couldn't keep up. When he reached the top of the mountain, he saw that his son had not been mistaken. Below him lay the most beautiful valley he had ever seen, and in its midst was a city of fine houses.

"See, Father, I told you," cried Benjamin, finally catching up to Mosiah.

"Yes, son, you did. Someday you will be a good scout," said Mosiah, patting the boy on the head.

"Are they Lamanites?" asked Benjamin.

"No, my son, they are not Lamanites or Nephites. They are strangers."

"Should we be afraid of them, Father?"

"No, Benjamin. I want you to go back to Amaleki and tell him what we have seen. Tell no one else and ask him to keep the people where they are until I return. I will see for myself who these strangers are. You are not to worry about me. Go now, my son, and see how well you can carry out an order."

Benjamin was off like the wind as Mosiah started to

pick his way down the opposite side of the mountain. It was mid-morning by the time he reached the valley floor. The closer he came to the city, the more cautiously he moved. It was his plan to find out all he could without being seen. He followed a little stream as it went meandering toward the village. There were trees and bushes to hide him. Suddenly, rounding a bend, he came face to face with three small boys, very much like his own son. They began chattering noisily in a language he couldn't understand, but from their friendly smiles, he was made to understand that he was welcome. He liked their intelligent faces so much that he allowed them to lead him into the village. He was a great curiosity, and soon a crowd had gathered around him. He tried to understand them, but there was not a single person who spoke his language. At last, he came to understand that this was the land of Zarahemla and a man named Zarahemla was king. Furthermore, he soon discovered that they were delighted with his visit and nothing was too good for him. They gave him choice food to eat and new clothes to wear. Zarahemla himself went with Mosiah to welcome his people to the land of Zarahemla.

CHAPTER 30

There was great rejoicing and feasting in the land of Zarahemla over the coming of Mosiah and his people. Immediately Mosiah began teaching the new people his language, and in a very short time they were able to speak with perfect understanding. Zarahemla and Mosiah learned to have great respect for each other, and they spent many hours together.

One day, as they sat talking, Zarahemla said: "You know, Mosiah, every time I see you, my heart is full of thanksgiving. The Lord was very merciful to send you and your people to us, with the plates of brass which contain the record of the Jews."

"Then, my friend, you people are Jews?" asked Mosiah, eagerly.

"Yes, indeed we are. Our forefathers came out from Jerusalem at the time that Zedekiah, king of Judah, was carried away captive into Babylon," answered Zarahemla, noticing his friend's growing excitement.

"Our forefathers lived in Jerusalem, too. Perhaps we have more in common than just our friendship. Lehi was warned by God to flee from Jerusalem in order to save the lives of his family. Zedekiah was king of Judah at that time. Perhaps our forefathers knew each other," said Mosiah with great feeling.

"My people," said Zarahemla with deep emotion, "journeyed in the wilderness, and were brought by the hand of the Lord across the great waters, into this land where you discovered us. We have lived here all these years. You see how numerous we have become. Nevertheless, we have had many wars and great numbers of us have fallen by the sword. We brought no records with us and, for that reason, our language became confused and gradually changed until, when you came, you couldn't understand us. We even drifted so far away from God that we denied Him. So you see, Mosiah, by being able to see the brass plates, we, too, can find eternal life."

There was great harmony between the people of Zarahemla and the Nephites, and they had such great faith in Mosiah that they appointed him to be their king.

The years passed swiftly in the land of Zarahemla, and with their passing, strong bonds of friendship and love grew between the people of Nephi and the people of Zarahemla. The Nephites had found happiness in their new home. But, in spite of their happiness, many of them grew restless when they thought of the land of Nephi. They longed to see it again, for they thought of it as the land of their inheritance. When they spoke of visiting their old home, Mosiah discouraged them. He knew that the Lamanites had overrun much of the land they would have to journey through and it was far too dangerous.

One morning, while Mosiah was still at home, his son, Benjamin, burst into the room, excitement flooding his cheeks with high color.

"Father, there is a crowd of men outside, waiting to see you. They have brought a large stone with engravings on it."

"Engravings? What kind of engravings?"

"The writing is in a strange language I cannot read," said Benjamin.

"Then I cannot read it either," said Mosiah, "for I have taught you all I know."

"I told them so, but they wouldn't listen. They have such faith in you, they believe you can perform miracles. Will you see them?" asked Benjamin with deep emotion, for his faith in his father was as great as theirs.

"Tell them to come in. If God wills it, He will find a way to make it possible for me to interpret the engravings."

In a few minutes, the stone was placed before Mosiah. Instantly, he saw that the writing was strange to him.

"Can you read it?" questioned the men, eagerly.

"Where did you find this stone?" asked Mosiah, ignoring the question.

"In a land far to the north," they said, waiting patiently for Mosiah to answer them.

For several minutes, Mosiah bowed his aging head over the stone, and they knew he was praying for God's help. They respected his prayer and were silent. Suddenly, it was as though a light shone upon the old man's face and he began to interpret what was written on the stone, by the gift and power of God.

The engravings gave an account of a man named Coriantumr and his slain people. They told of his first parents coming out from the tower at the time the Lord confounded the language of the people. The anger of the Lord fell upon them and their bones lay scattered in a land far to the north.

Coriantumr was discovered by the people of Zarahemla; he dwelt with them for the space of nine moons.

There came a day in the land of Zarahemla when the people bowed their heads in sorrow. Mosiah, their king, was dead, and he had been a great and mighty leader.

God had given him rare gifts of wisdom, courage, and faith. Through these gifts, he had successfully led the Nephites away from destruction, down into the land of Zarahemla. Through skillful leadership, he had united the people so closely that there had been peace and happiness throughout all his days. With his passing, his son, Benjamin, became king.

Shortly after the death of Mosiah, the people were rudely awakened at dawn one morning by the terrible war cry of the Lamanites. They were attacked so suddenly that many were slain before they could gather their forces for battle. Nevertheless, King Benjamin had foreseen possible trouble with the Lamanites and had made full preparations for war. The fighting continued for days, but at last King Benjamin and his army were successful in driving the Lamanites out of the land of Zarahemla.

After the battle, the people talked continually about the bravery of their king. They said: "Benjamin, our king, is a noble man. He saved our lives."

When Benjamin heard this, he said: "I did not save your lives. You were faithful to God's commandments and, as a reward He saved us from destruction."

Then Benjamin ordered a day of feasting and thanksgiving to God for His wonderful mercy. For a long time after this, the people lived in contentment and peace, except for a number of the Nephites who had grown anxious to possess the land of their inheritance. At last, one day, a certain number of them went up into the wilderness to return to the land of Nephi. Their leader was a strong and mighty man. But, along with these good qualities, he was hot tempered and very proud, and because of his pride and bad temper, he caused a bitter quarrel among them. It became so serious that they were all slain except fifty, who returned to the land of Zarahemla.

After this terrible experience, King Benjamin thought they would be content to live in the peaceful land of Zarahemla. But they were not. Soon they grew restless again and, this time, they took a larger number than ever and started on their journey into the wilderness. Amaleki had a brother who went with them, and he was never heard from again.

The morning sun fell on Amaleki's snow-white hair as he climbed the steps to the king's palace. He was old and weak, and now he wondered if he would have enough strength to reach the palace door. He was forced to rest frequently; as he rested, he watched the people who went up and down the steps. They were younger than he and moved easily, with little or no effort—at least, it seemed so to him. He noticed, too, that not a single soul offered to help him. As a matter of fact, no one seemed to even notice him. There had been a time when he had been important to his people; now, he was already forgotten. The thought depressed him and he turned and started up the steps again.

Just at that moment, the palace door opened wide and King Benjamin came running down the steps toward him.

"Amaleki!" he cried. "Amaleki, my dear old friend. Here, take my arm and lean on me. Why didn't you send word you wanted to see me? I would have come to you or, better still, I would have sent carriers to bring you here in style."

King Benjamin's welcome was so warm and his arm so strong that Amaleki scarcely noticed the rest of the steps. Soon he found himself seated in a comfortable chair and being refreshed with a tall, cool glass of goat's milk.

"I suppose you are wondering why I am here," said Amaleki.

"No, only overjoyed at seeing you again."

"I have been deeply troubled of late, knowing that very soon I must go down to my grave," said Amaleki.

"Have I done something to displease you?" asked the young king, humbly.

"No, no. If I am displeased with anyone, it is with myself, for I have no son. It has been the custom to hand Nephi's plates down from father to son. In some cases, they have been given to a brother, but I have no one. Now, if I had a son, I should want him to be like you. Knowing that you are a just man in the sight of the Lord, I should like to leave the plates in your keeping."

"I am greatly honored, Amaleki. Your trust in me will be justified, for I shall guard the plates with my life, if need be."

"Come with me to my house and I will deliver the plates to you. They are full and I have made an end of my writing. Tell my people to come unto God and believe in prophesying, in administering of angels, in the gift of speaking with tongues, and in the gift of interpreting languages. Oh, Benjamin, plead with them to continue in fasting and praying and, as the Lord liveth, they will be saved."

"I shall carry out your commands to the best of my ability and, through God's help, I shall preserve these records so that your voice and the voices of our fathers before you shall rise up from the dust to inspire a new nation to come unto God."

PART 3
The Land of Their Inheritance

CHAPTER 31

A shaft of golden sunlight fell across the palace floor and just reached King Benjamin where he sat in his huge armchair. He rested his head against the back of the chair. His eyes were closed, but he was not asleep, for the fingers of his right hand kept drumming a rat-a-tat-tat on the arm of his chair. In spite of the deep wrinkles about his eyes and mouth, he was still a good-looking man. He stood head and shoulders above the crowd. He was the tallest man in all the kingdom and his faithful followers said he was the most handsome.

A patch of bright sunshine fell upon the king's left hand and drew his eyes to see where the warmth came from. He smiled a bit grimly when he saw how old his hand looked as it lay there in the glaring light. He closed his eyes again, as if to shut out the unpleasant thought. No man in Zarahemla loved life more than King Benjamin, and strangley enough, he liked old age best of all. His splendid health and keen mind made this enjoyment possible. It was a mellow time of life. He had done his share in the workaday world and now he had time to reflect, wisely, upon the many things life had taught him. With the wisdom he had gained through his long years of service, he was able to give sound advice to those in need of his help. Yes, indeed, he liked old age. He liked the feeling of having time to do the many things he had left undone in the early years of his life.

Today, he was not as patient as usual. It was a day he had looked forward to for many years and yet dreaded its coming. Today he meant to give Zarahemla a new king. He had loved his people well and it gave him a heavy heart to place their welfare in another's hands.

He had sent for his three sons, one of whom he would appoint king to reign in his stead. They had kept him waiting for over an hour. He smiled to himself as he thought of his three fine sons, Mosiah, Helorum, and Helaman. Mosiah, his eldest son, bore the name of his grandfather and, more that that, he looked like him. King Benjamin loved and respected all three of his sons, but he felt a special tenderness for Mosiah. Perhaps the reason for this was because he was constantly reminded of his father.

King Benjamin's thoughts drifted to life in Zarahemla. For many years there had been no wars—not even a rumor of war. Throughout all the kingdom, there was peace and happiness. The people loved each other unselfishly, and above all, they loved God and kept His commandments faithfully. God smiled down on them and made them prosper and multiply in the land. They became so numerous that it was difficult to count them all.

In King Benjamin, the people had an excellent example to follow. He ruled them with a gentle hand and a loving heart. In all his dealings with them, he was honest and just. Not once, during his long reign, had he ever taxed them for his support or the support of any member of his household, but frequently he gave to the less fortunate. He worked with his hands and with his mind for their betterment.

Suddenly, a shadow fell across the open doorway.

Looking up, the old king saw his three sons entering.

"Ah, my sons, you have come at last," said King Benjamin, smiling pleasantly.

The three men crossed quickly to their father's side. After greeting him, they sat at his feet. King Benjamin looked at them with admiration, for they were fine-looking men. Mosiah and Helorum were as tall as their father, while Helaman was short but powerfully built. All three of them had dark hair and flashing black eyes.

"We are sorry to be late," said Mosiah, "but the messenger you sent had difficulty finding us. We were visiting the sick."

"May God bless you for your efforts. I wouldn't have called you if it hadn't been necessary, but my time grows short and I have much to say to you. I have taught you well and now you, in turn, must teach your children the things I have taught you. I have taught you the language of my fathers so that you might become men of understanding and know the prophecies which have been spoken by all the good men of God. I have taught you to read and understand the brass plates. Now, my sons, I would like you to remember that if it were not for these plates and the commandments of God, we would have been ignorant of His mysteries. If Lehi hadn't had the brass plates, it would have been impossible for him to remember all these things, and we would have lost the word of God. Oh, my sons, we would have been like the Lamanites. And now I say to you, all that you read in the brass plates and in the plates of Nephi are true. Read them often and teach them constantly to your people, for their welfare is in your hands."

For more than an hour, King Benjamin talked with his sons, telling them over and over again of their duties to God and man. At last, when he had finished, his sons left him so that he might have quiet and rest.

It was late afternoon when King Benjamin arose

from his couch, feeling more tired than when he had lain down. His thoughts disturbed him, for he remembered that he must appoint a new king at once. He knew that his days were numbered, and that soon he must go the way of all the earth. It made him sad to think of leaving his people and the precious land of Zarahemla. He found great enjoyment in living and his clean, pure life made his memories rich and satisfying. He felt the full weight of his responsibility in selecting the next king. The future of his people would depend largely on the kind of king who would rule over them.

After he had changed his linen and brushed his hair carefully into place, he went to his armchair and sat down heavily. He remembered that he had not always lived in Zarahemla; as a small boy, he had lived in the land of Nephi. He recalled the day his father, Mosiah, had told his family that the Lord had commanded him to take his wife and children and all those faithful to God's command-ments and leave the land of Nephi to seek a new home. He remembered much about their travels; most of all, he remembered that he had been the first to see the land of Zarahemla. It had been beautiful then, but it was more beautiful now. King Zarahemla and his people had wel-comed Mosiah and his followers and had loved them so much that they had made Mosiah king over all the land.

Suddenly, Benjamin knew that his son Mosiah was the one to be king. God had shown him the way. Now he was at peace with himself for the first time in many days.

King Benjamin had Mosiah brought before him and said, "My son, I want you to proclaim throughout all this land to all the people of Mosiah and to all the people of Zarahemla who dwell in this land, that they must come up to the temple. I want them to hear from my own mouth the name of the man who will be their new king."

"But Father," said Mosiah, with emotion, "you are king! They want no other."

"Thank you, my son," the old king said affectionately. "Since my days are numbered, it is necessary that I appoint a new man to reign in my stead. I have chosen you to be their ruler and their king. The people will love you so long as you are righteous and keep God's commandments. Think first of their welfare before your own."

"Father, I am deeply grateful to you for having chosen me king. I love our people. I shall try with all my heart and soul to be a good king and a son you can be proud of."

"I am not entitled to your gratitude. I did not choose you. You, my son, were chosen by the Lord our God. After I tell our people that you are to be their king, then I shall give them a name to make them known above all other people to come out of Jerusalem. I shall do this because they have been a faithful people in keeping the commandments of the Lord. This name I shall give them shall never be blotted out, except through sin. If they do fall into sin and become a wicked people, then the Lord will no longer preserve them by His matchless and marvelous power. It was only through His power that He saved our fathers from falling into the hands of the Lamanites and becoming victims of their hatred."

After King Benjamin had given his son Mosiah charge of all the affairs of the kingdom, he also gave him charge of the records which were engraven on the brass plates and the plates of Nephi.

"And now, my son," said the old king, "here is the sword of Laban and the ball or compass which led our fathers through the wilderness. It was prepared for them by the hand of the Lord that they might be led according to the strength of their faith. When they were unfaithful, they did not prosper or progress in their journey, but were often driven back and made to suffer. The Lord did this to make them remember their duty. Guard these things well and be faithful to the trust the Lord has placed in you. Go now and take the proclamation to the people, that they may prepare to gather at the temple."

Later the same day, Sara and Ena, two pretty country girls, sat talking in Sara's father's garden. As they sat under the pepper tree, they were disturbed by the clatter of horses' hooves and the sound of a horn. Unable to see the road because of the high stone wall that enclosed the garden, they jumped up and ran to the gate. It was Mosiah, mounted on a beautiful milk-white horse. He looked very dashing in his purple tunic and cloak of spun gold. The sight of him brought a warm flush to their cheeks and a sparkle to their eyes. Almost at once, Mosiah saw them and reined in his horse.

"Good evening, Prince Mosiah," said Sara timidly.

"Good evening," he answered, fully aware of the admiring glances the girls were giving him. "My father has sent me forth to bring the people a proclamation. Can I trust you to take the word to each of your fathers?"

"Indeed you can," said Sara quickly. "When we give our word we always keep it."

Mosiah smiled at the rebuke.

"What is a proclamation?" asked Ena, at last overcoming her shyness.

"From time to time my father, King Benjamin, has sent messages to his people but rarely, if ever, has he sent a proclamation. Now, a proclamation is like a message, except that it is a command that must be obeyed."

"I feel frightened," said Sara. "Has something terrible happened—a war or something?"

When Mosiah answered, his voice was gentle and reassuring. "There is no reason to be frightened. King

Benjamin has asked me to tell the people to gather at the temple. Will you ask your fathers to bring their wives, their daughters, their sons, and their children's children, until the entire family has been gathered together? That is all of the proclamation. My father will tell you his message when you reach the temple."

Bidding the girls good-bye, Mosiah rode off down the lane, rolling up great clouds of dust as he went. Soon he was completely hidden from view and the girls went back to sit on the bench beneath the pepper tree. They talked of the mysterious proclamation and about the handsome prince.

CHAPTER 32

"Father!" shouted Helaman, coming into the great hall of the palace.

"Here I am, son," said King Benjamin from where he sat reading at a small table close to the window.

"Mosiah is back!" said Helaman excitedly. "Already the people are gathering at the temple."

No sooner had Helaman spoken than Mosiah burst into the room, looking tired and dusty.

"Welcome home, my son," said the old king.

"I planned to be back before this. I made the journey in good time, but on the way back I had to ride carefully, as the roads were all crowded with our people, their donkeys, and the best of their flocks. Oh, it's quite a sight, Father."

"Why should they bring their flocks?" asked Helaman.

"Your brother said the *best* of their flocks, and they bring them so that they might offer them to God, as a sacrifice, according to the law of Moses. And you, Helaman, are to select the best animals in our flocks so that we, too, might offer them to God in thanks for His mercy and goodness. Mosiah, how did you find our people?"

"There is peace and happiness throughout all the

land. They are a faithful people, loving each other and God," said Mosiah.

"Already," said Helaman, "there are more people than our temple will hold, and yet they continue to come."

Benjamin's smile was warm and a bit mysterious, as if he knew something they didn't know. Finally, he drew them to the window and said quietly, "You can see the temple from here. Look, do you see anything new?"

"A tower!" said both sons at once.

"I had it built so that most of my people will be able to hear the sound of my voice. However, even then, some will not be able to hear me, so I am having my words written down in order that they can read my message."

Great admiration shone in the eyes of Mosiah and Helaman. How wise and clever their father was, making his plans and carrying them out before anyone else had even thought of it.

When the people were all gathered at the temple, they pitched their tents so that each door was toward the temple. This was done so that they might stay in their tents and hear the words of King Benjamin. When the king began to speak, the people felt their faith being strengthened, for they knew he was inspired by the Lord. He taught them many things, too numerous to be written.

"I have worked with my hands," said the king, "in order to serve you, that you might not be burdened with taxes. I tell you these things that you may learn that when you are in the service of your fellow men, you are really in the service of God. He has created you, and all that you have, you owe to Him. Yet, for all His goodness, He asks nothing except that you keep His commandments. He has promised that, if you will keep His commandments, you shall prosper in the land.

"I have asked you to gather at the temple to tell you that I can no longer be your teacher and your king. Even now, as I stand here, my whole body trembles, but the Lord God will support me, for He has commanded me that I should tell you that my son Mosiah is a king and ruler over you. And now, my people, I want you to do as you have always done. You have kept my commandments and the commandments of my father and now I ask you to keep the commandments of my son, or the commandments of God which shall be delivered to you by Mosiah. Do this and you will continue to prosper and your enemies will have no power over you."

King Benjamin continued to speak to the people from the tower, pouring out words of wisdom that sank deep into men's hearts, making them search their souls for hidden sins. He told them about a wonderful thing that had happened to him. One night, an angel of God came and stood before him and told him to awake and listen carefully to all that he had to tell him. The angel said that after a period of time had passed away, Jesus Christ, the Son of the Lord our God, would come to earth and His spirit would dwell in a human body. Then he told King Benjamin of the marvelous miracles Christ would perform—he would make the blind to see, the deaf to hear, and the dead to live again. The angel pictured how Christ would suffer, bleed, and die, and then, most glorious of all, he would arise from the dead and go among the people. Because of His death and resurrection, men would be given eternal life if they would but keep the commandments of God.

King Benjamin suddenly stopped speaking and looked down at the multitude. He saw that all those within the sound of his voice had fallen to the earth for fear of the Lord.

They cried aloud with one voice, saying: "Oh, have mercy and forgive us, for we believe in Jesus Christ."

After they had spoken these words, the spirit of the

Lord came upon them and their hearts were full of joy. King Benjamin stood for a long time, looking down from the tower upon his people below. He was very tired. It had taken great effort to talk for such a long time, and only through God's support had he been able to accomplish it. He stood enchanted by the picture his people made. Their brilliantly colored tents, spread out against a backdrop of green trees, completely encircled the temple. The bright sunshine caught up the colors and made them dazzling to the eyes. These were his people, peace loving and kind to one another. Suddenly, his eyes filled with tears as he thought that, perhaps, this would be the last time he would speak to them. He wondered if they had believed his words. For their own sakes, they must believe. In order to find out the truth, he sent among them and asked them.

With one voice, they answered: "Yes, we believe all the words spoken by our king. Furthermore, we believe the words the angel spoke to him regarding the coming of Christ. From this day forth, we will forsake our sins and always do good. We promise God to keep His commandments and be obedient to Him in all things."

These were the words that King Benjamin had hoped to hear, for he had promised to give his people a name that should never be blotted out, as long as they kept God's commandments. But he couldn't give them the name until they believed in Christ. Joy filled his heart as he began to speak once more: "From this day forth, you shall be known as *the children of Christ*. If you keep the promise you made to God, you will one day find yourselves at His right hand in heaven."

After King Benjamin had finished speaking to his people, he decided it would be wise to record all the names of those who had taken upon them the name of Christ and promised to keep His commandments. Great joy filled the old king's heart when he discovered that every person in the kingdom, except young children, had his name recorded. King Benjamin had his son Mosiah brought before him. He blessed Mosiah as king and ruler over the people. Besides giving him the kingdom, he made him the keeper of the records. Next, he appointed priests to go among the people to teach and constantly remind them of their vows to God. Mosiah was thirty years old when he became king. It had been 476 years since Lehi had left Jerusalem.

Three years later, when the air was mild and fragrant with springtime blossoms, King Benjamin died. He died as he had lived, with simple dignity and at peace with God and man. As his three sons, Mosiah, Helorum, and Helaman, stood looking down at their father for the last time, they thought he looked years younger. A faint smile just touched his lips.

"Our father was a great man," said Mosiah, quietly.

"Indeed he was," said Helaman. "No man ever deserved a richer reward."

"I was thinking, as I stood here looking at him, that perhaps he was already being rewarded. The expression on his face is an inspiration. He looks so happy that I find my belief in the hereafter strengthened," said Helorum, deeply moved.

CHAPTER 33

K ing Mosiah walked in the ways of the Lord, keeping all His commandments faithfully. He had great strength of character and his sincere love for his people made him place their welfare above his own. He believed it was good for them to work with their hands as well as their minds. Furthermore, he believed that the closer they worked with nature, the closer they came to God. Because of these things, he encouraged them to till the soil and to raise flocks and herds.

Now, Mosiah would not ask his people to do the things he himself would not do, so he, too, tilled the soil and used his hands in many ways. Mosiah supported himself and his family, just as his father had done. He didn't want his people to be burdened with taxes. He wanted every person to enjoy complete freedom.

The first three years of Mosiah's reign were happy, peaceful ones, but then one day a group of people began talking about Zeniff and the men he had taken with him to the land of Nephi. This had happened many years before, when Mosiah's grandfather had been king. After Zeniff and his followers left Zarahemla, they had never been heard of again. Some people wanted to try to find out what had happened to them. Finally, King Mosiah be-

193

came tired of their teasing and appointed sixteen strong men to journey up to the land of Lehi-Nephi and discover what had become of Zeniff's group.

The very next morning, they set out on their journey. Their leader was a strong and mighty man named Ammon. He was a descendant of Zarahemla. They did not know the right course to follow in order to reach the land of Lehi-Nephi, so they wandered in the wilderness for forty days. In the midst of their wandering, they came to a hill north of the land of Shilom.

"We will pitch our tents here," said Ammon.

"Are we near the land of Nephi?" the men asked him.

"All I know is that we are lost," said Ammon. "I want to leave you here, where you will be safe, until I locate the land of our inheritance."

Ammon took three of his brethren with him and set out immediately. They hadn't gone far when they came face to face with a man.

"Who are you?" they asked.

"I am king of the people in the land of Nephi and in the land of Shilom."

Without any warning, Ammon and his men were suddenly surrounded by the king's guards, who took them and bound them securely and threw them into prison. When they had been in prison two days, the king had them brought before him and the bands that held them were loosened.

"I have had you brought before me to answer a few questions. Perhaps you should have been put to death at once, but I decided to give you this chance. You see, I like your courage. Behold, I am Limhi the grandson of Zeniff, who came up out of the land of Zarahemla to inherit this land." As he spoke, he watched them carefully. "I want to know why you were so bold as to come near the walls of the city when I myself was with my guards outside the gate."

When Ammon saw that he was permitted to speak, he went quickly to the king and bowed low before him, saying, "O King, I am very thankful to God that I am alive and can speak. I will speak with boldness, for I am sure that if you had known me, you would not have bound me. I am Ammon, a descendant of Zarahemla. We have come up out of the land of Zarahemla to ask about our brethren, whom Zeniff brought from our land."

As King Limhi sat listening to the words of Ammon, a warm flush of pleasure lit up his face and he said, "Now I am convinced that my people in Zarahemla are still alive. My joy is great, and tomorrow my people shall rejoice. We are in bondage to the Lamanites and they tax us heavily. We know that you will deliver us out of the hands of the Lamanites, and we will be your slaves. It will be better to be the slaves of the Nephites than to pay tribute to the Lamanites."

Limhi called his guards and commanded them to set Ammon and his men free. He told them to go to the hill north of Shilom and bring the rest of the men to the city so that they might eat and drink and rest themselves from their long journey. When this was done, King Limhi sent out a proclamation among all his people, asking that they gather at the temple so that he might speak to them.

The next day, when his people were gathered at the temple, Limhi said: "Lift up your heads and be comforted, for the time has come when we shall no longer be in bondage to our enemies. You know how we are burdened down with heavy taxes. We are forced to pay, to the king of the Lamanites, one half of all the grain we raise, one half of the increase of our flocks and herds, one half of all else that we possess. If we refuse to pay, we lose our lives. It is no wonder that you, my people, are sad. Many of our brethren have been killed and their blood has been spilled in vain, all because of sin. If the people had not sinned, the Lord would not have let this great evil come down upon us. God has been very angry with us and, in his wrath, he let our enemies come upon us. The Lord promised this people that if they continued in sin, He would destroy them, and He has fulfilled His promise. But, behold, He has also told us that if we return to Him and serve Him faithfully, He will someday deliver us out of bondage."

King Limhi told them many things and the people listened eagerly. He told them about their brethren in the land of Zarahemla. Then he had Ammon stand up before the multitude and tell them all that had happened in the land of Zarahemla, from the time that Zeniff left until he himself came to the land of Nephi. When Ammon had spoken, King Limhi dismissed the multitude.

When all the people had gone to their own homes, King Limhi and Ammon started toward the palace. At first they walked in silence, each one busy with his own thoughts. Ammon was thinking of Zarahemla, of its peace and quiet and most of all of the happy people. Here, in the land of Nephi, there was a feeling of unrest. Because they were in bondage to the Lamanites, they were an angry, sorrowful people. And now, in the dusk of early evening, everything took on a strange look. The deepening shadows gave him an uneasy feeling.

"Ammon, can you read strange languages?" asked King Limhi.

"No, but why do you ask?" questioned Ammon.

"That is a long story, but I will tell you, briefly. Some time ago, I felt sore at heart when I saw how my people suffered because of the Lamanites. Wanting to free them, I sent forty-three men to the north, in search of our people who lived in the land of Zarahemla. I felt sure that, when they heard of our misery, they would come to our rescue."

"What became of the men?" asked Ammon with sincere interest.

"They became lost. However, they found a land of many waters, and in this land they found the bones of men and beasts and the ruins of mighty buildings. They brought back with them, among other things, twenty-four plates of pure gold. There are strange engravings upon them, and since no one in my kingdom can tell me what they say, I am very anxious to find an interpreter. Do you know such a person?"

"Yes, indeed I do," said Ammon. "He is our prophet and seer. God has given him a rare gift with which he can translate and interpret all languages. This instrument is called an interpreter. It is a gift that God gives only to choice men of the land."

When King Limhi heard Ammon's words, his heart was filled with joy and he gave thanks to God.

"There is, no doubt, a great mystery contained in these plates. These interpreters were undoubtedly prepared for the purpose of revealing such mysteries to the children of men," said King Limhi.

Early next morning, King Limhi had the plates brought to Ammon. These were the records of his people from the time Zeniff and his followers had come out of the land of Zarahemla. Ammon read the records with eagerness. At last, he was to know just what had befallen his brethren.

The first part of the record, written eighty years earlier, told of things already known by Ammon. It was an account of the first group of men to leave Zarahemla. Their leader had been a quarrelsome man and because they forgot the Lord, they let him stir them up until they shed each other's blood. Zeniff and the others who had not been killed returned to Zarahemla. Zeniff gathered together a large group and set out once again for the land of Nephi. After many hardships, they came to the land of Shilom. Here on the hill they pitched their tents and waited while Zeniff and four strong men entered into the city of Lehi-Nephi. They went to speak to the Lamanite king, whose name was Laman. He was just as cunning and sly as the first Laman, who had lived hundreds of years before.

Now, Laman and his people were lazy. At times, when they had neglected tilling the soil, there was famine in the land. Therefore, he smiled at Zeniff and offered to enter into a treaty with him whereby the Nephites would be given back the land of their inheritance. Furthermore, they were to be given the land of Shilom. Immediately, the Lamanites withdrew from the land and the Nephites moved in. They set to work repairing the walls about the city and building new buildings. Soon the city of Shilom and the city of Lehi-Nephi began to be beautiful once more. They tilled the soil and raised flocks and herds, and because they loved God and kept His commandments, they prospered and multiplied.

Twelve years passed and Zeniff and his people grew stronger day by day. King Laman watched them with growing uneasiness. It had been his plan, from the first, that as soon as they became prosperous, he would bring them into bondage, so that the Lamanites might glut themselves with the riches of the Nephites. Therefore, in the thirteenth year of Zeniff's reign in the land of Nephi, the Lamanites came upon the people while they watered their flocks and began to slay them, taking their animals and their grain. When Zeniff heard about their treachery, he asked God for guidance and strength. Since the Lamanites far outnumbered the Nephites, King Laman felt very bold. They had forgotten God long ago, so they did not know His power. God answered the prayers of His people and made them so mighty that they killed ten Lamanites for every Nephite until, at last, the Lamanites were driven out of the land.

Once more, Zeniff and his people began to prosper. For twenty-two years there was peace and happiness, but at the end of that time, the Lamanites made war on them once more. Their hatred for the Nephites was black and terrible to see. Since the time Lehi left Jerusalem, their hatred had grown and had been passed on to their children for four hundred years. They blamed the Nephites for all their misfortunes. Zeniff and his people were well prepared for them, and once again they drove them out of the land. Zeniff grew old and died and his kingdom was passed on to his son, Noah.

It was a dark and tragic day for the people in the land of Nephi and Shilom when Noah became king over them. He was wicked and hard-hearted, caring only for his sinful pleasures and comforts. He knew that his people were prosperous, that they lived in beautiful homes, and that many of them had gold and silver and precious stones. When he saw them in their fine clothing, he became greedy and wanted what they had, so he appointed high priests to help him tax the people. They took one-fifth of all their possessions. Then King Noah set to work, planning great buildings for his workmen to build. First, they built a palace for the king and his many wives. His throne was made of the finest wood and decorated with gold, silver, and precious gems. The seats which were set apart for the high priests were higher than all the other seats and decorated with pure gold. A breastwork was built before each seat so that they might rest their arms while speaking. A great tower was built near the temple. It was so high that from it one could see the lands of Nephi,

Shilom, and even Shemlon, the land of the Lamanites. The Nephites planted grapes and spent much time in making wine, adding drunkenness to their other sins. The people worked hard to support King Noah and his priests in their laziness and sinful ways. They forgot God and thought only of their own greatness, boasting that fifty of their men could stand against thousands of Lamanites.

There was a man in the kingdom that watched with sorrowful eyes and a heavy heart while King Noah and his wicked priests led the people into sin. Even the best of the people no longer knew God or kept His commandments, and so Abinadi, for that was the man's name, began going among the people, secretly teaching them. God saw his work and was pleased. Now, Abinadi was strong in body and quick in mind, so God made him His prophet. After a while, King Noah heard of his prophecies and had his guards seek him out and bring him before the throne. Abinadi was unafraid and spoke plainly before the king and his priests. He told them that the sin they lived in was unforgivable in the sight of the Lord. Furthermore, he told them that unless they repented and turned to God, they would be visited with pests, all manner of diseases, famine, terrible storms, and wars, wherein much blood would be shed. He told them, too, that they would become as beasts of burden, having packs lashed to their backs and driven before their masters. So great was King Noah's anger that he had Abinadi turned over to the priests to decide his fate.

From among the priests, a young man came and stood before the king. This man was Alma, a descendant of Nephi. He began to plead with the king to spare Abinadi's life. He had heard all the words spoken by the old prophet and he knew that he had told the truth. Alma knew that he and his people were wicked. As King Noah listened to Alma's pleading, he grew very angry and ordered him out of the kingdom. Then, as soon as Alma had gone, the wicked king sent his army after him to kill him. Alma ran as fast as he could and hid himself away so that the king's men could not find him. He remained hidden for several days, writing all the words that Abinadi had spoken.

As soon as Alma had gone, the king ordered his guards to surround Abinadi and cast him into prison. After three days, King Noah had him brought before him.

"I have brought you to me," said the king, "to give you another chance. If you will deny your prophecies and also take back your words about our wickedness, I will set you free."

"That I will never do," said Abinadi in a firm, clear voice. "All that I have spoken is true."

When the king heard these words, he ordered Abinadi to be burned alive. While the old prophet suffered the agonies of burning, he continued to prophesy, telling the king that he, too, would be destroyed by fire. But the sinful king and his cruel priests only laughed and mocked him.

CHAPTER 34

I hope I am not disturbing you," said King Limhi, coming into the room where Ammon sat reading the record.

"Do come in," said Ammon. "I can read later."

"No, I won't disturb you. I know how anxious you are to learn the history of our people." With these words, he walked out of the room and Ammon turned back to the records and continued to read about Alma.

Alma repented of his sins and went among the people secretly, teaching them the words of Abinadi. Many of his people believed him and went to a place called Mormon. There was in Mormon a fountain of pure water, and since there was a thicket of small trees nearby, Alma hid here in daytime from the searchers of the king. Many of his followers came to hear his words. After teaching the people the way to enter the kingdom of heaven, he began to baptize them. They were called the church of God.

Alma appointed priests to teach the people. He told them there must be no quarreling. They must have a single purpose: the teaching of God's word. They set apart one day in each week to worship God. The priests were not to depend on the people to support them, but for their labor, they were to receive the grace of God.

Alma commanded that each one give according to his possessions, and to those who had nothing, help must be given. They must give of their own free will and good desires toward God. This was to support the needy. All their meetings were held in Mormon, in order that King Noah would not learn of their whereabouts. They knew that he would surely destroy them if he found them.

But behold, the king had already discovered that many of the people had moved out of his kingdom. He sent his servants to watch them. Therefore, on the day they gathered to worship God, King Noah discovered them. He sent an army to destroy them. Alma, being alert, discovered what the king intended to do, so they took their tents and their families and fled into the wilderness. There were 450 souls.

The king's men looked everywhere for the people of the Lord, but without success. Finally, they gave up the search and returned to the land of Nephi. They were frightened that the king would be angry when they came back empty-handed. Perhaps he would even kill them. However, they were greatly surprised when they found the king waiting for them. He was glad to have them back because there was rebellion in the kingdom. The larger part of the people remained loyal to King Noah, but a small group had openly expressed their unwillingness to support a king who taxed them heavily and used their labor to support him in his wickedness.

Now, the leader of this smaller group was named Gideon. He vowed that he would rid the people of the evil king. He drew his sword and went to find King Noah. When the two men had fought for a short time, King Noah saw that Gideon meant to kill him, so he gathered up his royal robes and ran as fast as he could go. He ran and ran until he reached the very top of the tower. Gideon ran after him as fast as he could go. When the king saw that he was running after him, he began to plead with him to spare his life. Then, casting his eyes about for some place to hide, he saw to his horror that the Lamanites had gathered their armies and were even now entering the land of Nephi. Gideon, who had reached the top of the tower, turned his eyes toward the place where King Noah was pointing with a trembling finger.

"The Lamanites are coming to kill us," said King Noah. "This is no time for us to fight each other; we must unite our forces and flee from the land."

"I agree with you," said Gideon. "I shall deal with you later."

King Noah commanded the people to take their wives and children and flee from the Lamanites. But the Lamanites ran after them and overtook them and began to kill them. When King Noah saw what was happening, he ordered the men to leave their wives and children and flee before the Lamanites. Many of the men refused to leave their families, saying that they would rather perish. Then they asked their fair daughters to stand before the Lamanites and plead with them to save their people. The Lamanites were charmed by the beauty of the Nephite women. In fact, they were so impressed by their pleading that they decided to spare their lives. They took them captive and carried them back to the land of Nephi, telling them they might possess the land on certain conditions. They must deliver up King Noah into their hands. Furthermore, they must give the Lamanites one-half of all they possessed and continue to do this from year to year.

It was not long before the king of the Lamanites discovered that among his captives was Limhi, one of King Noah's sons. He was not at all like his father. He was kind and just. Gideon knew that Limhi would not destroy his father, although he was aware of his evil deeds. Gideon was determined that King Noah and his priests should pay for their crimes, so he sent men to overtake them in the wilderness. They had not gone far when they came upon the men who had left their wives and children to flee with King Noah.

"Where are the priests and King Noah?" asked Gideon's men.

"We destroyed King Noah by fire. We wanted to return to the land of Nephi, and when King Noah commanded that we stay with him, we grew very angry and destroyed him. We would have destroyed the priests as well, but they ran away," answered one of the men.

When they reached the land of Nephi and brought the news of King Noah's death, they appointed Limhi to be their king. He began, at once, to establish peace. The Lamanites withdrew from the land of Nephi, but the king put a heavy guard about the land so that the Nephites could not escape. The Lamanites were happy at the prospect of living upon the labor of the Nephites. They would not have to work and could spend all their time hunting and fishing. For two years, Limhi and his people lived in peace with each other and the Lamanites.

One day, a terrible thing happened. It had been the custom of the Lamanite girls to go to a place in Shemlon, to dance and sing and enjoy themselves. One day, the wicked priests of King Noah discovered them. They hid themselves and watched them dance. Each day after that they continued to watch, until at last, when there was only a small group, they came out of their hiding place, captured the girls, and carried them away into the wilderness.

When the Lamanites found that twenty-four of their daughters were missing, they immediately blamed Limhi and his people. With terrible anger, they began to prepare for war. Fortunately, Limhi saw their preparations from the tower and hid his people in the forest where

they could take the Lamanites by surprise. When the Lamanites came, the people of Limhi fell upon them and
killed them. At last, the people of Limhi began to drive
the Lamanites before them.

When the Lamanites were driven from the land, King
Limhi's people found the king of the Lamanites lying in a
field with the dead. He was not dead, but only wounded.
They bound up his wounds and took him to King Limhi,
saying, "O King, we have brought you the king of the Lamanites. Let us slay him."

"No," said King Limhi. "There has been enough
bloodshed already." Then, turning to the king of the Lamanites, he said, "Why did you break your word? Surely
you remember the oath you gave me that you would not
come upon us in war, if we would pay you half of all we
possess. We have kept our word, and yet you have broken
yours."

The king of the Lamanites grew very angry and said,
"I have broken my word because your people have carried away the daughters of my people. I grew so angry
that I went before my army and led them in war against
you."

Now, King Limhi had heard nothing of all this and
he, too, grew angry when he heard what his people had
done. Immediately he commanded that they search the
homes for the Lamanite daughters, and punish the guilty.

When Gideon heard about the search, he said to the
king, "I pray thee, wait. Do not search the people, for they
are free of guilt. Don't you remember the wicked priests
of your father, Noah? They are in the wilderness and they
are the ones who have stolen the Lamanite daughters. O
King, tell the king of the Lamanites so that he will be
satisfied, for even now the Lamanites are returning to
make war on us, and you know that we are few in
number compared with them. Let us make peace while

there is yet time, for surely all the words of Abinadi are coming true. If we had only listened to the words of God, and turned away from sin, then we would not be suffering as we are today."

King Limhi turned his kindly eyes on Gideon and thanked him for his wisdom. And when he had told the king of the Lamanites about the wicked priests and that they must be the guilty ones, the king of the Lamanites said, "Let us go forth without weapons and meet my people. I give you my promise that they will not kill you."

When the Lamanites saw that the people of Limhi were without weapons, they took pity on them and returned with their king, in peace, to their own land.

King Limhi was both grateful and happy to have peace. His people were very dear to him and he grieved for those who had been killed. After a while they took new heart in their work, but there were dark days ahead for them. It was well that they didn't know how great their suffering was to be, or they may have welcomed death.

In a short time, the Lamanites began to stir up their anger against the Nephites. They did not dare kill them because the king had given his word. But they went into the borders of the land where the Nephites worked in the fields and, without warning, they would strike them on their cheeks and put heavy loads on their backs and drive them as though they were dumb animals. Their suffering was great and there was no way they could escape. The Lamanites had them completely surrounded on every side.

When they could stand it no longer, they went to their king and asked if they might go to war against the Lamanites. Limhi hated war with all his heart and soul, but at last he gave them permission to go into battle. But their enemies were victorious. They were beaten so badly that the cries of the mourners could be heard throughout the land—wives mourning for their husbands, mothers for their sons, sisters for their brothers. At the sight of so much grief, Limhi let them go into battle a second and third time. But each time, they were beaten, and their suffering became terrible to see. The Lord's word was fulfilled. They began thinking about Abinadi and his promise that if they would turn to God, he would help them. They humbled themselves, even to the dust, and submitted to the yoke of slavery, allowing themselves to be beaten and driven to and fro, according to the wishes of their enemies. They began to cry to God for help. So great were their cries that they lasted all day long. The Lord was slow to hear them because of their sins. Finally, he heard them and began to soften the hearts of the Lamanites, so that they made their burdens lighter. In a small way, they prospered so that at least they were not always hungry.

The king did not dare to go outside the walls of the city unless he took his guards with him, fearing that he might fall into the hands of the Lamanites. It was here that Ammon and his men found the king.

CHAPTER 35

After Ammon had finished reading the record of Zeniff and his people, he sat for a long time, thinking of many things. In all that had happened to the people, there was one thing that stood out clearly—as long as they kept the commandments of the Lord, they prospered and were happy. Even after they fell into sinful ways, the Lord had been slow to anger and continued to let them prosper for a time. While the Lord had been slow to anger, yet He was just as slow to forgive. However, of late, He began to soften the hearts of their enemies, making their burdens just a little lighter. All at once, an idea flashed through Ammon's mind—an idea so simple and yet so startling that it brought Ammon erect in his chair. It came to him that God was using him as an instrument to bring freedom to Limhi and his people. It all seemed very clear to him now. For a long time, while at Zarahemla, he had been thinking of the people that had gone with Zeniff many years before and were never heard of again. He just kept thinking of them and pleading with his king, Mosiah, to let him go in search of them. At last, the king gave him permission to take sixteen strong men and go in search of them. Now he knew there had been some force, stronger than himself, that had led him to do these things.

The Lord had worked in a mysterious way his wonders to perform.

Through the open window came the cries of women and children weeping for their dead; the cries of the suffering people, bearing burdens too great for them; and the cries of all the people, pleading with God for forgiveness and mercy. Their cries touched Ammon's heart and he went in search of Limhi.

"Oh, there you are," said Ammon, coming upon Limhi just outside the palace.

Ammon talked to Limhi about ways of freeing the people. Then they called the people together, in order that they, too, might have a voice in plans for their freedom. They decided that the only way to rid themselves of the Lamanite yoke would be to escape into the wilderness.

When the crowd had been dismissed, Gideon came and stood before the king, saying: "O King, you have listened to me before and always with profit. Now I wish you would listen to me again, for I have a plan."

"Speak, man, speak! What is your plan?" questioned the king anxiously.

"My plan," said Gideon excitedly, "is to gather our women and children, our flocks and herds, and all other things that we can carry with us and escape. We can go this very night, through the secret passage in the back wall of the city."

"Aren't you forgetting," said the king, "that an army of Lamanites is guarding every foot of the wall?"

"No," said Gideon. "But according to your custom, you send a tribute of wine to the guards. When they are drunken, they fall asleep easily. Tonight I will take the wine to them, and when they are asleep, we can escape through the secret pass. We will go into the wilderness and travel around the land of Shilom."

The king listened to Gideon and liked what he heard. He sent out a proclamation to all the people, telling them of Gideon's plan and commanding them to be ready that very night. He sent the Lamanites more wine than ever before. The Lamanites were delighted with the extra tribute and drank deeply and freely of the wine. Soon they fell asleep, and the people of Limhi escaped into the wilderness with their flocks and herds and as many precious things as they could carry with them. They made their way around Shilom and headed toward the land of Zarahemla, with Ammon and his men leading the way.

After many days of travel, they saw the beautiful land of Zarahemla. For the first time since they had left the land of Nephi, Limhi began to worry. He was suddenly afraid that King Mosiah would turn them out of his land. But when he told Ammon of his fears, Ammon laughed at him and said:

"Do not be afraid. You are Mosiah's people. He loves you just as dearly as he does any of us. You will see how glad he will be to welcome you home."

Ammon was right, for King Mosiah was overjoyed to have them home and they became his subjects. He was filled with joy to receive the records which were found in the land of many waters.

When the Lamanites discovered that the people of Limhi had escaped into the wilderness, they grew very angry and sent a great army to overtake them and bring them back. After they had followed them for two days, they could no longer see their tracks and then they became lost in the wilderness.

Limhi expected to see Alma and his followers when he reached the land of Zarahemla, but no one had seen them. Where could they be? Perhaps they had lost their way in the wilderness, or perhaps, after escaping from the wicked King Noah's army, they had been overtaken by the Lamanites and destroyed. This thought made Limhi sad and sick at heart, because he loved his people very much. However, if Limhi had only known that Alma and his people were safe and were even then entering the borders of Zarahemla, there would have been no need for sadness.

When Alma and the people of the Lord fled before King Noah's army, they went into the wilderness. On the morning of the eighth day, they climbed to the summit of a low mountain range, and there below them lay a beautiful little valley. Alma thought it was the most pleasant spot he had ever seen. The valley floor was carpeted with rich green grass, and in its center lay a tiny lake, shimmering in the golden sunlight.

"This is the place," said Alma. "Here we will be safe for a while."

After so many days in the wilderness, the little valley looked like heaven to the travel-worn people of the Lord. When they reached the valley floor, they found the water crystal clear, ice cold, and pure. They called their new-found valley the land of Helam, and the city where they pitched their tents they also called Helam. Immediately they began to till the soil and build fine buildings. The Lord was pleased with their labors and made them prosper in the land. Now, the people loved Alma so much that they asked him to be their king.

"No," said Alma, "I will not be a king over you. We are all equal in the sight of the Lord. But I will teach you and lead you in the ways of the Lord our God."

There was another reason why Alma felt he could not be king. He still remembered when he had served the wicked King Noah as one of his evil priests. Alma had repented and had walked in the straight and narrow path.

But still he wondered if God had fully forgiven him his past sins.

Alma spoke again, saying, "The Lord has freed you from the evil King Noah, and I want you to value your freedom and trust no man to be a king over you."

Alma became their high priest, and anyone who taught or served the people in any way received the right to do so through him. He taught them to love and help one another. Although God was pleased with the people of the Lord, still he wanted to try their faith. Therefore, he let the Lamanites come upon them.

You will remember how Limhi and his people escaped from the land of Nephi, and how the Lamanite army tried to find them, only to become lost in the wilderness. They wandered from place to place until, at last, they found the priests of Noah. Since the leader of the priests was called Amulon, they had named the land after him. The priests grew frightened, thinking that the Lamanites would kill them. Suddenly, Amulon thought of a way they might be saved, so he sent their wives to plead for them.

"Oh, hear us, our fathers," said the priests' wives. "We are your lost daughters and we love you, but we are also the wives of the priests. We beg you to spare the lives of our husbands."

Now, when the Lamanites saw that it was really their lost daughters, and that they were happy with the priests, they did not destroy them. The priests joined the Lamanites and traveled with them in the wilderness, in search of the land of Nephi. After they had wandered for many days, they came to Helam.

It happened that some of the people of Alma were in their fields, tilling the soil, when they saw the Lamanites approaching. They were overcome with fear, for the Lamanite army greatly outnumbered Alma's people. When they saw them coming, they took to their heels and ran as fast as they could to the city of Helam. When they told Alma, he was unafraid. He asked them to pray to God for His help in their terrible hour of need. While the people prayed, Alma went forth alone to meet the Lamanites. He soon discovered that they were lost, and he promised to guide them back to the land of Nephi if they would spare the lives of his people. However, after Alma had shown them the way, they didn't keep their promise. They set guards about the land of Helam. The Lamanite king made Amulon, the wicked priest, ruler over them. However, he was subject to the will of the king of the Lamanites.

The Lamanites began to be a mighty people. They ruled the lands of Amulon, Helam, Shemlon, Shilom, and Nephi. In all these lands, the Lamanite king made Amulon and the rest of the wicked priests teachers over the people. They taught the Lamanites the language of Nephi and how to keep their records. They taught them many useful things, but they forgot to teach them the most important thing of all—that God lives and expects us to keep His commandments. They were a friendly people to each other. Soon they began to grow rich, and with their riches, they became cunning and delighted in all manner of wickedness.

"Mother, why does Amulon hate my father, Alma?" asked Ruth, a young girl whose eyes were too sad for her years.

"Alma and Amulon were once King Noah's priests, and Amulon remembers that your father turned against him and tried to save the life of the prophet Abinadi. Amulon is still a wicked man, my child, and he will try in every way to make your father and all of us suffer," explained her mother.

"Did you know," asked Ruth, "that Amulon has commanded us to stop our prayers to God, or he will put us to death?"

Alma's wife, a beautiful woman in spite of the deep lines of care, sighed heavily and answered, "Ruth, my dear, his command won't stop us from praying in our hearts. God will hear us just as well as though we spoke aloud. In fact, He has already answered our prayers by making us strong enough to carry our burdens without getting tired."

Just at that moment, Alma opened the door and came to where Ruth and her mother sat talking. There was a glow about his face that made his wife and daughter look at him carefully.

"Alma," said his wife, "you look very happy— perhaps I should say more alive and glowing than I have ever seen you. Tell us what has happened."

"The Lord has just spoken to me," said Alma, seating himself in front of them. "He has told me that this very night we are to gather our flocks, our grain, and all we have, and on the morrow He will lead us out of bondage. Come now, let us do as the Lord has commanded."

In the morning, the Lord caused a deep sleep to fall upon the Lamanites. Alma and all his people, together with their flocks and their possessions, went safely out of the land of Helam. After they had traveled twelve days, they came to the land of Zarahemla. Mosiah received them with joy.

CHAPTER 36

It was springtime in the land of Zarahemla, and the air was heavy with the perfume of blossoming trees. Throughout all the land, there was rejoicing and thanksgiving over the coming of the people of Limhi and the people of Alma. They were gathered in two great groups. All the descendants of Zarahemla were called the people of Zarahemla, and all the descendants of Nephi were called the people of Nephi. Now, the people of Zarahemla greatly outnumbered the people of Nephi, but the Lamanites outnumbered both of them, two to one.

King Mosiah made Alma the spiritual leader of the people and gave him the right to baptize them and establish churches in the land. Alma worked faithfully, baptizing all those who believed in Christ and establishing churches with priests and teachers over each church. There were seven churches, since one church could not serve them all.

Today, Alma was visiting his friend Mosiah at the palace. They were seated in the king's favorite spot, near a huge window that overlooked the city. King Mosiah was watching his old friend with anxious eyes. Something was troubling him. He longed to help him, but he was at a loss to know what to do.

"Zarahemla is beautiful in springtime," said Alma, avoiding the subject that saddened him.

"Zarahemla is beautiful at all times of the year, but I think she outdoes herself in the springtime. This is a great people and a glorious land," said King Mosiah with pride.

"Yes, yes," said Alma absently.

"I'm sure you didn't come to discuss the springtime, or even this precious land of promise. Tell me, old friend, what bothers you?" said Mosiah, in a voice warm with understanding.

Alma sighed heavily and said, "You know as well as I do of the wickedness of a number of our young people. They refuse baptism and even deny Christ. I came to you once asking that you deal with them, but you put the responsibility on me. I prayed earnestly to God for His guidance. His voice came into my mind, telling me that all those who would repent and confess their sins should be numbered among His people, but all those who would not repent of their sins should be dropped from His church."

"Have you carried out God's command?" asked the king.

"Yes, indeed I have," said Alma quickly. "A great many unbelievers have repented and confessed their sins and are now members of the church. However, the number of unbelievers grows larger each day. It makes me very sad, but something else has happened that overshadows this. I need you to deal with it."

"I shall be glad to help you in any way I can," said King Mosiah, anxious to be of service to his unhappy friend.

"Thank you," said Alma. "A terrible thing has happened. The unbelievers have begun tormenting the people of the church. They steal from their flocks and herds and destroy their crops. There are five young men who ride together at night and commit all sorts of sins."

As Alma talked on, the king's anger grew, until at last he brought his fist down heavily on the arm of his chair and shouted, "I'll deal with them. I won't have my people mistreating each other. Today I will send a proclamation, warning them that they must stop their wickedness or answer to me. You can be sure, my friend, I won't deal lightly with them."

"There is something I must tell you, although I dread speaking the words aloud," said Alma, greatly disturbed. "The five young men who are the leaders in this wickedness are your four sons and my son, Alma." Alma waited for the king to speak, but when he was too shocked to reply, Alma continued: "These sons of ours have silver tongues. They flatter the people until, in their pride, they are easily led into sin."

The king sat with bowed head, saying nothing, and Alma sought for magic words to comfort him in his great disappointment. Now, Mosiah was a just man, and he had thought until now that his sons were following in his footsteps.

A few days later, on a dark, moonless night, five young men rode along the countryside, mounted on five spirited black horses, bent on destruction. Their talk was loud and boastful. Young Alma was making light of those who believed in Christ, when suddenly, the earth began to tremble violently—so violently that they were thrown to the ground. They saw an angel descending from heaven in a cloud. He spoke to them in a voice of thunder. The five young men were so frightened they failed to hear his words, but he spoke again and this is what he said:

"Alma, arise and come here. Why do you do these evil things against the church of God? The Lord has heard the prayers of His people, and your father, Alma, has also prayed with great faith, asking God to give you a knowledge of the truth. For that reason, I have come to convince you of the power of God. Behold, my voice shakes the earth. You can see me and you know that I am sent from heaven. I say to you, go your way and do not destroy the church."

With these words, the angel disappeared. Alma and the four sons of King Mosiah fell again to the earth, so great was their astonishment. They had seen the angel with their own eyes and heard his voice, which was like thunder. They had felt the earth shake beneath them and they knew that it had all come through the power of God. When Alma tried to arise, a strange thing happened. He found that he was too weak to move. He could not even raise his hands. He tried to tell the king's sons, but he could not talk. When they saw that he was helpless, they picked him up and carried him to his father. When they told Alma all that had happened, he rejoiced and gathered a great multitude together, that they might see what the Lord had done for his son.

"Will all the priests come forward?" asked Alma. "I should like you to fast and pray that the Lord will open the mouth of my son and let him speak again. And also, we will ask that his limbs might again be strong, in order that the people can see the goodness of God."

They prayed and fasted for two days and two nights. At the end of that time, young Alma arose and began to speak to the people, saying, "I have repented of my sins and the Lord has forgiven me. I am born again of the Spirit. I walked in darkness, but now, I have seen the marvelous light of God. My soul was in great torment, but now, I am without pain."

From this time forward, Alma and the four sons of King Mosiah began to teach the people. They traveled throughout all the land, telling the people what they had seen and teaching the word of God. All five of them became instruments in the hands of God, bringing many to a knowledge of the truth.

At dusk one day in late summer, Mosiah walked in his garden. It was his custom to come here each day during the twilight hours. Here, away from the rest of the world, he walked and talked with God. He had solved many a problem in this peaceful spot, but this evening his heart was especially heavy. At last, weary with the burden of his thoughts, he sank down on a garden bench and buried his face in his hands. For many days, his four sons had pleaded with him to let them go up to the land of Nephi, to teach the Lamanites the word of God. For the first time in his life, he had known fear. He knew now that he was afraid of loneliness—afraid that he would never see his sons again, and most of all, that the Lamanites would destroy them. As the evening shadows closed in on him, he slipped from the bench and knelt beside it.

"Oh, Lord God," he prayed, "should I let my sons go up to the land of Nephi, to teach thy word to our brethren, the Lamanites?"

As he continued to kneel beside the bench, the voice of the Lord came into his mind, saying, "Let them go, for many shall believe in their words and they shall return alive. I will deliver your sons out of the hands of the Lamanites." Mosiah arose, feeling more rested and happy than he had done for many days. He went to the palace and told his sons that their wish was granted. Immediately they set out upon their journey.

Mosiah watched them go, and with their going, he knew he had no son upon whom to confer his kingdom or the records. Therefore, he took the brass plates, the plates of Nephi, and all other records, together with the interpreters, and conferred them upon young Alma. He commanded him to care for them and also to keep a record of his people, handing it down from one generation to another, just as had been done since Lehi left Jerusalem.

A few days after the king's sons had left the land of Zarahemla, Mosiah sent throughout all the land, among all the people, asking them to tell him whom they wanted to be their king.

The people answered, "We want Aaron, your son, to be our king and our ruler."

It was with a heavy heart that Mosiah told the people Aaron could not be their king, since he had left the kingdom. Neither could any of his other sons. He had much to say against having a king. In order that they would all hear what he had to say, he sent his written word among all the people. He told them he would be their king until his death, and at his passing, he thought it wise to appoint judges to judge the people according to their law, given them by God. The people were convinced. After much thought, they appointed young Alma to be the first chief judge. He was also the high priest of the church. He walked in the ways of the Lord, keeping His commandments and judging the people fairly. Throughout all the land, there was peace and happiness.

Alma's father passed away, at the age of eighty-two, having lived to fulfill the commandments of God. A few days later, King Mosiah died at the age of sixty-three, just 509 years from the time Lehi left Jerusalem. Thus ended the reign of the kings over the people of Nephi, and thus ended the days of Alma, who was the founder of their church.

CHAPTER 37

A lma, as head of the church and first chief judge of Zarahemla, was kept very busy—so busy, in fact, that there were seldom enough hours in a day to do all the things that needed his attention. He was a good man, kind and just. He loved his people dearly and watched over them with tender care. The people, on their part, returned his love and respect; nevertheless, he was on trial because he represented the new form of government. They sometimes wondered if they would be sorry they had given up their rule by kings. They watched and waited for the first sign of success or failure. They didn't have long to wait, for a man named Nehor soon put him to the test.

One day, word came to Alma that there was a man going up and down the land, telling the people that the priests and teachers of the church should not belittle themselves by working. The people should support them. Furthermore, he taught that God had made them all and no matter what they did, He would love and forgive them. This was an easy belief to follow, and many of the people who were weak found his ideas to their liking. This man was Nehor. Soon he broke away from the church and started a new one, based on his teachings. He made the people support him with all sorts of riches and expensive clothing. For a long time, there was no word of Nehor. Alma had almost forgotten about him when, suddenly, the news was brought to him that Nehor had killed a man. The whole land of Zarahemla was stirred by the news. The law said a life for a life. If Alma let the sin go unpunished, it would lead to other crimes and many of them would be slaves again. They remembered Mosiah's reign and the freedom they had enjoyed under his protecting care.

Alma learned that the man who had been killed was his good friend Gideon—the same Gideon who had led Limhi and his people out of bondage. He learned, too, that Gideon had come to the defense of the church of God and had told Nehor he was leading the people away from the true church. Nehor became angry and struck Gideon several blows. Gideon was an old man, and being old and weak, he died. Alma commanded that Nehor be brought before him, that he might be judged according to the law.

Alma was seated by a long table, busily recording the history of his people, when the door opened and they brought Nehor before him. He looked up and for a moment, he was so surprised that he sat speechless, observing the man before him. Nehor was a great giant of a man. His eyes were as cold as steel and just as hard. His huge mouth was curled into an evil smile. At last, Alma's gaze rested on Nehor's hands. Never in all his life had he seen such huge hands, and now they were restlessly opening and shutting as though they would like to be about Alma's neck. The guards who brought him in had fallen back and were now huddled together for protection. There was no fear in Alma's eyes, only righteous anger. The guards marveled at his courage, and when he spoke, his voice was clear and steady:

"Nehor, you have taken a man's life. What have you to say for yourself?"

"I was forced to defend myself against an old man and his crazy ideas," said Nehor boldly.

"It must have taken all the courage you had to defend yourself against a weak old man." Alma spoke with disgust.

Suddenly, Nehor threw back his head and laughed loudly, thinking it a good joke. And then, just as suddenly, his mood changed to black fury. He beat upon his chest and shouted, "Nehor is not afraid of any man—not even you, Chief Judge."

He stepped close to Alma and thrust his evil face forward. Alma met his cruel eyes without fear, while the guards trembled violently at a safe distance.

"Are you guilty of killing Gideon?" asked Alma. His voice had a strange effect on Nehor, for at that instant the great giant suddenly became a weakling. He began begging for mercy. Alma knew that it was through the power of the Lord that Nehor was given over into his hands.

"You have shed the blood of a good man, a man who has done much good among this people. The law says, a life for a life. Therefore, I condemn you to die."

They carried him to the top of the hill Manti, and there, before he died, he confessed that what he had taught the people was not the word of God. But his death did not put an end to sin. The vain, proud people continued to break away from the church and they did many cruel things to the children of God.

The fifth year of the rule of the judges was long to be remembered, because it was a year of great bitterness and heartbreak. When the people of the church could no longer stand the abuse of the unbelievers, they went to war against them. The unbelievers were driven out of Zarahemla, but they were not defeated. They joined with the Lamanites and came back into the land of Zarahemla. A terrible war was fought, in which thousands were killed.

The first year following the war was a time of suffering, both in mind and body, for the people of Zarahemla. There was scarcely a family in all the land who hadn't lost a loved one. Their fields of grain had been beaten into the earth by the armies. Their flocks and herds were almost destroyed. The cries of hungry children were heard on every hand. They became a humble people and turned to God in their hour of need, and He heard their prayers and blessed them.

By the eighth year of the reign of the judges, they had become a prosperous people. Many of them had become worldly, thinking only of their riches. Alma watched them with a heavy heart, and wondered how they could forget their suffering and their need for God so quickly. At last, desperate in his desire to help them before the Lord grew angry, he gave up his position as chief judge in order to spend all his time as high priest of the church. He appointed a faithful elder as chief judge, to rule in his stead. This man's name was Nephihah.

Alma spent all his time teaching the people and bringing them to the remembrance of the goodness and mercy of God. He traveled throughout all the land of Zarahemla, and finally his labors began to bear fruit—the people turned to God and began to keep His commandments once more. Then Alma went over into the valley of Gideon and successfully taught the people God's word. Hundreds of them were baptized and rejoiced in being members of the true church. From the land of Gideon, he went to Melek, and the people blessed him for bringing the gospel to them.

When Alma left Melek, he did so with a light heart and a sense of deep satisfaction. It was a pleasant morning in early fall, and Alma was happier than he had ever been. He knew it was because he was spending his time bringing the people the word of God. He breathed deeply of the fresh, pure air as he turned his footsteps north, to the city of Ammonihah. Part of the journey led through a forest. Through the trees, he caught sight of many wild animals, but he was unafraid, for he knew he walked with God. He traveled for three days and then, at last, he saw the beautiful city of Ammonihah. Even before he entered the city, he felt a strange, unfriendly spirit. It was so strong that he hesitated, wondering if he should turn back. However, he soon overcame his doubts and entered the city and began at once to preach to the people.

Little did he know that Satan had already taken hold of the hearts of the people. Because of this fact, they would not listen to his words. At last the people said: "We know you are Alma, the high priest of the church, but we do not believe in the things you teach; therefore, you have no power over us. We know, too, that you are no longer chief judge over this people, and for this reason we demand that you leave our city."

The people said many evil things to Alma. They spit on him and cast him out. Sick at heart, he turned his footsteps toward the city called Aaron. As he walked along, he was weighed down with sorrow because of the wickedness of the people of Ammonihah. Suddenly, an angel appeared to him. It was the same angel he had seen as a young man, when he and Mosiah's sons had ridden out to destroy the property of the people of the church. This time, however, he was not afraid, but his heart was filled with joy. He knew the angel was there to help him.

The angel spoke, saying, "You are blessed. Lift up your head and rejoice. You have great cause to rejoice, for you have been faithful in keeping the commandments of God from the time you received my first message. I am sent now to command you to return to the city of Ammonihah and preach again to the people. Tell them that if they do not repent, the Lord will destroy them."

As soon as Alma received the message, he hurried back to the city. But this time he entered by another way. He was very hungry, and he remembered that he had had nothing to eat for many days.

Alma said to a man standing near the entrance, "Will you give a humble servant of God something to eat?"

"Good evening. I have been waiting for you," said the man, quietly.

"Waiting to see me?" asked Alma, astonished. "But you are a stranger. How could you possibly know me?"

"You are Alma, a holy prophet of God," answered the man, smiling at Alma's confusion.

"That is my name, but how do you know me? Who are you?" asked Alma, tired of the riddle.

"My name is Amulek and I am a Nephite. Early today, an angel appeared to me and told me to wait here for you. Come with me to my home. I will feed you. Your presence will bring a rich blessing to my house."

Alma followed Amulek to his home, still astonished by all that had happened. When he had eaten Amulek's bread, he thanked God for His wonderful power and he asked that Amulek's house be blessed. Now, Alma stayed with Amulek for many days, until at last the word of God came to him, saying: "Go forth and preach my word to this people. Take Amulek with you and have him testify of the things he has seen. Call upon the people to repent. Tell them if they don't repent, I shall be very angry with them—so angry, in fact, that I will destroy them."

They went forth and began to preach to the people of Ammonihah. Alma reminded them of the promise God had made to Lehi when he reached the promised land.

He said that if this people would keep His commandments and walk in the straight and narrow path, they would prosper in the land. But if they would not keep His commandments, He would destroy them. Alma pointed out how God had kept His promise. He reminded them also of the curse that fell upon the Lamanites because of the wickedness of Laman, Lemuel, and the sons of Ishmael.

The words of Alma and Amulek fell upon deaf ears and hardened hearts. The more they preached to the people of Ammonihah, the more wicked they became. With their wickedness came a deep hatred for these holy men of God. They tried to slay them, but they could not, for Alma and Amulek were filled with the Spirit of the Holy Ghost. Then they took them and bound them fast and threw them into prison. The judges of the land came to the prison each day to abuse Alma and Amulek. Their suffering was so great that Alma called upon God to free them from the hands of their enemies. Lo and behold, God sent His mighty power, and they stood up and the cords that bound them fell away as if they were nothing. The earth trembled so violently that the walls of the prison began to crack and crumble. At last, the whole prison fell to the earth, leaving Alma and Amulek safe and free. All the others who were in the prison lost their lives. The Lord had granted this power unto Alma and Amulek, according to their faith in Christ.

When the people in the city of Ammonihah heard the great noise and felt the trembling earth, they ran forth in a great multitude to the prison. They could scarcely believe their eyes when they saw their strong prison in ruins. Every living creature was dead except Alma and Amulek. Suddenly, they were struck with fear and turned and fled before the two holy men of God.

CHAPTER 38

A lma and Amulek turned their backs on the city of Ammonihah and left the wicked people to their own devices. They traveled slowly back to the land of Zarahemla.

"I am without a home," said Amulek.

"My home shall be your home," said Alma, placing a friendly hand on his companion's shoulder.

In the eleventh year of the reign of the judges, after many years of peace, a cry of war was heard throughout the land. The armies of the Lamanites came into the city of Ammonihah and began to slay the people and destroy the city. Before the Nephites could raise an army large enough to drive them out, they had destroyed most of the people and had taken the rest captive. There was not one living soul left in the entire city. And thus, the word of the Lord was fulfilled. For years to come, it was a place of ruin and complete desolation.

Early in the fifteenth year of the reign of the judges, there was peace and plenty throughout all the lands of the Nephites. Much of the credit was due to Alma and his good friend Amulek. They spent all their time going among the people, teaching them in the ways of the Lord and stirring them to remember God's loving mercy to the faithful and His terrible anger against those who sinned. Their labors were well rewarded, for most of the people were humble and faithful to God and to each other.

Today, Alma was following the trail that led away from Gideon and southward, toward the land of Manti. It was high noon and the day was hot and still. Where the sun touched his hands and face, it felt scorching hot. He was hungry, but there was no sign of shade, and he disliked the thought of eating his bread and cheese in the burning heat of the sun. He knew that at the bottom of the slope the path turned and led into meadow country. Here, the trail was bordered on either side by two rows of willow trees, their lacy branches interlocking with each other, making a long tunnel of green. The very thought of this cool, inviting spot brought a smile to his lips. The smile disappeared when he remembered the stories he had heard concerning the mishaps that had befallen certain travelers. On several occasions, bands of Lamanites had surprised lonely travelers, robbing and beating them. In spite of the stories he had heard, he decided he must get out of the burning rays of the sun at any cost. As he made the turn, he came into full view of the little meadow valley, with its graceful willow trees. It was like a fairyland, with a thin veil of mist hanging over it, making it all seem a bit unreal. Here and there were pools of sparkling, clear water. It was a paradise for birds and all living creatures who loved God's great outdoors.

Alma stopped to rest and to look for any signs of Lamanites, knowing they could easily hide among the shadowy willows. As soon as he reached the willow lane, its cool freshness seemed to give him new strength. He chose a spot under a huge willow tree and sat down on the ground to eat his meal. Suddenly, he was alert to a sound among the trees. He sat silent, almost afraid to

breathe. When the sound came again, he knew that whatever it was, it was walking toward him. In fact, it was very
near. The fingers of his right hand found the handle of his
hunting knife and closed upon it. Suddenly, the head of a
donkey poked through the drooping branches of the willow tree.

When the donkey saw Alma, he was so surprised that
he sat down on his back legs and cried, "Hee-haw! Hee-
haw! Hee-haw!"

"Don't be a foolish old fellow, I'm not going to harm
you," said Alma, laughing at the comical donkey.

At that moment, he noticed a short broken rope
around the donkey's neck. Furthermore, he noticed a
pack on its back. He had been so occupied with the donkey, he failed to hear the voices of men approaching. As
soon as he heard them, he went to the edge of the trail
and looked southward. There, coming toward him, were
four men. Immediately he returned to the donkey and
took hold of its rope.

"Come, little donkey, I need you to make friends for
me," Alma said, and he led the donkey to the path.

Instantly, the men caught sight of him. To his great
surprise, one of them called his name. He saw then that
they were the four sons of King Mosiah. Ammon, the eldest, was the first to reach him. They were all overjoyed
to see each other again. They had shared a wonderful experience together. These were the five men to whom the
angel had appeared fourteen years before, and had
caused them to forsake their sins and walk in the ways of
the Lord.

"Is this your donkey?" asked Alma.

"Yes, it is," they answered. "He broke away from the
pack train. But come, we have better things to talk about
than the runaway donkey."

"Where are you going?" asked Alma.

"We are returning to Zarahemla. It won't seem the same without our father or mother. Come, sit down and tell us all about the things that have happened since we have been among the Lamanites."

Alma was only too glad to give them a full account of the happenings of their people in and about the land of Zarahemla. When he finished, he asked that they tell him of their labors among the Lamanites.

Alma rejoiced at seeing his friends again. But his joy knew no bounds when he learned that they had walked in the ways of the Lord since the angel had appeared to them. They had prayed and fasted often until, at last, through their great faith, God had given them the power of prophecy. They were men of great understanding, and through their constant study of the records, they had come to know the word of God. And when they taught His word, it was with authority from on high. For fourteen years they had labored among the Lamanites, and because of their good example and their knowledge of the truth, they had had great success in converting them to the gospel. The sons of Mosiah had met with many hardships. Often, their lives were in danger and they had suffered, both in mind and body. They had been hungry, thirsty, tired, and discouraged. But, through their prayers and God's watchful eye, they had overcome great obstacles.

CHAPTER 39

A lma and the sons of Mosiah talked all through the day and far into the night. As if by special arrangement, just as twilight was fading into night, a full moon rose in a cloudless sky, blessing them with its white, silvery light. Now, as the others lay sleeping, Alma lay wide awake. He was thinking of all they had told him about their experiences with the Lamanites, beginning fourteen years earlier. Ammon had done most of the talking.

When the sons of Mosiah and those who went with them had reached the Lamanite borders, they had prayed and fasted. They asked God that His Holy Spirit would be with them, so that they might impart the truth to the Lamanites. They asked Him also for courage in their labors. Their job required a great deal of courage, because the Lamanites were a wild and hard-hearted people. They hated the Nephites with a fierce and terrible hatred. But, with faith in God, the sons of Mosiah parted company, each going in a different direction. They prayed that they would meet again when their labors were completed.

Ammon went to the land of Ishmael. This land was named after the sons of Ishmael, who joined with Laman and Lemuel and became known as the Lamanites. Just as Ammon entered their land, he was set upon by several men. They bound him and took him to their king. This was the practice they always followed when they captured a Nephite. It was left to the pleasure of the king to decide the fate of the victim.

Lamoni was king over the land of Ishmael and when he saw Ammon, he looked at him suspiciously and asked, "What are you doing in my land? Do you wish to live here, among my people?"

Ammon answered him, "Yes, I should like to live here among your people, perhaps until I die."

The words of Ammon pleased King Lamoni so much that he ordered that the ropes that bound him be loosened.

"I will give you one of my daughters to be your wife," said King Lamoni, smiling at the surprised look on Ammon's face.

"I do not wish so great an honor. I shall be very happy to be your servant," said Ammon, humbly.

King Lamoni, like the rest of his people, had been taught from early childhood to hate and distrust the Nephites, but in spite of himself he found it pleasant to talk with Ammon. Yes, he even liked him. However, he meant to test him, so he said, "Take Ammon to my servants who tend my flocks. I want him to help them."

Ammon was delighted. He liked working outside. He had often tended his father's flocks. He knew, too, that in this way he would have an opportunity to teach the word of God. Little did he know that, in a very short time, he would find himself in real danger. He prayed silently for God to provide a way to touch their hearts, so that they would listen to the truths he wanted to teach them.

Water for the flocks and herds was scarce in the land of Ishmael. For this reason, more than one man's animals had to use the same watering place. On the morning of the third day, Ammon and the other servants drove the king's flocks to the place called Sebus. It was a pleasant morning and as Ammon watched the thirsty animals drink the clear, cool water, he felt happier than he had for a long time. He was deep within his own thoughts when he realized that something was happening to the animals. Looking up, he saw a number of strange Lamanites scattering the flocks. This was the custom of certain bands of Lamanites. They would wait at the watering place and scatter the animals in all directions, in the hope that they could drive off part of them for themselves.

The king's servants began to cry out in fear, saying, "The king will surely slay us as he has done with our brethren who lost the flocks in the same manner."

Ammon saw at once that the servants were too frightened to even try to get the animals back. Therefore, with a prayer in his heart, he said with firm conviction, "Do not be afraid, for we can easily get the flocks back again, if we work fast."

Ammon's words so encouraged them that they ran around the flocks and brought them back to the water. But the wicked men were still there and came forth to scatter them again.

"Encircle the animals," said Ammon, "and see that they do not run away, while I go forward and talk with these men."

King Lamoni's servants hurried to do as Ammon commanded. There was something about his voice that made them feel that they could trust him. When he walked toward the men who stood on the banks of Sebus, the king's servants watched him with fear and trembling.

When Ammon was within speaking distance, he called out to the wicked Lamanites: "Stand aside and let us water our flocks! If you do not, you will be sorry, for some of you may be destroyed."

The men roared with laughter. They were great in

number and they thought that anytime they wished, one of them could go forth and kill Ammon. But there was something they did not know—Mosiah had been promised by the Lord that his sons would be delivered out of their hands. Nor did they know the great power of the Lord when one has faith like Ammon.

When Ammon saw that the men did not mean to let them come near the water, he took his sling and began casting stones at them. Six of their number were struck and fell to the ground, while not one single stone hit Ammon. When the wicked Lamanites saw what was happening, they picked up huge clubs and came forward to kill Ammon. But when they raised their clubs, Ammon smote them with his sword and they were unable to harm him. They were so astonished at his great power that they turned and ran away. Then he returned to the king's servants, and together they watered the flocks and drove them home to the king's pastures.

The servants hurried to the king to tell him what had happened. He was so astonished that he asked them whether Ammon was really a man or the Great Spirit.

"We don't know, but we do know that he cannot be killed by the king's enemies."

When Ammon came to the king, he found him in great distress. He was afraid to speak. But Ammon, knowing what was in the king's mind, told him not to be afraid.

"How did you know my thoughts? Who are you? Are you the Great Spirit who knows all things?" asked the bewildered king.

"I am not," answered Ammon.

"If you will tell me how you get your great power, I will grant you anything you ask for," said the king, with great excitement.

Now, Ammon, being a wise man and entirely unselfish, said, "Will you listen to my words, if I tell you how I got this great power?"

"Yes," answered the king. "I will believe anything you tell me." And thus he placed himself in Ammon's hands.

"Do you believe there is a God?" asked Ammon.

"I don't know what that means."

"Do you believe there is a Great Spirit?"

"Yes," said Lamoni.

"This is God," said Ammon. "Do you believe this Great Spirit, who is God, made all things in heaven and earth?"

"Yes, I believe that He created all things on earth, but I do not know about heaven."

"Heaven is a place where God and all His holy angels dwell."

The king sat silent, trying to understand the marvelous things he had heard. At last, when he spoke, his voice was full of faith: "I believe all that you have told me. Are you sent from God?"

Ammon said to him, "I am a man, and man was created in the image of God. I am called by Him to teach your people to know what is just and true."

Then Ammon told him all about the creation of the world, down to the time that Lehi left Jerusalem, and of how Laman and Lemuel and the sons of Ishmael had rebelled.

The king believed all that he heard and he began to cry to the Lord, saying, "Oh, Lord, have mercy on my people. Bless us, as you have the Nephites."

As soon as the king had spoken these words, he fell to the earth as if he were dead. The servants carried him to his wife and laid him upon his bed. He lay as if he were dead for two days and two nights. His wife, his sons, and his daughters wept aloud because of their great loss.

On the second day, the servants said to each other, "Our king is dead and we must bury him. Let us go and tell the queen."

"No," said the queen, when they told her. "The king is not dead."

The servants were surprised to hear the queen's words and they looked at each other, as much as to say, "Our queen is mad. Her great grief has destroyed her reason."

Now, the queen knew their thoughts, so she commanded, "Go bring Ammon the Nephite to me. You men who tend the flocks have said he is a true prophet of the Great Spirit. He will know what to do."

When Ammon came, he was overjoyed to learn what great faith the queen had.

"The king is alive. At this time tomorrow, he will arise from his bed," said Ammon.

Now, Ammon knew that the Lord had used this means to take away the veil of darkness from the mind of the king and to fill his being with God's holy light. The queen sat by her husband until the next day. Then, just as Ammon had said, the king arose from his bed.

"You are blessed, my queen. I have seen a wonderful vision. I saw the Redeemer and I know that He will come to earth and save mankind."

Then he prayed until he was overcome and fell to the earth again. In a few minutes, the queen, Ammon, and all the king's servants fell to the earth. They lay as though they were dead. There was one who did not fall. Her name was Abish. For many years, she had known about the ways of the Lord. Her father had had a remarkable vision. She thought that if all the people could see the king and queen and all the others lying on the ground, they would believe in the power and goodness of the Lord. Therefore, she ran from house to house, until a great multitude had gathered about those lying on the ground. They began to quarrel with each other. Some said that great evil had befallen the king and his household because he had let the Nephite stay. Others said that the Nephite had brought them the Lord's holy light. In the multitude were some of the men who had scattered the king's flocks. Seeing Ammon lying on the ground, one of them came forward and raised his sword to kill him. Suddenly, he fell dead. This so frightened the crowd that no one dared come near those who lay on the ground, except Abish. She ran to the queen and touched her hand. To their surprise, the queen arose and began praising the Lord. She took Lamoni by the hand and he and all the servants arose.

From that day forth, their hearts had been changed. They had no further desire to do evil. A great many of the people became baptized and a church was established in the land of Ishmael. The Lord began to pour out His spirit upon them, because of their repentance.

CHAPTER 40

A few days later, on a rain-swept morning, King La-moni and Ammon were rolling along in a chariot drawn by two fine, white horses. The rain had stopped and the clouds began to lift, letting the sun stream through, touching the tiny raindrops on the leaves and changing them into brilliantly colored jewels. Ammon breathed deeply of the cool, fresh air and thought that the rich, green fields and woods were the most beautiful sight he had ever seen. In spite of the rough roads, the ride gave him great pleasure.

"You are a skillful driver," said Ammon. "I notice you miss most of the ruts."

"Oh," said King Lamoni, "it's easier than you think. See how the rain has marked each rut clearly. Something has been puzzling me, Ammon."

"Something about me?" asked Ammon.

"Yes," answered Lamoni. "When I asked you to come with me to the land of Nephi that you might meet my father, who is king over all the land of the Lamanites, you objected. You said you must go to the land of Middoni, because your brother Aaron and two of his friends were in prison there. Tell me, how did you know this?"

"God told me," said Ammon, simply.

Lamoni turned and looked at Ammon in surprise at the matter-of-fact way in which his friend spoke of God— just as though He were one of their companions. And, indeed, He was. His Spirit was with Ammon wherever he went.

Suddenly, they heard the rumble of another chariot coming toward them. Looking up, Ammon saw two beautiful, cream-colored horses drawing a chariot trimmed in gold and precious stones. The rays of the sun made it glitter so brightly that he raised his hand to protect his eyes.

"It is my father," said Lamoni, as the chariot came to a stop beside them.

"Well, at last, I see you," roared the old king. "What kept you away from my feast?"

Patiently and with great feeling, Lamoni told his father all about how Ammon had converted him to the faith. For this reason, he had not been able to come to his father's palace. When his father heard his son's words, a terrible anger seized him.

"Where are you going with this Nephite son of a liar?" questioned the old king.

"To Middoni, Father," answered Lamoni quietly.

"And why do you go to Middoni?" he asked sharply.

"To free Aaron and his two friends from prison."

"I've never heard of them before. Tell me who they are and why they should concern you," demanded the king in a great, thundering voice.

"This is Ammon, Father, and it is his brother and his friends who have been cast into prison. I go to plead with the king of Middoni in their behalf," said Lamoni, watching his father carefully. The old man was not only his father but his king as well. He ruled his kingdoms with an iron hand and many a king had been destroyed by him.

When the king heard his son's words, color flooded his face. He grew so red that Ammon expected to see him explode into a thousand pieces. For a few seconds he was unable to speak, and when he did, his words were fierce with anger.

"You go to free the Nephites, children of liars? How dare you? They robbed our fathers and now their children have come among us to deceive us, that they may again rob us of our property. I command you, as your king, to slay Ammon with your sword. Furthermore, I command you to stay away from Middoni. Turn around and go back with me to Ishmael."

Lamoni had always been more than a little afraid of his father—especially when he was angry. But now, to his great surprise, he felt calm and unafraid.

"I will not slay Ammon," answered Lamoni. "Neither will I return to the land of Ishmael. I am going to Middoni to set the prisoners free. I know that they are just men and holy prophets of the true God."

When his father heard this, he drew his sword and raised it, as if to kill his son. Suddenly, Ammon came forward and said to him: "You must not kill your son. Nevertheless, it would be better that he died than you. He has repented of his sins, but if you should go in your anger, your soul could not be saved. If you slay your son, you will shed innocent blood."

While Ammon was speaking, the old king drew his sword and came dangerously near where Ammon was standing.

"I know," said the king, fiercely, "that if I kill my son, I will shed innocent blood. It is you who will destroy him."

In a wild rage, the king rushed toward Ammon, striking him again and again with his sword. But Ammon withstood all the blows; in fact, he didn't seem to mind them at all. At last, Ammon raised his sword and struck the arm of the king, making it useless. When the king realized what had happened—that he was now at the mercy of the Nephite—he began to plead for his life.

"Spare my life," he moaned, "and you shall have whatever you want, even if it be half my kingdom."

"If I spare your life, you must let Aaron and his friends go free. Furthermore, you must allow your son, Lamoni, to keep his kingdom and have a free hand in ruling it. Now, O King, if you will grant these things, I will spare your life."

The king was astonished at Ammon's words. He fully expected him to demand riches and power. But Ammon had asked for neither. In fact, he hadn't asked for a thing for himself. This was a strange man, thought the king. In that moment, he knew how great was the love of the Nephite for his son, Lamoni. It warmed his heart and he forgot his hatred for the Nephites.

"Yes, yes," cried the old king. "I will grant all you have asked for and more. Come with me to the land of Nephi and dwell among us."

"Thank you," said Ammon, "but I go to Middoni first to free my brother from prison, and then I shall return to Ishmael, to finish my mission there."

Lamoni's father made Ammon promise to come to the land of Nephi later, then the three of them parted good friends.

The king of Middoni was happy to see King Lamoni. He gladly granted their request to set Aaron and his friends free. In a short time, the prisoners were brought to them. Ammon scarcely knew his brother; he was so thin and pale. All three of them were naked, and where the ropes had bound them, their skin was raw and bleeding. Ammon felt sick at the thought of how they must have suffered. When Aaron and his friends had been clothed and fed, the two brothers sat down to have a long visit. When they had finished, they said good-bye and departed in opposite directions.

Ammon returned with Lamoni to the land of Ishmael and spent all his time going among the Lamanites, teaching them the word of God. Hundreds of them were converted and joined the church. King Lamoni sent his messengers throughout all his kingdom, telling the people that they were free to worship according to their desires.

After Aaron left Middoni, he was led by the Spirit to the land of Nephi—yes, even to the king, ruler over all the lands except Ishmael.

"O King," said Aaron, "I am the brother of Ammon. If you will spare our lives, we will be your servants."

With these words, Aaron and his friends fell upon their knees before the old king.

"Arise," said the king. "Your lives are spared, and all I ask in return is that you teach me about the ways of the Lord."

It came to pass that the king, the queen, and all their servants became converted to the teachings of Aaron. The old king sent out a proclamation to all the Lamanites in his kingdom. He told them that Aaron and his three brothers were to be free to teach the people from house to house and in their churches. Furthermore, the people themselves were to be free to worship as they pleased. After this proclamation, thousands were converted to the gospel of Jesus Christ. They wanted to be given a name that would distinguish them from the nonbelievers of the Lamanites. From that day forth, they were known as the Anti-Nephi-Lehies.

One day, when the four sons of Mosiah chanced to meet, Ammon said to them: "We have met with great success in all our missionary labors. We have entered into their houses and taught them. We have taught them in the streets and upon their hills and in their temples. We have been cast out, mocked, spit upon, stoned, and cast into prison. But, through the power and wisdom of God, we have always been delivered. We can now see the fruits of our labors. They are many and we can see their sincerity because of their love toward one another and toward us. There never has been such great love in all the land—not even among the Nephites. We have great reason to rejoice."

CHAPTER 41

The converted Lamanites, known as the Anti-Nephi-Lehies, were in grave danger. When they became members of the true church of God, they had buried their weapons of war and vowed never to take them up again, even in defense of their own lives. Now, the wicked Lamanites knew this, and they took advantage of it by stealing from their flocks and herds and their storehouses. They killed many of them for no reason at all. When Ammon and his three brothers saw this work of destruction they were very sad, for they loved the people dearly, and they, in turn, loved the four brothers. The Lamanites treated them as though they were angels of God, sent to save their souls.

"O King, let us gather these people of the Lord and go down to the land of Zarahemla. There we will be with the Nephites, out of the hands of our enemies," said Ammon.

But the king said, "The Nephites will destroy us because of our past sins against them."

Then Ammon said, "I will ask the Lord. If he tells us to go to Zarahemla, will you go?"

"Yes," said the king, "if the Lord tells us to go, then you can be sure we will go. We will offer ourselves as their slaves, until we have paid them back for our many sins against them."

"No," said Ammon, "that is not the way of the Nephites. Many years ago my father, Mosiah, established a law forbidding slavery. Therefore, let us go down and rely on their mercy."

But the king said to Ammon, "Go and ask the Lord. If He says to go, we will obey Him. Otherwise, we will perish in our land."

The Lord answered Ammon, saying, "Get this people out of this land, so that they will not be destroyed! Satan has a great hold on the hearts of the Lamanites. Blessed are the Anti-Nephi-Lehies, for I will preserve them."

They began at once to gather all the people of the Lord and all their flocks and herds. Then they went into the wilderness which divided the land of Nephi from the land of Zarahemla.

"My brothers and I," said Ammon, "will go to Zarahemla. You remain here until we return. We will prepare the hearts of the Nephites, so that they will receive you into their land."

The four sons of King Mosiah set out immediately for the land of Zarahemla. It was on this very journey that they met Alma. They had talked for hours and they were overjoyed at meeting their friend. Early next morning, Alma awakened Ammon and his brothers.

"It is sunrise," said Alma. "It is time for us to begin our journey to Zarahemla."

"Do you mean you are going with us to Zarahemla?" asked Ammon, smiling his pleasure.

"Yes," answered Alma. "I thought perhaps I could help you, since I am high priest, but if you would rather go alone, I will understand."

Now, Ammon and his brothers were delighted at the prospect of having Alma with them. They had wanted to ask him to join them, but they had hesitated, since they knew he was doing missionary work among the Nephites. When they reached Zarahemla, they went at once to Alma's house.

"I would like you to share my home with me," said Alma.

The brothers were grateful for the invitation, since their father and mother had both passed away.

"First, we must see the chief judge of the land," said Ammon.

The chief judge was deeply touched by the story of the conversion of the Lamanites known as the Anti-Nephi-Lehies. When he learned that they needed protection from their enemies, because they would not take up arms to protect themselves, he was anxious to help them. He sent a proclamation throughout all the land of the Nephites, asking the people what they wished to do to help their brethren.

"We will watch over them," said the people, "and protect them from their enemies. They can have the land of Jershon as the land of their inheritance. We will give them protection by placing our army between them and the wicked Lamanites."

Now, Jershon was a beautiful land in the east by the sea. It joined the land Bountiful. Alma and Ammon returned to the Anti-Nephi-Lehies where they waited in the wilderness. They were grateful to learn of the generosity of the people of Zarahemla. When they entered Jershon, they blessed the land and began at once to build their homes. They were honest and upright in every way, and they were firm in the faith of Christ to the very end. The Nephites learned to love them and they became a highly favored people.

One afternoon, during the seventeenth year of the

reign of the judges, Alma and his good wife sat in their comfortable living room. Alma had been reading, but now he pushed the record from him and leaned back in the chair and closed his eyes. After a few minutes he sat up and watched his wife mending his tunic. Because of his great love for her, he thought her beautiful. She wasn't really beautiful at all, but rather plain. She felt his eyes on her and, looking up, she smiled at him. There was magic in her smile. It changed her plain features into sweet loveliness and made her dark eyes sparkle.

"You're not forgetting your appointment with the chief judge, are you?" she asked.

"No," replied Alma.

"You look troubled. Is this meeting worrying you?" asked his wife.

"Yes," said Alma. "He is an evil man."

"Of whom do you speak?" she questioned.

"Korihor!"

"Korihor," she said. "I don't believe I have heard of him."

"He is a wicked man. He denies the prophets of our God and he goes so far as to deny the coming of Christ. He says there is no God, and that those of us who claim there is only do so in order that we can live from the labors of the people."

An angry flush crept into the cheeks of Alma's wife. No one knew better than she that he had never allowed anyone to support him, even when he spent most of his time going among the people, teaching them the ways of God. There had been times when he and his family had gone hungry to help others. When Alma saw her anger, he soothed her by putting his arm tenderly about her shoulders.

"Well, at last this man has gotten himself arrested,

and he is to be judged this very afternoon. Now, I must go. The chief judge wants me to hear what Korihor has to say for himself."

Alma reached the bar of justice before the prisoner. At last, when they brought him in, he was very angry. Alma studied his face and found it evil and cowardly.

Korihor said, "I deny that there is a Christ or that there ever will be one, but if you will show me a sign, I might believe. Surely, your God is powerful enough to give me a sign."

"You need no sign," said Alma, "for all about you bears testimony of God. How dare you tempt Him by asking for a sign? Think well, before you make Him angry. Now, do you still want a sign?"

The corners of Korihor's mouth curled into an evil smile as he said, "Yes, I shall deny all these things, unless you show me a sign."

"I am very sorry to learn how hard-hearted you are. Since you deny the Spirit, which teaches all of us what the real truth is, you may lose your soul. But perhaps it is better that one man lose his soul, than the many that you are leading astray by your lying. Now, if you dare deny again, God will strike you dumb. You will never open your mouth again to destroy this people." Alma's voice was low and pleading. He was deeply grieved over the terrible thing Korihor was demanding.

But Korihor threw back his head and laughed. "I do not believe there is a God," he said. "And, furthermore, you do not know there is one either. Show me a sign, if you can."

"Very well," said Alma. "You shall be struck dumb, and I say this in the name of God. From this day forward, you shall not speak again."

When Alma had said this, Korihor found that he was dumb. He tried and tried to speak, but no words would come. Then he pulled on his tongue, but that did not help.

The chief judge said to him, "Are you convinced now of God's power?"

Korihor wrote these words in answer: "I know that I am dumb. I cannot speak. I know that no one but God could have such power. Behold, I have been deceived by the devil, for he appeared to me in the form of an angel. I have taught his words. Alma, ask God to forgive me that I may have this curse taken away."

Alma said, "If this curse was taken away, you would again lead the people astray. Therefore, it shall remain until the Lord wills it otherwise."

From that day forward, everyone knew of Korihor and the terrible curse that had been placed upon him. All those who had heard his words were frightened and began to repent. They feared that the Lord would strike them dumb also. Now, Korihor went from house to house, begging for his food. One day, while he begged on the street, he was run down and killed. Thus he came to a sorrowful end, because of this sin in denying God.

CHAPTER 42

"A re you tired, my son?" asked Alma, anxiously watching his son Shiblon throw himself on the ground beneath a giant tree.

"I am leg weary. I should be ashamed to admit it when you, who are twice my age, seem as fresh as when we left Zarahemla early this morning," answered the young man.

"I am used to walking and you're not," said Alma pleasantly as he seated himself on the trunk of a fallen tree. "I never see you walk anyplace if you can possibly get there on horseback. My missionary labors have kept me walking constantly."

"I suppose you have been in every nook and corner in all of the Nephite lands," said his son with admiration.

"Oh, my son," said Alma. "I wish that I were an angel so that I could speak unto all the ends of the earth. I would speak to every soul and cry repentance, with a voice that would shake the earth. But I am a man and I must be content with this human body the Lord has given me."

"In my opinion, Father, you're a man above all other men. You not only preach the gospel, but live it as well. Every night and morning, I ask God to make me the kind of man you are," said Shiblon earnestly.

At the sound of his son's words, Alma's heart skipped a beat. This was one of those rare moments that every parent hopes for, but few experience. His son approved of him and wanted to be like him. Suddenly, in that moment of great joy, a painful thought saddened him, for he had a confession to make to his son. Would Shiblon turn away in hatred when he heard his father's words? He had meant to tell his sons, but he had put it off, always hoping for just the right time.

"I have a confession to make, which I should have made long ago. Perhaps when you hear it you will no longer wish to be like me. I had a wasted youth. I went about the countryside, with the four sons of King Mosiah, bent upon the destruction of the true church of God," said Alma, burying his face in his hands.

"Don't be sad, Father, I know the story," said Shiblon.

"You know? But how?" asked Alma, scarcely believing what he heard.

"My mother told me. She told it so effectively that my brothers and I grew up thinking it was one of the most beautiful stories we had ever heard. I like best the part where the angel descended in a cloud and spoke with a voice of thunder."

"God bless your dear mother. She was wiser than I. All these years, I have been dreading to tell you," said Alma.

"But why?" asked Shiblon.

"I was afraid that when you knew, you would hate me, and I couldn't bear the thought of losing your love and respect," explained Alma, with deep emotion.

"In reality it made us love you more and gave us a living testimony of the truthfulness of the gospel."

Alma felt that a heavy burden had been lifted from

his heart. He silently thanked God for giving him such a wonderful wife.

"Thank you, my son. I am a happier man for knowing that you share my secret. As soon as you have rested, we must be on our way down the mountain to the waterfall. It is there that I told the others to join us," said Alma.

"We are going to Zoram, aren't we?" asked Shiblon.

"Yes."

"How many are going with us?"

"The three sons of Mosiah, Ammon, Aaron, and Omner. I am leaving Himni to take over my duties in the churches of Zarahemla. Furthermore, I am taking you and your younger brother, Corianton, and two friends," explained Alma.

"But what of Helaman?"

"I am leaving Helaman, my eldest son, to look after your mother and sisters. We will spend the night at the waterfall, and from there the eight of us will make the journey together to the land of Zoram."

"I have never been to Zoram. Is it far away?" asked Shiblon, sitting up.

"Yes, my son, it is far away. It lies east of the land of Zarahemla, nearly bordering on the seashore. It is south of the land of Jershon and borders the wilderness, which is full of Lamanites."

"Is it true, Father," asked Shiblon, "that the Nephites who live in the land of Zoram have turned against God and now worship idols?"

"Yes," replied Alma. "They were once strong believers in God and His son, Jesus Christ, but now they have fallen into sinful ways and they threaten our security."

"But how can that be?" asked Shiblon.

"The Nephites fear that the Zoramites will make friends with the Lamanites. This would be a means of bringing great loss to the Nephites. Now, my son, we know that preaching the word of God has a way of leading people to the things that are just—it has a more powerful effect on the minds of people than the sword or anything else. That is why we mustn't lose any time in reaching them with the word of God."

After several days of travel, Alma and his seven missionary companions reached the land of Zoram. The first things they saw were the fine buildings and the beautiful churches. Going inside a church, they saw a strange thing. In the middle of the church was a high platform, far above their heads. One at a time, the people of Zoram climbed to the top of the platform and raised their hands above their heads and prayed aloud to a strange god.

"Holy god," they prayed, "you have made it known to us that there is no Christ and we shall be saved while all around us shall be cast into hell, for which we thank thee, amen."

When Alma and the other missionaries heard these prayers, they were surprised beyond all measure. Every man offered the same prayer. The place where they prayed was called the Holy Stand. When all the people had said this prayer, they returned to their homes and never spoke of their god until the next week, when it was prayer day again. When Alma saw this, he was very sad. He knew that they were wicked people. Their hearts were set upon gold and silver and all worldly goods. They wore costly clothes. Their fingers were covered with rings and upon their arms were bracelets. About their necks were ornaments of gold and silver and precious gems. Their hair hung down in ringlets. When the Zoramites saw the travel-worn clothing of the missionaries, they drove them out of the church, for only the rich were admitted.

From the church, Alma and his brethren went their separate ways. They taught the word of God from house to house and in the streets. The poor people gathered around them, eager to hear again the word of the Lord. They had been forbidden to worship in the fine churches. They had once kept the commandments of God, for they were Nephites, too. The missionaries taught the poor people repentance and how to seek forgiveness. The poor Zoramites worried because they had no church to worship in. But the missionaries comforted them. They told them that they could worship in their hearts, and God would hear their prayers and bless them for their faithfulness.

Now, when Alma and his companions had preached the word of God to all the Zoramites, they left Zoram and went over into Jershon, the land of the Anti-Nephi-Lehies. The Nephites called this people by a new name—the people of Ammon.

After the missionaries left Zoram, the rich people grew very angry at the poor, who had accepted the word of God. They drove them out of Zoram. These poor people followed the missionaries to Jershon. They were made welcome by the missionaries and the converted Lamanites. When the ruler of the Zoramites heard where they had gone, he sent word to the people of Ammon that they must drive his people out of their land. He made many threats against them, but the people of Ammon were not afraid. They welcomed the poor people of Zoram. They fed them and gave them clothing and lands for their inheritance.

When the Zoramites heard what they had done, their anger was terrible. Immediately they went into the wilderness and began to mix with the wicked Lamanites. Soon the Zoramites and the Lamanites began to make preparations for war against the people of Ammon and the Nephites.

The people of Ammon gave up the land of Jershon and went over into the land of Melek, so that the armies of the Nephites could use Jershon for a battleground. Alma and Ammon and their brethren returned to Zarahemla, after bringing many Zoramites to repentance.

When Alma reached home, he saw the sudden look of anxiety in his wife's eyes.

"Are you ill, my husband?" she asked him tenderly.

"No, I am not ill—I'm just tired and old," he answered.

Now, Alma's wife had never heard him use the word *old* in connection with himself. He had always had good health, and so much energy that one was apt to take him for a much younger man than he was. Now, as she looked at him, she saw deep lines of worry. His tired, drawn expression made her count his years. He was, indeed, an old man. However, the next morning he arose from his bed looking as though years had fallen away from him overnight. As soon as he had eaten his breakfast, he called Helaman to him.

"My son Helaman," he said, "I am leaving you the records that have been entrusted to me. You are to keep a record of this people on the plates of Nephi. Here are the brass plates, which contain the records of the holy scriptures. I command you to guard them well. They are to be handed down from generation to generation until they go forth to every nation, kindred, tongue, and people. Keep them shining brightly."

"I shall do as you command. Father, what is this that looks like a compass?" asked Helaman.

"It was given to Lehi, to guide his people to the promised land. They called it a ball or director. It has also been known as the Liahona. It worked for them when they had faith, but when they doubted God's power, it stood still. My son, see that you take care of these sacred things. Go unto this people and declare the word of God. And now, farewell," said Alma.

Next, he sent for Shiblon and praised him for his faithfulness in the mission field.

"I have had great joy in you," said Alma, "because of your faith and patience among the Zoramites. May the Lord bless your soul and receive you at the last day into His Kingdom, to sit down in peace. My son, farewell."

Before he sent for his youngest son, Corianton, he sat for a long time, sick at heart, because of the things he was forced to say to him. When at last he sent for him, he said:

"Shiblon has set a good example for you, but you did not follow it. You, Corianton, did not listen to my words. You grew proud and boastful of your own strength and wisdom. And this is not all, my son. You have committed a terrible sin in the eyes of the Lord. Go before the Lord in prayer and ask His forgiveness. You, as the son of the high priest, should set a good example for the people to follow. Oh, my son, humble yourself and go among the people and preach the word of God. Amen."

The sons of Alma went among the people, teaching them. But Alma himself couldn't rest, and he, too, went forth crying repentance to all those who would listen.

CHAPTER 43

I n the beginning of the eighteenth year of the reign of the judges, the sound of war echoed and reechoed throughout all the precious land of promise. The icy fingers of fear reached out and gripped the hearts of all the people. They knew what a terrible thing war was. The Zoramites joined the Lamanites and became Lamanites. Furthermore, they joined forces with the Amalekites, who were a wicked people. The Lamanites gathered their forces by the thousands in the land of Zoram.

When the Nephites saw that they were coming to destroy them, they began making preparations for war. They gathered their armies in the land of Jershon. It was the plan of the Nephites to protect their lands, their houses, their wives and children from the hands of their enemies. Above all, they wished to preserve their liberty, so that they might worship God according to their own desires. In this hour of peril, they thought of the black hatred the Lamanites held for their brethren, the Anti-Nephi-Lehies, or the people of Ammon, as the Nephites called them. The people of Ammon would not take up arms even to save their lives. Therefore, if the Lamanites came upon them, they would be destroyed. However, the Nephites had made up their minds to protect them at any cost. They gave them lands for their inheritance, outside the battlefield. In return, the people of Ammon gave a large share of their produce to support the army.

The man appointed to be the chief captain over the Nephites was Moroni. Now, the chief captain took command of all the armies of his people. Moroni was only twenty-five years old—a strong, handsome man, loved and respected by all his people. With Moroni leading them, they felt sure of victory. He met the Lamanites in the borders of Jershon. When the armies of the Lamanites saw that the people of Nephi had been prepared with breastplates, arm shields, head shields, and thick clothing, they were seized with terror. The Lamanites were naked, except for a skin that they wore about their loins. And because of their nakedness, they did not dare to fight the well-armed Nephites. The Lamanites went into the wilderness. They made a long journey toward the river Sidon, in order to come into the land of Manti and take possession of it before Moroni knew where they had gone.

But Moroni, being a wise leader, sent spies into the wilderness to watch their camp. He remembered Alma and his prophecies. Therefore, he sent men to request that Alma pray and ask God where the armies of the Nephites should go to defend themselves against the Lamanites. Alma did as Moroni requested and the word of the Lord came to him, saying:

"The armies of the Lamanites are marching about the wilderness. They plan to come into the land of Manti, because it is the weakest city of the Nephites."

As soon as Moroni received the message, he knew just what to do. He placed his armies so that they encircled the Lamanites; no matter which way they turned, they found part of Moroni's army. But the Lamanites, seeing that they were surrounded, began fighting fiercely.

Since they had double the number of men, it began to look for a while as if they would win the battle. But Moroni's voice came to his men, saying:

"Fight men, fight! Think of your women and children. Our cause is just because we fight to protect our liberty, our lands, our homes, and above all, the right to worship God as we choose. Death would be better than to become slaves of the Lamanites."

When the men heard these words, they fought with new courage. When the Lamanites saw that they were being defeated, terror seized them and they stood helpless before the Nephites.

"Stop!" shouted Moroni. "We have beaten them and there is no need to shed more blood. You know that you are in our hands and we do not wish to kill you. We came only to defend our liberties, not to shed blood or take you as our slaves. The Lord has been good to us and delivered you into our hands. We shall set you free, because of our religion and our faith in Christ."

Moroni made the Lamanites promise never to come against them again in war. When they had made this promise, the armies of both the Lamanites and the Nephites returned to their own homes. Thus ended the record of Alma, which was written upon the plates of Nephi.

During the golden autumn of the nineteenth year of the reign of the judges, Alma came to Helaman and said, "Do you believe what I have told you about the importance of the records of our fathers?"

"Yes, Father, I believe," said Helaman.

"Do you believe in Jesus Christ, who shall come?" asked Alma, again.

"Yes, I believe all the words you have spoken," said Helaman.

"Will you keep my commandments?" asked Alma.

And Helaman said, "Yes, I will keep your commandments with all my heart."

"You are blessed and the Lord shall prosper you in this land," said Alma. "But I have something to prophesy to you. It must be kept secret until the prophecy is fulfilled. Therefore, write down what I shall tell you."

Helaman did as he was told and this is what he wrote: "I see that this very people, the Nephites, in four hundred years from the time that Jesus Christ shall come to this land, shall lose their faith. There shall be wars, famines, and bloodshed, even until the people of Nephi shall be entirely wiped out. This will come true because they will lose faith in God. They will fall into darkness and all manner of sin. But, if any remain and are not destroyed in that great and terrible day, they will be numbered among the Lamanites. Yes, and they shall become like them—all except a few who shall be called the disciples of the Lord. The Lamanites will hunt these disciples down and slay them."

After Alma had said these things to Helaman, he gave him a blessing. Then he sent for his two other sons and blessed them. Furthermore, he blessed the church and all those who should stand fast in the faith.

That very afternoon, Alma said farewell to his family. He walked out of Zarahemla and took the road that led to Melek. When many days had passed and there was no word from him, his good wife and sons began to worry.

One evening, Alma's wife called her three sons to her and said, "Your father has been gone for the space of many days. I am worried about him."

"But, Mother," said Helaman, "Father has often stayed away from home for long periods of time."

"Yes, I know," answered his mother, "but always before, he sent me messages telling where and how he was. This time there has been no news from him, from any source."

Corianton, who probably loved his mother more tenderly than any of her children, saw the deep lines of worry on her pale face. He was deeply touched and went quickly to her side, placing an arm about her thin shoulders.

"Don't worry, little mother," he said. "We are sure to find him."

She smiled at her youngest son and said, "Thank you, Corianton. I need all three of you. I want you to organize a searching party. Go into every nook and corner of this great land and search for your father. We know he set out for Melek. If you do not find him in the Nephite country, search the lands of our enemies."

Alma's sons were only too willing to obey their mother, for they loved their father and respected him above any other man. In spite of their efforts, winter, spring, summer, and fall came again and still there was no word of Alma. His children watched their mother grow thin and fade away into a tiny old lady, with eyes that were always searching for her lost Alma. But then, one day in late autumn, Helaman, Shiblon, and Corianton saw a change come over their mother. Her eyes were no longer haunted by searching. There was a shining look about her and one sensed a feeling of quiet peace.

"Mother," asked Shiblon, "have you received good news about Father?"

"No, I have received no news, and yet, I have a message for you. You are not to continue the search."

"But why?" asked her sons.

"Because," she answered, "your father is no longer with us. God has taken him home."

"But Mother," said Helaman sternly, "we have found no evidence of his death or his burial."

"You know that your father was a righteous man."

"Yes, we know this," they answered.

"I believe," said their mother, with quiet devotion,

"that God needed Alma. He has taken him up by the Spirit, or buried him by His own hands, even as He did Moses. Now, the scripture says that the Lord took Moses to Himself and so, I suppose, He has also received Alma in the Spirit. Because of this, we know nothing about his death and burial."

Alma's children accepted their mother's belief and the word went forth throughout all the church of Alma's reward for his righteous living. With their father as an example, the three sons of Alma went out among all the people of Nephi and preached the word of God. There was great need for teaching the people, because they had become rich and proud of their worldly possessions.

CHAPTER 44

From among the Nephites came a strong, handsome man with evil, dark eyes. Amalickiah, for this was the name of the man, loved worldly possessions with all his heart. He wanted to be a rich man more than anything else on earth. At last he became rich—not because he earned it, but because he learned to trick the vain, proud people. However, after he became wealthy, he was still not satisfied. He wanted power, so that he could control the lives of the people about him. The more he thought of it, the more he liked the idea. He must become their king, and after he had become king of the Nephites, he would then find a way to become king of the Lamanites, too.

Amalickiah set to work immediately to influence the people. He told the lower judges that they were too good to work under the chief judge, and that if they would appoint him king, he would place them in charge of the courts of the land. To each group of people, he made promises and said many flattering things, until they began to believe him. Many of them left the church and soon forgot God's mercy. They also forgot to keep the commandments of God, and this made them easy prey for the wicked Amalickiah.

When Moroni heard that Amalickiah wanted to be

265

king, he became very angry and said, "This man is dangerous. It is time that all those who believe in Christ unite to preserve their liberty."

Then Moroni took off his coat and tore a strip of cloth from it and wrote this message: "In memory of our God, our religion, our freedom, our peace, our wives, and our children." When it was written, he fastened it to the end of a pole. Then, putting on his armor, he carried the pole forward. He bowed himself down to the earth and prayed to God for His blessings of liberty to rest upon his people, so long as there should be a band of Christians to possess the land. When he had poured out his heart to God, he went forth among the people, waving the torn part of his coat. From every direction people ran to him and offered their services in the cause of freedom.

Now, when Amalickiah saw that most of the people had joined Moroni, he became frightened. He knew that those who joined with him were doubtful of the justice of their cause and would probably desert him at any moment. Therefore, he took those who would go with him and started for the land of Nephi.

When Moroni learned that Amalickiah was headed for the Lamanite territory, he thought it wise to cut them off before they joined forces with the Lamanites. He ordered his men to bring them back and put Amalickiah to death. They did as they were commanded, but Amalickiah and a few of his men escaped and were soon in the land of Nephi.

Never before had the people of Nephi been so closely united as they were at this time. They worked unselfishly for the common good of all the people. Even though the threat of a Lamanite war hung over them, yet their joy knew no bounds. They kept the Lord's commandments faithfully, and He poured out rich blessings of peace, happiness, and prosperity.

Shortly after Amalickiah fled to Nephi, the land of the Lamanites, Ammon came to Zarahemla. He came to see Moroni. Although Moroni was many years younger than Ammon, yet they had much in common. When they were together, they forgot the difference in their ages.

"How are your people, the converted Lamanites?" asked Moroni warmly.

"Oh, Moroni," said Ammon, "they are a wonderful people—always rejoicing in the goodness of God. If all the people in this precious land of promise were as faithful as they are, there would be no war."

"Much of the credit is due to you and your three brothers. You spend all your time reminding them of God's blessings and teaching them in the ways of the Lord."

"I have brought you news," said Ammon. "It seemed so important that I decided to bring it to you myself. It is about Amalickiah."

"Amalickiah?" questioned Moroni.

"Did you know he is king of the Lamanites?" asked Ammon.

"King of the Lamanites?" repeated Moroni. "Why, that's impossible."

"In the few weeks he has been in the land of Nephi, he has lied, tricked, and murdered his way to the throne. Now he is king of all the Lamanites, in all their lands. He had his servant slowly poison the Lamanite leader of the army. When he was out of the way, Amalickiah took over the leadership and marched to the city of Nephi. When the king came out to meet them, Amalickiah had one of his servants stab the king to death. But, through clever planning, no one knew that he had had any part in the treachery. He told the Lamanites that the king's servants were responsible for his death. When the servants of the king heard these lies, they became frightened and fled to my people in the land of the Nephites. Knowing that Amalickiah would incite the Lamanites to war against us, I decided you should know of these things."

"Thank you, Ammon," said Moroni. "I will need to speed up our preparations for war. But tell me, what has become of the Lamanite queen? Has she been murdered?"

"Amalickiah is a clever man, and wicked through and through. With his silver-tongued flattery, he won the heart of the queen and she is now his wife."

"Amazing," was all that Moroni could say, so great was his bewilderment.

Ammon was right in thinking that Amalickiah would stir up the Lamanites to make war on the Nephites. At that very moment, he had men appointed to speak to the Lamanites from their towers. These men told them how they had been robbed and cheated by the Nephites. They kept on building their hatred until they were eager to make war on the Nephites. All Amalickiah's plans were being fulfilled. He was now king of the Lamanites, and he felt that he must become king of the Nephites, too. He gathered a great army and, following Moroni's methods of protecting his men from arrows and stones, he had them dressed in armor. He pictured to his men that soon the Nephites would be their slaves, and they would have nothing to do but live from the labors of the Nephites.

Amalickiah appointed his chief captains from among the Zoramites. They were, in reality, Nephites, and they knew well the strength of the Nephites and their weakest cities.

At the end of the nineteenth year of the reign of the judges, the Lamanite army moved toward the land of Zarahemla, by way of the wilderness. While Amalickiah had been lying, cheating, and murdering his way into power, Moroni, on the other hand, had been preparing the minds of his people to be faithful to the Lord their God. He began at once strengthening his army and building small forts, throwing up banks of earth and placing timbers on top of the banks for the protection of his army. He also built walls of stone to encircle their cities and the borders of their lands. In the weakest places, he stationed a greater number of men. The Nephites kept on working, under Moroni's guidance, until all their lands and their cities were well protected. Moroni gave all his time preparing to preserve their liberty, their lands, their wives, their children, and their peace. He wanted the Nephites to be faithful to God.

Moroni was a strong and mighty man. He hated bloodshed, but he taught the Nephites to defend themselves against their enemies. He also taught them never to give an offense, and never to raise the sword except against an enemy, to preserve their lives. If all men had been, and were, and ever would be like Moroni, the very powers of hell would be shaken forever. The devil would never have a chance to gain power over the hearts of men.

Moroni was a man like Ammon and his brothers, and like Alma and his sons. They all preached the word of God, and through their labors, the people became humble and served the Lord faithfully. The people were brought so close together, through their faith, that for the space of four years they lived in perfect peace and harmony among themselves. Yet, in spite of this fact, they were compelled to fight with their brethren, the Lamanites. And their wars with the Lamanites never ceased for the space of many years.

Amalickiah sent his Lamanite armies to attack the rebuilt city of Ammonihah. This was the wicked city that God destroyed many years before, and the Nephites had just started to rebuild it. Amalickiah considered it one of the weakest spots in the Nephite territory. Therefore, he expected little or no trouble in capturing it, and once it had fallen into his hands, he would have a stronghold from which to storm other cities. But a great surprise was in store for him. He hadn't considered the brilliant mind of Moroni or his clever preparations for war. Moroni's wisdom and inspired leadership gave him the power to foresee the plans and movements of the Lamanites. Amalickiah had no way of knowing how well the lands and cities of the people of Nephi were fortified.

When the Lamanites approached the city of Ammonihah, they were amazed to see the deep ditches and the high ridges of earth piled up around the city. Suddenly, the Nephites began casting stones and shooting arrows into the unprotected Lamanites, and hundreds of them dropped dead while only fifty of the Nephites were wounded. The Lamanites fought wildly, trying to tear down the walls of earth in order to gain entrance to the city. But the more they fought, the more terrible their loss became. At last, they fled back into the wilderness. When Amalickiah heard of their terrible defeat, his face grew dark with anger.

"Moroni will live to regret this day," said Amalickiah. "I shall kill him with my own hands."

Amalickiah soon discovered that this threat could not be accomplished as easily as he thought. Time after time he sent his armies to attack the Nephite cities, but each time they suffered heartbreaking defeats, while the Nephites fought without danger from behind the ridges of earth.

For the space of four years, the Nephites lived in peace with each other. Although they were compelled to defend themselves against the Lamanites, still, they enjoyed great happiness. Not since Nephi's day had the people been so united or so faithful to God's commandments. Little did they know that their peace was not to last.

In the twenty-fifth year of the reign of the judges, Nephihah, chief judge over the people of Nephi, died and his son Pahoran was appointed to take his place. A group of people, claiming to be of royal blood, came to Pahoran and demanded that he alter the law.

"No," said Pahoran, "I shall not alter the law in any respect."

"We do not believe in free government," they said. "We want a king and we intend to have one."

All those who wanted a king to rule over them were known as king-men; those who wanted liberty and freedom were called freemen. The quarreling between the two groups grew very bitter and hostile. When Moroni heard of the uprising he was deeply grieved, for he knew that the Nephites' strength lay in their unity. They had fought together to preserve their liberty, and the disloyalty of the king-men shocked him deeply. He loved all his people but, being a soldier, he knew what dangers lay in rebellion. They must be suppressed as quickly as possible. Therefore, he called out his army and sent them forth to battle against the king-men. In a very short time, four thousand of the king-men were slain and their leaders thrown into prison. Those who were left promised to support and fight for their liberty and freedom.

CHAPTER 45

I n the twenty-fifth year of the reign of the judges, Moroni stood atop the lookout tower, which gave a view of the great city of Zarahemla and all its border lands. It was the last day of summer and the heat had settled down like a heavy blanket, shutting out every breath of air. But Moroni was unaware of the heat, for he was sad and worried. He was sad because he had had to deal so harshly with the king-men and because so many of them had been killed. He hated bloodshed, but he knew it was God's will that the people of Nephi should be free. As leader of the army, it was his duty to preserve their freedom. He was worried because this was a critical time for such trouble to break out among the people of Nephi. For Amalickiah had again stirred up the hearts of the Lamanites against the Nephites. He was gathering soldiers from all parts of his land, arming them and preparing for war. He had sworn to slay Moroni with his own hands.

Just at that moment, there was a clatter of running feet coming up the stairway that led to the tower. Turning around, Moroni saw a curly-headed child. When the boy reached the landing, he called out, "Hello, Chief Captain Moroni!"

"Hello, there! Who are you?" asked Moroni, smiling at the small boy.

"I'm nobody important, but I bring you a secret message," said the boy with pride.

"If you were chosen," said Moroni, "to bring me a secret message, then you must be someone very important—someone I can trust."

"Yes sir, everyone knows that I can be trusted. My name is Helaman, son of Helaman and grandson of Alma," said the boy, boasting a little.

"Well, my lad, you have a great deal to live up to. Your grandfather was a great man in the ways of the Lord, and your father is following in his footsteps," said Moroni kindly.

"I know that, sir," said the boy politely. "I am trying to be like them."

"Fine," said Moroni. "And now, tell me, what is this message that is so important and secret?"

"Teancum, leader of one of your armies, sent me to tell you that, while you have been putting down rebellion here at home, the Lamanites have come into the land of Moroni, which borders on the seashore. Amalickiah has driven the people out and killed many of them. He has taken over the city."

Now, Moroni had been afraid that this very thing would happen. Nevertheless, the news came as a shock. He closed his eyes and prayed that God would be merciful to his people whom the Lamanites had captured. Suddenly, he looked at young Helaman searchingly. He seemed to be an honest child, but still, there was something strange about his story.

"Helaman," said Moroni, "the city of Moroni lies far to the east—so great a distance, in fact, that a small boy like you couldn't possibly travel so far."

"Oh, sir," said Helaman, "the message was relayed to me. You see, sir, there are a number of men stationed at different places along the way, and it is their duty to get the messages through to you. I am stationed only a few miles out of Zarahemla. You see, sir, I am one of the younger men."

Moroni smiled at the manly little fellow, who was trying so hard to be grown-up.

"Take this message to Teancum and Lehi: Say that I will join them as soon as possible."

"Yes, sir," said Helaman, and he was off like the wind.

Before Moroni could gather his army and move them from the west to the eastern seashore, several of the Nephite cities fell into the hands of the Lamanites. Amalickiah, the wicked king of the Lamanites, lost his life, and Ammoron, his brother, became king in his place. When the Nephites lost one of their cities, it seemed impossible to retake it again, because the cities were all so well protected with walls of stone and great ridges of earth. But to Moroni nothing seemed impossible. His faith in God was firm and strong and he knew that his cause was just—the cause of freedom. As soon as he arrived, he saw clearly that they would have to lure the Lamanites out of the cities in order to take them. He accomplished this through cunning and daring and Mulek was retaken and a great victory was won.

As the fighting continued week after week and month after month, the Nephites captured a large number of prisoners. Moroni ordered his men to preserve the lives of the prisoners, so that they might exchange them for Nephites who had fallen into Lamanite hands. In the twenty-ninth year of the reign of the judges, Ammoron sent word to Moroni that he wished to exchange prisoners. Moroni was overjoyed at this news and sent a message to Ammoron, saying:

"It is you and your brother, Amalickiah, who came

against my people in war. If you do not repent and withdraw your armies into your own lands, you will bring down the anger of that God whom you have rejected, and He will destroy you. I will not exchange prisoners, except on condition that you will deliver to us a man, his wife, and his children for one prisoner. Now, behold, if you do not agree to this, I will come against you with my armies; yes, I will do more than that, I will arm my women and children and I will follow you to your own land, which is the land of our first inheritance. I will give you battle until you are destroyed from off the face of the earth."

When Ammoron received Moroni's message, he was very angry and he wrote him, saying:

"I am Ammoron, a descendant of Zoram. But now, I am a bold Lamanite. Your fathers did rob the Lamanites of the right to govern. If you will lay down your arms and subject yourselves to be governed by those to whom the government rightly belongs, then I will cause my people to lay down their arms. You say we have rejected your God, but we know no such God and neither do you. If there is such a being, then He has made us as well as you. If there is a devil and a hell, perhaps He will send you to dwell with my brother, whom you have murdered. We have waged this war to obtain the Lamanites' right to the government. And now I close my letter to Moroni."

When Moroni received this message, he was very angry. He knew that Ammoron was aware of his lies.

"I will not exchange prisoners with Ammoron," said Moroni fiercely. "Now I know that my people are held in the city of Gid, under heavy Lamanite guard."

Moroni stopped speaking and sat lost in deep study. His men, knowing he wished to be alone, left the room quietly. Several minutes passed, and then a light knock came on his door. But Moroni had no eyes or ears for anyone or anything. The knock came again and then, without waiting, the door opened and a tall, young boy entered the room and stood watching Moroni with profound respect.

At last, Moroni spoke aloud to himself. "What shall I do?"

"Ask God," said the boy.

Moroni was startled at the sound of a strange voice and said sternly, "Who are you and what are you doing here?"

"I am Helaman, son of Helaman and—"

"And grandson of Alma," finished Moroni, smiling.

"Then you remember me?" asked Helaman, surprised.

"Yes, indeed I do, although it has been a long time since I last saw you. You have been growing so fast, I didn't know you at first," said Moroni.

"I can do a man's work now," said young Helaman proudly.

"What can I do for you?" asked Moroni kindly, but still aware that his time was precious.

"I have come here, sir, to offer my services in our fight for freedom. Shall we pray together?"

Moroni sat amazed at this boy, who always surprised him with his courage and faith. Without saying another word, Moroni knelt down with Helaman and asked God for guidance. While Moroni prayed, God's voice came to his mind and suggested a way to free the Nephite captives.

"Helaman, will you search among my people for a man who is a descendant of Laman, son of Lehi?"

"Yes," said Helaman, happy to be of service.

In a short time Helaman returned, bringing a Lamanite with him.

"What is your name?" asked Moroni.

"My name is Laman, and I am a descendant of the

first Laman, who came out of Jerusalem 537 years ago."

"Good," said Moroni. "But how did you come to join my forces? Do you believe in freedom for all the children of men?"

"I do now, sir. But that is not why I am here. When the wicked Amalickiah had my king murdered, he blamed me and the king's other servants. We were forced to flee out of our lands. However, my coming among your people and my people, the Anti-Nephi-Lehies, was a great blessing to me. Here, I learned of the coming of Jesus Christ. I am deeply grateful for this knowledge, and now, if I can be of any use, I am here to serve you."

While Laman talked, Moroni studied him carefully. He had the feeling that here was a man good and true. The Nephite and the Lamanite were united in common brotherhood. Moroni outlined his plan to Laman, and when he was through, the two men clasped hands in warm friendship.

That evening, under cover of darkness, Laman, with a small number of his men, set out for the city of Gid, where the Lamanites held the Nephite prisoners. Within a few feet of the city gates, a voice cried out on the still night air:

"Halt! Who goes there?"

"Fear not, for behold, I am a Lamanite," said Laman. "We have escaped from the Nephites while they sleep. We have taken their wine and brought it with us."

The Lamanites were very fond of wine, especially wine made by the Nephites, so when they heard Laman's words, they received him with joy.

"Give us your wine that we may drink, for we are very weary."

But Laman teased them, "Let us keep our wine until we go against the Nephites in battle."

But these words only made the Lamanites more anxious than ever to drink the wine, and they said, "We are weary. Let us drink the wine now, and by and by we will be given more wine to strengthen us for the battle."

"Here it is," said Laman. "Drink it if you wish."

They drank the wine freely and smacked their lips over its pleasant taste. Now, the wine was strong, on purpose, so that the Lamanites would fall into a deep, drunken sleep. They drank and drank and made merry. When they were all asleep, Laman and his men returned to Moroni and told him what had happened.

"You have done well," said Moroni. "Now my men will carry weapons of war to the city of Gid, and while the Lamanites sleep, we will arm the Nephite prisoners. Even the women and children who are able to use a weapon of war will be armed."

The men moved quietly and swiftly to the city of Gid, where they gave the weapons to the Nephite prisoners in profound silence. Not a single Lamanite awakened. Now, the Nephites could have slain the drunken Lamanites, for they lay in a deep sleep. But Moroni had ordered his men to spare them. He had no desire to shed the blood of his enemies—only to free his people. He had obtained just what he wanted. Next morning, when the Lamanites awakened, they were shocked to find that they were surrounded by Nephites outside the city and by their prisoners from within. Moroni ordered them to lay down their weapons; when this was done, he took them prisoner.

After Moroni had everything well in hand, he sent for Laman and said, "You played your part wonderfully well and I want to thank you from the bottom of my heart."

It was a well-known fact that Moroni gave his compliments sparingly, and only to the few who really deserved them. Laman knew this, and when he heard Moroni's words and felt his warm handclasp, he straightened his shoulders with pride.

"Thank you," said Laman. "I believe that the Lord our God is well pleased with the work you did last night. You set the Nephite prisoners free and captured the Lamanite guards without losing a single soul. You are the wisest and greatest man I ever knew."

"Any wisdom or success I may have is given me by the mercy of God," said Moroni humbly. "Laman, my friend, I am sick unto death of war and bloodshed. I wish we were done with it, so that we might turn our energies to preparing the minds of the people for the coming of Christ."

"Is He coming soon?" asked Laman eagerly.

"I don't know the time or place of His coming, but I believe it will be soon. Perhaps some of our children will live to see Him. Laman, I pray God that we may be worthy of His great sacrifice."

"Amen," was all Laman could say, so deep was his emotion.

And thus ended the twenty-ninth year of the reign of the judges.

PART 4

The Savior Comes
to the Promised Land

CHAPTER 46

At dawn, Helaman arose and walked through the quiet streets of Zarahemla. When he reached the marketplace, he sat down beside the fountain and watched the birds taking their morning bath. At this early hour, when all was quiet and peaceful, Helaman felt very close to God. It was as though all he needed to do was to reach out and clasp His hand. However, soon the marketplace would be alive with activity. Already some of the shopkeepers were stirring about, preparing for the day's trade. Soon Helaman was so deep within his own thoughts that he forgot the birds and the shopkeepers, until the first rays of the morning sun stretched out long ribbons of light that touched the rising mist from the fountain and changed it into a brilliantly colored rainbow. He was always amazed at the wonders of God's creation.

"Good morning, Helaman, my friend," said a cheerful voice.

Helaman looked up to see Hagoth. He had known Hagoth all the days of his life. He was a good man, although sometimes his lively imagination led him to do foolish things. But Helaman loved him in spite of his faults, and now his voice was warm and cheerful as he said, "Good morning, Hagoth. What brings you to the marketplace so early?"

"I came in search of you. Your good wife told me I would find you here."

"What can I do for you?" asked Helaman, anxious to serve his friend.

"I have come to say good-bye. I am moving to Bountiful, on the borders of the West Sea," explained Hagoth excitedly.

"But why?" asked Helaman, with deep feeling.

"I am a very curious man. I look at the mountains and wonder what lies beyond them. I keep on looking until my curiosity becomes so great that I am forced to go in search of the answer. Did you know that fifty-four hundred men, together with their women and children and all their possessions, left the land of Zarahemla and went into the land northward? They were curious like me," said Hagoth, as the light of adventure came into his eyes.

"But they left Zarahemla many days ago. Surely you will not set out alone to overtake them," said Helaman, deeply concerned for his friend's welfare.

"No, Helaman, I shall not follow them. I have done many foolish things in my day, but with the passing of the years, I like to think that I have gained some wisdom," said Hagoth.

"Indeed you have," Helaman hastened to reply, feeling guilty for doubting the wisdom of his old friend.

"As I told you earlier, I am moving to Bountiful. There I shall build a great ship. It will carry the curious beyond the narrow neck of land, to the new country that lies northward," replied Hagoth.

"But why should they leave this precious land of promise? This is the land of their inheritance. Why should any of our people want to go into a strange land full of unknown dangers?" Helaman was frowning and feeling more tired than he had in a long time.

Hagoth looked carefully at his good friend and said cheerfully, "The Nephites have tried for many years to hold the Lamanites back from the land northward. King Mosiah once said that this land and the land that lay beyond the narrow neck was all a part of our inheritance. Zarahemla has become crowded. Many of our people would have a much better chance in the new country. If Lehi had felt as you do, our people would still be in Jerusalem."

The warm, red blood flooded Helaman's cheeks as he heard Hagoth's rebuke.

"Thank you, Hagoth," said Helaman, "you are right, of course. Good luck to you, and may God bless you in your shipbuilding."

Days, weeks, and months went by without a single word about Hagoth and then, one day in early summer, the news came that Hagoth had built a great ship and launched it into the West Sea. There was great excitement and many of the Nephites went aboard and sailed away with their wives and children and many provisions. As soon as they were gone, Hagoth began to build other ships.

One bright, sunny morning, the people of Bountiful were aroused by the sight of Hagoth's first ship returning. No sooner had it docked than many others swarmed aboard. When they had loaded their provisions, they set out again to the northland—but they were never heard of again. It was thought that they were drowned in the depths of the sea. Hagoth wondered if this would be the end of his shipbuilding, but the people were unafraid and many of them sailed forth into the land northward.

One cold, bleak day in winter, Helaman and his son Nephi went walking. It was Helaman's habit to walk with long, quick steps, but today his steps were slow and short, in order to make it possible for his young son to keep up with him. Nephi was very proud that his father had asked him to go along. He wasn't exactly sure where they were going. He kept thinking about it as they walked along. He didn't want to bother his father with foolish questions, but finally his curiosity was so great that he was forced to ask, "Where are we going, Father?"

"To Chief Captain Moroni's house," replied Helaman.

"Did he invite us, sir?"

"Yes, indeed he did. He sent a written message, asking us to come today."

"How soon is he going to die?" asked Nephi, catching hold of his father's hand.

The question so surprised Helaman that he stopped and looked at his son and asked rather sternly, "Whatever gave you such an idea?"

"I heard Mother telling Great-uncle Shiblon that Chief Captain Moroni was dying."

Nephi's eyes had grown so large and sad that Helaman put his arm around the boy's shoulders and drew him close to his side.

Helaman said, gently, "We all hope and pray that he will live, but he is very sick. I think he is the greatest man of our time. I want you to see him in the hope that you will follow in his footsteps."

Nephi looked up at his father and asked gravely, "What makes him a great man, Father?"

The question was so surprising, coming from one so young, that Helaman was silent for a few moments, and when at last he spoke, it was with a voice of sober judgment.

"There are a number of things that make this good man great. First, he has been faithful in keeping God's commandments. Second, he has served God's people, always placing their welfare first. His brilliant mind and tender heart have ever been used in serving his people. He has led us to many glorious victories over our enemies."

After Helaman finished speaking, they walked along in silence. Helaman was thinking of his friend Moroni, of how much he had come to mean to him. The very thought of his passing brought a pang of sorrow to Helaman's heart. It was so great that it bordered on despair.

Nephi was thinking, too—very serious thoughts for one so young. His father had said that he would like him to walk in the footsteps of Moroni. He loved his father and wanted to please him. He tried to remember all the things that Helaman said made Moroni great. But try as he would, all he could remember was that Moroni kept God's commandments. He began saying the commandments to himself. He was happy that he had learned them so well. Some of them he didn't understand, but he could ask his father later.

"Here we are at Moroni's house," said Helaman, stopping to open the garden gate.

"It's a very old house, isn't it?" asked Nephi.

"Yes, but a very beautiful and sturdy one."

They walked up the path and stood beside the door—but before Helaman could lift the knocker, the door was opened by Moroni's son, Moronihah. He took them to his father's bedroom.

Moroni lay in his bed, the covers drawn up to his chin. His eyes were closed and his face was drawn with deep lines against the pain. He was not an old man, but life had taken a great toll of his strength.

"Father, Helaman and his son are here. They came as soon as they received your message," said Moronihah.

Slowly, and with difficulty, Moroni opened his eyes.

When he saw Helaman, a faint smile just touched the corners of his mouth.

"Helaman, son of Helaman and grandson of Alma," said the sick man.

"Why, sir, you remember the day we first met. I'm afraid I was given to boasting." Helaman spoke softly, remembering the happy day when he had first taken a message to Chief Captain Moroni atop the lookout tower.

"You can well afford to be proud with forefathers like Helaman and Alma. And this is Nephi, son of Helaman, grandson of Helaman, and great-grandson of Alma. Promise me that you will follow in your father's footsteps. We need more men like your father. Come, lad, what do you say?" asked Moroni.

But Nephi was silent. His eyes were on the floor and a hot, red flush had spread over his face. Helaman, greatly disturbed over his son's behavior, reached out and placed a firm hand on his shoulder.

"Our friend Moroni has asked you for a promise. What have you to say?" asked Helaman.

At last, Nephi spoke without taking his eyes from the floor. "I should like to please you, sir, but I can't."

Moroni was so surprised that he raised his head from the pillow to get a good look at the boy and asked firmly, "Why not? Don't you love and respect your father?"

"Oh, yes, sir. I love and respect him very much, but you see, sir, I can't promise, because I've already promised my father that I would walk in your footsteps."

Nephi's words surprised and touched Moroni so deeply that his eyes filled with tears and he said with deep emotion, "God bless you both."

Moroni was so tired by the effort he had made that he sank back against his pillow and closed his eyes. Helaman, worried by the thought that they were staying too long, looked up to ask Moronihah whether they should leave, but he was not in the room. Helaman had been so absorbed in the words of his old friend that he had not seen Moronihah go. Moroni opened his eyes again and asked Nephi to come close to his bed. He began talking to him in a low, quiet voice, telling Nephi of the coming of Christ and pleading with him to always keep God's commandments, that he might see Him when He came to the promised land. He told the boy that no man would know the hour or the day of His coming, but it would be soon, and he believed that Nephi would live to see Him in the flesh. Then he told of the signs that would point to the Savior's birth and death.

Turning to Helaman, he said, "My son, Moronihah, has been made chief captain of the army. Very soon now, your Uncle Shiblon will confer upon you the sacred records and other precious things that have been handed down from generation to generation. The two of you can be a great influence for good among our people. There are many dark days ahead for you, and I want you to promise a dying man that you two will be loyal to each other and true to the faith. Meet often and help each other solve the problems that confront you. Do you promise?"

"Yes, as God is my witness," said Helaman gravely.

"There is something else I must tell you," said Moroni. "There is a band of robbers—a secret organization, bent upon enslaving our people. They mingle among the people in such a way that they cannot be found. Your next-door neighbor might be one of them and yet you would never know, so beware and ever keep on guard. Remember that this is the land of our inheritance and God meant it for all of us and not for just the few. And, now, good-bye."

Three days later Moroni died, and thus ended the thirty-sixth year of the reign of the judges.

CHAPTER 47

In the thirty-ninth year of the reign of the judges, Shiblon died and Helaman became keeper of the records. He took this new responsibility very seriously. He had heard from his father and grandfather how important these records were, how they had been handed down from one generation to another. He began at once to teach the people from the records, all except the part that Alma said must be kept secret.

The year following Shiblon's death, Pahoran died. Now, Pahoran had been chief judge over all the Nephites for many years. He was a just man and he had served the people with honesty and wisdom. Three of his many sons came forward and declared their right to the judgment seat. The people took sides and began quarreling with one another. The conflict became so bitter that finally all three of Pahoran's sons lost their lives.

While the people were quarreling among themselves, the Lamanites were arming and preparing for war. The wicked Coriantumr, a descendant of Zarahemla, broke faith with his people and with God. The king of the Lamanites knew him to be a mighty man who could stand against the Nephites with his strength and cunning. The king believed that, by sending Coriantumr at the head of his army, he could gain power over the Nephites. Coriantumr, flattered by the king's appointment, eagerly led the Lamanite army to the land of Zarahemla. Along the way there was little opposition, and when they were opposed, they quickly cut their way through. The Nephites were so busy quarreling over the judgment seat that the Lamanites were at the gates of the great city before they knew what had happened. The Lamanites had made the march with so much speed that the Nephites had had no time to prepare for their defense.

Coriantumr quickly cut down the watch by the entrance to Zarahemla and marched with his whole army into the city, slaying everyone who opposed him. They took possession of the city so quickly that the Nephites scarcely knew what had happened. When Coriantumr saw how easily he had taken possession of the strongest city in all the land, his heart took courage and he decided to make war on all the Nephites. Therefore, he headed toward the city of Bountiful. He was determined to cut his way through so that he might obtain the northern land. Thinking that the Nephites' greatest strength lay in the center of their country, he began his march without giving them time to gather their armies.

But, behold, this march of Coriantumr's through the very center of the land proved a great blessing to Moronihah, because he had fortified the borders, never dreaming that the Lamanites would dare come into the great city of Zarahemla. When Moronihah discovered this, he immediately sent forth an army to head them off before they could reach the land of Bountiful. He gave them such a battle that they were forced to retreat back toward Zarahemla, and again Moronihah cut off their retreat. Great numbers were slain, and among them was Coriantumr. The Lamanites could not retreat, neither on the north nor the south nor the east nor the west, for they were completely surrounded by the Nephites.

Moronihah took possession of the city of Zarahelma

again and the Lamanites, who had been taken prisoner, were permitted to leave in peace. Thus ended the forty-first year of the reign of the judges.

After Moronihah had established peace between the Nephites and the Lamanites, the Nephites began to think of their government, and again they began quarreling among themselves. Finally, Helaman was appointed chief judge and ruler over his people.

When Helaman returned home and told his wife, a very frightening thing happened. No sooner had he spoken than all the blood drained from her face, leaving it an ashen gray. She closed her eyes and would have fallen, but Helaman caught her in his arms and half carried her to a chair. Then he knelt beside her and rubbed her wrists and hands.

"Are you ill?" he asked her tenderly.

"No, I'm afraid."

When he looked into her eyes, he saw how terror-stricken she was.

"*Afraid?* Afraid of what? Surely you know that I would not let anything harm you."

"I am not afraid for myself. It is for you," she said quickly.

"But why?" he asked.

"Already, three men have lost their lives over the judgment seat. We know that at least one of them was killed by a member of the secret band of robbers. You must know that they will not stop killing until they themselves have placed a man on the judgment seat. Oh, Helaman, for my sake, please give it up. I couldn't bear living without you."

Helaman placed a loving arm about her and said gently, "But, don't you see, that is my reason for accepting the appointment? While I am judge, I intend to find out all about this band of robbers and bring them to justice, before they have time to get control of the government. Think what it would mean to be ruled by such wicked men. As soon as they had us in their power, we would become slaves. It is the right of all men to be free and to worship as they please."

"But I'm afraid! Even now they are probably lying in wait for you, and at the first opportunity they will kill you," said his wife with great agitation.

"They will not succeed, for God is with us. Your faith has never failed us before. Pray now, and ask God to guide us in this righteous cause."

They knelt down and prayed together. When they were through praying, Helaman's wife was no longer afraid. Had she been able to hear what was going on in the little cottage next door, she would have known that God was already preparing the way for Helaman. One of Helaman's servants, with his good wife, lived in the little cottage.

The servant's wife sat on a low stool with her elbows resting on her knees and her face cupped in the palms of her hands. She was anxiously watching her husband darken his skin with cinnamon bark. By skillfully shading certain parts of his face more than others, he completely changed his features. How clever her husband was! He could easily pass for a Lamanite in his borrowed clothing and dark skin.

"There, wife, how do I look?" he asked.

"Must you go tonight?" she asked, ignoring his question.

"I have told you that tonight is the night the robbers plan to kill Helaman. With my help, his life will be spared. Gadianton, who now is leader of the secret band of robbers and murderers, has flattered them with his fine speeches. He has led them to believe that were he chief judge of the Nephites, he would give the robbers power and authority over the people. Being evil, they eagerly uphold him, thinking how nice it will be to have slaves and riches."

"How do you know their plans?" she asked in a dull, flat voice.

"They think I am one of them. I have been mingling with them for the past six nights," he answered.

"If they find out you are not a Lamanite, they will kill you," she said, with heartbreak in her voice.

"Many of the robbers come disguised. They don't trust each other. Most of them are Nephites who go among the people of the church, deceiving all they meet. Tonight, I will meet Helaman's would-be murderer."

At midnight, on a dark street that led to Helaman's house, the servant waited among the shadows. At last, he heard the sound of approaching footsteps. He said a silent prayer, pleading with God to help him do the right thing.

When the robber drew near, Helaman's servant gave him the secret sign. Immediately, the robber trusted him and the servant said to him, "Let us go forth unto the chief judge of the land."

Now, this pleased the robber very much, for he believed that Gadianton had sent this man to help him. At a moment when the robber was least expecting it, the servant attacked him and destroyed him. Then he ran and told Helaman all the things he had seen and heard and done. But when Gadianton found that the robber did not return, he became afraid that he himself would be destroyed. Therefore, he and his band fled from the land by a secret way into the wilderness. When Helaman sent men to take them, they could not be found. Had Helaman known, at that moment, that Gadianton would one day almost completely destroy the people of Nephi, he would have continued to search.

Several years passed in comparative peace and plenty. The people of the church kept God's commandments and they prospered far beyond their rarest dreams. In spite of their prosperity, thousands upon thousands left Zarahemla and migrated into the land northward. Many of the people of Ammon, who were Lamanites by birth, joined them. Soon the north land was inhabited from sea to sea. They even spread into the Land of Desolation. Now, it received this name because it was without timber, and because they found many bones of people and animals. They were a strong, hardy people and soon set to work making houses of cement. After a while, they sent for shiploads of timber to be brought from Zarahemla. All the people who saw the new land were eager to inherit it.

In the fifty-third year of the reign of the judges, Helaman lay sick unto death. He had served as chief judge of the land for many years and the people had been happy with his judgments. He had ever been honest and just in all his dealings. He had followed the leadership of his father, Helaman, and his grandfather, Alma. He loved God and believed in Jesus Christ, who would soon come to the promised land.

Today he had sent for his sons, Nephi and Lehi, to give them his final blessing and to confer on Nephi the sacred records and to make him chief judge of the land.

"Father," said Nephi, "we are here."

"Is there something we can do for you?" asked Lehi with deep concern.

He lifted one of Helaman's hands and held it in both his own, trying to warm the icy cold fingers. Both young men were devoted to their father and tried to pattern their lives after his.

"Come closer to me, Nephi, I have something I wish to tell you both and my breath grows short. Keep God's commandments and tell the people that I have given you the names of our first parents who came out of the land of Jerusalem. When you think of your names, remember the ones you were named after, and when you remember them, remember their works and that they were good men. Do good, but do not boast about it. Do these things to lay up a treasure in heaven that will last forever and will not fade away. In this way, you will obtain the precious gift of eternal life. Oh, remember, remember, my sons, the words of King Benjamin when he told his people that the only way whereby man can be saved is through the atoning blood of Jesus Christ. Remember that He is coming to redeem the world and that He will come to the promised land, just as the prophets have foretold. You can be sure that as long as you follow in His footsteps, the devil shall have no power over you. And now, farewell, my sons."

With these words, he sank upon his pillow, closed his eyes, and died with a deep sense of peace. As his sons looked down at their father, Helaman, son of Helaman and grandson of Alma, their faith in Jesus Christ was renewed and they believed that someday they would join him in a far better place than this.

CHAPTER 48

With Helaman's passing, the Gadianton robbers began to feel secure once again. They left their hiding
places in the wilderness and drifted back to Zarahemla in
small bands. They were careful not to let the people
know who they really were. They posed as God-fearing
men in order to win the confidence of the people of the
Lord. For years they had watched the growing strength
and power of the Christians, but the thing they were most
jealous about was their prosperity—their numerous
flocks and herds, their gold and silver and precious
things, their fine houses and costly clothing. Greedy for
power and an opportunity to share in the wealth of the
Nephites, they played a waiting game. They realized that
they would have to destroy the Nephites' faith in God in
order to gain power over them. Little by little, they
planted seeds of doubt in the minds of the Christians. At
first, they sought out the weakest and began flattering
them. They told them how clever they were to become
wealthy and that all the praise was due them and not God.
In a very short time, evil had its way, and many of the
Nephites became boastful and proud. Soon they forgot
God and thought only of their own importance.

From afar, the Lamanites watched the Nephites grow

297

weak and corrupt. They, too, had an eye on the rich lands
of Zarahemla and the vast wealth of their lifelong
enemies. They watched and planned—gathering a vast
army. At last, the day came when they marched to the
great city of Zarahemla and captured it once again. Before
Moronihah could gather his forces, they had captured
half of the Nephite cities. Soon, however, Moronihah so
strongly fortified the remaining cities that the Lamanites
were unable to capture them.

In the sixty-second year of the reign of the judges,
Nephi gave up the judgment seat to Cezoram. Nephi had
become weary because of the sins of his people. The laws
had become so corrupt and the people so wicked and
proud that he felt he was wasting his time trying to rule
over them. He called Lehi, his brother, to him and
suggested that they spend their time for the remainder of
their days preaching the word of God. Lehi was eager to
comply with his brother's request. They started at once
among the people of Nephi, beginning in the city of
Bountiful. They went from one city to another until they
had been among all the Nephite people.

One hot day in midsummer, Nephi and Lehi took the
road leading away from Mulek and toward Zarahemla.
They had not gone far when they met Moronihah, leading
a small band of men. This group's duty was to inspect the
battle lines. Moronihah ordered his men to rest while he
talked with his old friends.

"You two have been a great blessing to our people.
Hundreds have listened to your words and repented of
their sins. They are now working to right their wrongs by
carrying the word of God to others. We have gained in
strength and are able to unite to defend ourselves against
the enemy. Where do you go now?" asked Moronihah.

"To Zarahemla," answered Nephi.

"Zarahemla!" said Moronihah, in astonishment.

"Have you forgotten that Zarahemla is in the hands of the Lamanites?"

"No, we have not forgotten," said Lehi, "but it is our duty to bring God's message to all our brethren."

"May God protect and reward you for your faithfulness," said Moronihah, with admiration for their courage.

Two days later Nephi and Lehi reached Zarahemla. To their surprise, there was no one to stop them from entering the city. When they began preaching, many of the Lamanites listened to them eagerly. They were so convincing and sincere that eight thousand of the Lamanites were baptized and convinced of the wickedness of the traditions of their fathers.

From Zarahemla they went to the land of Nephi, the home of the Lamanites. As soon as they reached the land of Nephi, they were taken by the Lamanites and cast into prison—the same prison in which Ammon and his brethren had been cast by the servants of Limhi.

After many days had passed, the Lamanites gathered about the prison for the purpose of slaying Nephi and Lehi. But a marvelous thing happened. Suddenly there was a circle of fire about the brothers, and the Lamanites dared not harm them for fear they would be burned. Nevertheless, Nephi and Lehi were not burned, although they stood in the midst of the fire.

"Behold," said Lehi and Nephi, "it is God that shows you this marvelous thing and try as you will, you cannot slay us."

No sooner had they spoken than the earth began to shake. It shook so hard that the walls of the prison looked as though they would tumble to the earth, but they did not fall. At that moment, a cloud of terrible darkness settled down upon them and the Lamanites were overcome by awful fear.

Then they heard a voice that seemed to come from

above the cloud of darkness, saying, "Repent, repent and do not try to destroy my servants whom I have sent you to declare good tidings."

Now, when they heard this voice, they realized that it was not a voice of thunder, nor a loud voice, but a still voice of perfect mildness, as if it had been a whisper. It seemed to pierce the very soul. In spite of its mildness, it shook the earth. The great cloud of darkness settled down more closely than ever.

The voice came again, saying, "Repent, repent, for the kingdom of heaven is at hand. Seek no more to destroy my servants."

The earth shook again and the walls trembled. For the third time, the voice came and spoke marvelous words—words that cannot be spoken by man. The walls trembled again and the earth shook so hard that it felt as if it were going to be torn apart. The Lamanites wanted to run away, but they couldn't because of the cloud of darkness which overshadowed them. They could not move, so great was their fear.

It so happened that there was one man among the Lamanites who wasn't a Lamanite at all, but a Nephite by birth. He had once belonged to the church of God. All at once, he discovered that he could turn about and that he could see through the cloud of darkness. He saw the faces of Nephi and Lehi, and they shone so brightly that they looked like angels. He saw that their eyes were raised to heaven and they seemed to be talking to some being whom they saw.

Now this man, whose name was Aminadab, cried out to the multitude and told them to turn and look. And, behold, they found that they could turn and they, too, saw the faces of Lehi and Nephi.

The multitude asked Aminadab, "What does all this mean? Who are these men talking to?"

Aminadab answered, "They are talking with the angels of God."

"What shall we do," they asked, "that this cloud of darkness may be removed?"

Aminadab said to them, "You must repent and cry to the voice until you have faith in Christ. When you have this faith, the cloud of darkness will pass away."

They did as Aminadab told them to do, and the cloud of darkness disappeared. There were about three hundred souls who saw and heard all these marvelous things. They were so inspired by what they saw and heard that they went forth throughout all the land, telling their brethren about these great wonders. They were so convincing that the greater part of the Lamanites were converted. As soon as they were converted, they put away their weapons of war and even put aside their hatred of the Nephites. And it came to pass that they gave back to the Nephites the land of Zarahemla and all the other lands that were once Nephite territory.

The Lamanites had become, for the most part, more righteous than the Nephites. Realizing this, the Lamanites went into the land of Zarahemla and preached to the Nephites there. They talked with such power and authority that many were brought down to the depths of humility and became humble followers of God and the Lamb.

Many Lamanites, together with Nephi and Lehi, went into the land northward, preaching to the people there. There was peace in all the land. The Lamanites went wherever they wanted to, whether it be in Lamanite or Nephite territory. The Nephites were equally free to travel wherever they wished. All the people were free to trade and carry on whatever business they chose. Both the Lamanites and the Nephites soon had plenty of gold, silver, and all manner of precious metals. This was true in both the land to the north and the land to the south.

The Lord blessed the people everywhere. He blessed their lands and their flocks and herds so that they produced abundantly. He gave them ideal weather and freed them from pests and disease. Above all, He gave them peace. They grew so rich that they could not count their possessions. Little by little, they forgot the days of their wickedness and how God cursed them with wars—when almost everyone mourned for the dead. They forgot their suffering from hunger and cold and thought only of their riches and their own importance. Yes, little by little, they began to turn away from God, until, in the sixty-seventh year of the reign of the judges, an awful thing happened. Cezoram and his son were murdered in the judgment seat and the Gadianton robbers seized control of the government of the Nephites. It was a dreadful thing. It was as though a horrible blight had fallen upon the land, destroying all it touched.

The secret band of robbers trampled underfoot and turned their backs upon the poor and meek followers of God. From the very day these wicked leaders took office, the faithful knew they were facing everlasting destruction.

In the sixty-ninth year of the reign of the judges, Nephi stood upon the deck of a great ship, watching the shores of Bountiful come into view. A wave of tenderness swept over him as he saw once again his native land. He had been away for a long time—perhaps too long, since his preaching had fallen on deaf ears. The people of the north had rejected all his work. They were so bitter against him that he could not stay among them. He hoped and prayed that the people of the south were still faithful to God's commandments. He had much to tell them about the coming of Christ, which would be soon—very soon.

"All ashore that's going ashore!" cried a loud voice as the passengers hurried from the ship.

"Nephi, my friend, how are you?"

Nephi looked up to see Moronihah pushing his way through the crowd to greet him. How good it was to be home! He had so many questions to ask his friend, but Moronihah made him talk about the north land and his experiences there.

"Now you must tell me about the people at Zarahemla. Are they still faithful?" insisted Nephi.

"I wish I could spare you disappointment, but you must know sooner or later, so it might as well be now. Our people are in an awful state of wickedness. The Gadianton robbers have taken over the government. They use their power and authority to set aside the commandments of God. They condemn the righteous because of their righteousness, and let the guilty and wicked go unpunished, because of their money," said Moronihah gravely.

Nephi was depressed by this black news, and for a few moments he was silent. Then Moronihah spoke again: "Now that you have returned, I feel sure you can find a way to humble them and bring them to repentance."

"Thank you, my friend, but I am not sure that I can reach their hearts any more than I did the people of the north land," said Nephi in a sorrowful voice.

"God will show you the way, my friend," said Moronihah.

Nephi set out almost at once for Zarahemla. As he journeyed toward his home, he considered carefully all he saw and heard. He saw signs all about him of God's generous blessings to his people. Never in all his life could he remember a time when there was so much prosperity. He talked to many people along the way, both the poor and the rich, and to his own heartbreak he discovered that their wickedness was even greater than Moronihah had pictured.

"Oh, God," he cried out in agony, "how long will you be merciful to this wicked people?"

When he reached Zarahemla, his family welcomed him with warmth and understanding. He went into his garden and wearily climbed up the steps of his tower. When he reached the top, he almost stumbled and would have fallen had it not been for a bench that caught his weight.

The main highway that ran through the city of Zarahemla passed Nephi's garden gate. The tower where he stood was next to the gate. He beheld the beautiful city with sadness. When he thought of his people, the Nephites, and how wicked they had become, his heart was swollen with sorrow. In his grief, he poured out his heart to God.

Now, it happened that some men passing on the highway stopped to listen to his mourning. They ran and told the people what they had seen and the people came in multitudes.

When Nephi saw the people below, he cried out to them, "Why have you gathered here? Have you come that I may tell you of your sins? Woe to you because of your wickedness. Unless you repent, you shall perish. Even your lands shall be taken from you and you will be destroyed from off the face of the earth. I know these things are true. The Lord God has made them known to me."

The people were very angry, because many of them belonged to the secret band of robbers. They realized that Nephi had it in his power to stir the people to righteousness, and they would lose their hold over them.

One day, as Nephi poured out his heart to God,

there came a voice saying, "Behold, you are Nephi and I am God. I say to you in the presence of my angels, that you shall have power over this people, and shall smite the earth with famine and destruction according to their wickedness."

Nephi went forth and told the multitude what God had said to him. They grew so angry that they tried to slay him, but the power of God was with him and they could not harm him. He was taken by the Spirit and carried away from them. Thus ended the seventy-first year of the reign of the judges.

CHAPTER 49

The day was hot and still. Nephi and Lehi had climbed
to the top of Nephi's tower, hoping the air would be
cooler there. The brothers were very much alike. Both of
them had the same burning desire to teach the people
and bring them to repentance. They had given their entire lives in the service of God and His son, Jesus Christ.

"Famine is a terrible thing," said Lehi, watching his
brother with dark, searching eyes.

"Yes, it is," said Nephi.

Lehi waited for Nephi to continue; when he was silent, Lehi said: "From here we can see the great city of
Zarahemla and all the surrounding lands. Look at the
trees and the flowers. Their leaves have withered and
dried and are falling to the ground as if winter were approaching, yet it is only midsummer. Beyond the city lie
the grain fields that will never make grain because they
are too dry. They will not even make feed for our flocks
and herds. If that does not move you, stop and listen to
the cries of the hungry."

"Are you accusing me of something, brother? Your
anger hasn't reached your voice, but it shows clearly in
your eyes." Nephi was disturbed.

"People say you asked the Lord to send this famine.
It has lasted over two years. Don't you think they have suffered long enough?" asked Lehi.

"Do you remember how the Gadianton robbers were making war on the people of God and destroying them by the sword? When I saw that soon all of us would be killed, I cried to the Lord, saying, 'Oh, Lord, do not let this people be destroyed by the sword; rather, let there be a famine in the land, to stir the people to remembrance. Perhaps it will bring them to repentance and save them from complete destruction.' My prayer has been answered. I hoped you would understand."

"Forgive me, Nephi. I didn't know your reason for asking for a famine. The people have sent me to plead with you to ask God to take it away before they all perish. They have repented and have swept away the Gadianton robbers from among them. They are meek and humble once more," said Lehi sympathetically.

When Nephi saw how humble and repentant they were, he knelt down and prayed, asking God to save them from the famine. His prayers were heard. Rain began to fall upon the earth and it brought forth an abundant crop. The people rejoiced and praised the Lord. No longer did they seek to destroy Nephi; now they loved and respected him, knowing that he was a true prophet. In the seventy-sixth year of the reign of the judges, the people of Nephi began to prosper once again.

The next few years were blessed ones. All the people who put their trust in God became rich and powerful. But, with their riches, they began once more to be lifted up in their pride. How foolish, how vain, how evil, how slow they were to do good, and how quick to listen to the words of the evil one! It seemed that unless the Lord visited them with death and terror and famine, they would not keep His commandments.

One day, in the eighty-sixth year of the reign of the judges, Nephi was working in his garden. It was a garden to be proud of. It was not only beautiful, but productive

as well. He grew fruit in abundance and supplied the
house with vegetables. He loved flowers, and his lily garden was the talk of Zarahemla. He did much of the work
himself, but of late he was beginning to feel the weight of
his years. He was on his knees transplanting a purple vio-
let when he heard someone running up the garden path.

"Nephi, Nephi, where are you?"

Without looking up, he knew it to be the voice of his
wife, and he called out to her, "Here I am, my dear. It is
hot today. You should not excite yourself."

"I have terrible news," she said breathlessly.

"Come, let us sit on the garden bench while you tell
me," said Nephi.

"You know the widow Ruth and her daughter Ila,
who live all alone near the marketplace?"

"Yes," came Nephi's simple reply.

"Last night, after dark, they were taken captive by the
Gadianton robbers," she said excitedly.

"But the Gadianton robbers have been wiped out,"
he said, deeply disturbed.

"We all thought they were, but the roots of evil grow
deep and strong. It is almost impossible to destroy them
completely. It seems that a number of Nephites have
joined with the wicked Lamanites and call themselves Lamanites. This wicked group has searched out the hiding
places of the Gadianton robbers and learned many of
their secret plans." Her voice told clearly how frightened
she was.

"How long have you known this?"

"Not until today, when I heard of the capture of Ruth
and her daughter. Many people have been robbed and
beaten. They have been afraid to tell, for fear the robbers
will kill them," she answered.

"But tell me about their capture. Are you sure it was
the robbers?" he asked in a troubled voice.

"Last night," said his wife, "a boy was passing the widow's house when he saw four hourses tied to the hitching post. Thinking it strange, he crept up to the house and looked in and saw that the men were masked and struggling with the mother and daughter. He turned and ran back to the marketplace and gave the alarm. Six men mounted their horses and started for the widow's house. When they arrived, the house was empty, but they rode after them as fast as they could go. The robbers heard them coming and, knowing that the captives slowed them down, they left them behind and rode on. It was a terrible experience for Ruth and her daughter."

"Thank God for their safe return," said Nephi softly.

"Listen," she said. "Do you hear that voice?"

"Yes," he answered. "Is it the voice of Samuel, the Lamanite prophet?"

"Yes. I stopped to listen to him on my way home. The wicked Nephites drove him out of the city and refuse to let him enter again. Now, he sits upon the wall and cries out to them. Many have stopped to listen and I believe their hearts grow soft."

"What did he prophesy today?" Nephi asked, as his eyes grew bright with interest.

"Samuel told the people that when five years have passed, Christ will come to earth. He said God would send a sign to tell us of His coming. There will be great lights in the heavens and there will be one day and a night and a day as if it were one day, without darkness. The sun will rise and set, but darkness will not come; when this happens, we will know that Jesus Christ is born. Oh, Nephi, do you believe he is a true prophet of God?"

"Yes, dear, he is a true prophet. God has told me these things, too. But go on, what else did he say?"

"He told us of another sign—the sign of His death.

When He dies, the sun shall be darkened and refuse to give light. The moon and the stars shall be dark, too. There shall be no light upon the face of the earth for three days, from the time of His death until He shall rise again from the dead. For the first few hours, there shall be wind, terrible thunder, and lightning; the earth shall shake and tremble. Many mountains will be laid low and many of the valleys will be lifted up into mountains. In the darkness, many graves shall be opened and give up their dead, and these saints shall appear to many. He said that God had told him these things, in order that the people might have a chance to prepare themselves for the coming of Christ."

"These signs have been foretold by the prophets of God since the beginning of time. Remember that Lehi saw His coming, in a vision, nearly six hundred years ago," said Nephi.

Just at that moment, the bell in the church nearby began tolling a mournful note. It seemed to spread out over the air and settle down heavily upon them. Now, the bell only rang to call the saints to worship on Sundays or to tell of a death or some other tragedy. Since this was not Sunday, Nephi looked at his wife in alarm.

"Do not look so startled, my husband. It will ring every evening, at dusk, to warn the children to come home. With the Gadianton robbers among us again, they are not safe on the streets after dark."

"It saddens me to think of such wickedness. I hope Samuel, the Lamanite prophet, can reach their hearts and bring them to repentance before our civilization is destroyed from off the face of the earth. Tomorrow I shall take Nephi, our eldest son, with me to baptize all those who will lay down their sins and believe in Christ."

Early next morning, Nephi arose at dawn and ate

breakfast with his wife in their kitchen. It had been their custom for many years to have an early breakfast together. It gave them an opportunity to talk over their plans for the day, as well as to share each other's problems. The quality of their love and devotion was a rare thing to see. It stood as an example and inspiration to all married couples.

"The fire on the hearth feels good this morning," observed Nephi.

"It does indeed, but in a few hours we will need to seek the coolness of the garden."

"I see our eldest son coming up the path. We are going to hear the Lamanite prophet, Samuel," he told her.

Nephi and his son, Nephi III, found Samuel speaking from the wall. He had touched the hearts of many, and when the people saw Nephi, they asked him to baptize them. But there were a great number who did not believe and were angry with Samuel. They cast stones and shot arrows at him, but the Spirit of the Lord was with him and they could not hit him. When they saw this, they were very angry and said they would capture him and bind him. Samuel heard them and dropped from the wall and fled out of their land. He went to his own country and began to preach and prophesy among his own people. He was never heard of again among the Nephites.

All day long and far into the night, Nephi baptized the Nephites who believed in Samuel's words. As he worked, he prophesied and performed great miracles.

Now, the ninety-first year of the reign of the judges passed away and it was six hundred years since Lehi had left Jerusalem. It was the very time the prophets had foretold the coming of Christ, and the people were anxiously awaiting the signs.

In the very midst of all this excitement, Nephi conferred the records upon his son, Nephi III, and went out of the land of Zarahemla. Where he went, no man knew. He disappeared just as Moses and Alma before him had done. His wife and children believed that God had taken him up to heaven as a reward for his faithfulness. They did not grieve, but rejoiced in his blessing.

CHAPTER 50

The ninety-second year of the reign of the judges was a time of great anxiety for the people of the Lord. They watched and waited in breathless anticipation for the birth of the Savior. Throughout all the ages, prophets of God had told the people that there would be certain signs that would tell of His coming. Samuel, the Lamanite prophet, had told them that in five years they could expect the Savior's birth. It was now time for His coming, and yet there had been no signs. Those whose faith was not strong began to doubt the prophets. Perhaps they had been misled, they told themselves. This thought cast them down into the depths of despair. However, to those of strong faith, there was no doubt. They watched and waited with great courage.

On the other hand, the wicked rejoiced. Although they said that the prophets were liars, really they were afraid that the prophets told the truth and that they would be punished for their sins. So now, when the signs failed to appear, they took new heart and began threatening the people of the Lord. They told them they were deceivers, and should be punished by death unless the signs soon came to pass.

When Nephi, son of Nephi and grandson of Helaman, heard their threats, he grieved over their wickedness. So great was his sorrow that he went into the hills and bowed down to the earth and cried out to God. He prayed all day long for his people who were about to be destroyed because of their faith in the prophecies. Just as day was ending, the voice of the Lord came to him, saying:

"Lift up your head and be of good cheer. Behold, the time is here, and on this night shall the sign be given, and on the morrow, I shall come into the world to fulfill all that has been spoken by the mouth of my holy prophets."

Nephi praised God for His goodness, then he arose and started back to Zarahemla. He was no longer tired. New strength seemed to fill his physical body while his soul was lifted up in joy. Never before had he felt such great happiness. The sun would soon be setting, but in spite of that fact, it would still be light.

About halfway down the mountainside, Nephi became aware that the sun had set; yet it was as light as midday. He looked down at the beautiful valley below him and saw the great city of Zarahemla spread out in all its glory. The dazzling white light caught up the gold dome of the temple and made it stand out among all the other buildings. There were no shadows. The light seemed to fill every nook and corner of the entire valley. It was a wonderful sight to behold and, in that moment, he bowed his head and praised God once again. He must hurry, he told himself. His people would need him. He would go at once to the temple.

In order to get to the temple, he had to pass his own house. His young son, Nephi the fourth, saw him just as he was passing by and ran after him as fast as he could go.

"Wait, Father, wait, I've something to tell you." Catching up to his father, he grasped him by the tunic.

"I'm in a hurry, my boy. Tell your mother I will be at

the temple," he said, freeing himself from his son's grasp.

"But Father, I wanted to show you something. Look, the sun has set, but it does not grow dark. Mother says this means that the Holy Baby is born. May I see him?"

Nephi, touched by his son's eagerness, caught the child up in his arms and carried him into the garden, placing him on a bench beside him. With great patience, he explained how the new baby would be born in a far-off land. But, someday, He would visit them in the precious land of promise.

"Run to your mother, now," Nephi said. "I am needed at the temple. I must baptize all those who will surely be convinced of the truthfulness of the gospel, now that they have seen the holy signs."

"But, Father, what will we do about going to bed?" asked the little boy, looking very puzzled.

Nephi smiled down at his son and said, "Go to bed and you'll see how easily you will go to sleep, if you just ask God to bless you this night. You see, son, this is a holy night and all children everywhere will be blessed with heavenly peace." Then, kissing his son on the forehead, he hurried away to the temple. When he reached it, he found a great multitude talking excitedly. They were astonished to behold God's sign of dazzling white light when there should be darkness.

There were many who had not believed the words of the prophets. Now they remembered how they had planned to destroy those who had believed. The very thought of their wickedness made them so afraid that they fell to the earth as if they were dead. They knew, now, that the Son of God would soon appear. All the people on the face of the whole earth, from the east to the west, both in the land north and in the land south, fell to the earth in astonishment. They knew that the prophets had told them of these things for many years.

There was no darkness all that night, and when morning came, the sun arose in its proper order. They knew it was the day that the Lord should be born. When the sun set that evening, it remained light again. The people knew that the words of the prophets had been fulfilled. A new star appeared—the most brilliant star in all the heavens. It came to mark the great event of the coming of the Savior.

Nephi went forth among the people, with many other Christians, baptizing those who repented of their sins. Once again there was peace in the land. Nephi proclaimed to the people that the time should be counted from the day of the Christ Child's birth. And thus began the year one.

One evening, Nephi's little boy came running to him where he sat by an open window reading from the plates of Nephi, and said, "Oh, Father, have you seen the new star?"

"Yes, my son. It was sent to guide the wise men to the birthplace of the little Lord Jesus."

"Is Grandfather Nephi one of the wise men?" asked little Nephi.

Nephi looked at his young son in amazement, for he believed that the little boy had forgotten his grandfather. The child had been so deeply grieved by his disappearance that when he had stopped talking about his grandfather, Nephi felt sure he had forgotten him. Now he was made aware that the child remembered only too well.

"What makes you think that your grandfather is one of the wise men?" asked Nephi gently.

"He has been gone such a long time. One day, he told me all about this new star. He said it would light the place where the little Lord Jesus lay. I believe that God spoke to Grandfather and told him to go find the baby. Do you think I am right, Father?"

"Perhaps you are. We have searched everyplace, in all the land of promise, and he is nowhere to be found. Yes, my son, perhaps he has gone in search of the Christ Child."

Many years passed away. At first, while the people remembered clearly the miracle of light that foretold the birth of the Savior, they remained humble and willing to keep God's commandments. During this time, there was peace throughout all the precious land of promise.

But Satan watched and waited for an opportunity to lead the Nephites astray. At last, some of the people began to be vain and proud of their riches. This was the opportunity Satan had been waiting for. He began clouding men's minds, telling them that there never had been the miracle of light—that it was only a trick to deceive them. Soon they doubted what they had seen and heard. These disbelievers joined with the Gadianton robbers and became wild and sinful. They lived in secret places in the mountains, coming out to rob and kill the Nephites.

There were many Lamanites who had been converted to the church, and they had ever been firm and faithful to God and His commandments. Satan had no power over them. Nothing could shake their faith in God and His Son Jesus Christ. Now, it happened that the Lord was so well pleased with these righteous people that He gave them a great miracle to show them how much He loved them. Suddenly, their dark skins were changed to white, and they became a delightsome people. They joined with the Nephites and were called Nephites. So great was their joy that they set aside a day of thanksgiving and praising God.

As the years passed, the robbers increased in number and grew more wicked. They lived upon the work of the Nephites. They robbed them of their animals, their grain, and all the things they produced. When the

Nephites tried to resist them, they killed them and plundered their houses. So great was the slaughter of the Christians that it looked as if they were all going to be destroyed. However, in spite of their suffering, they grew close to the Lord.

One day, in the twentieth year from the birth of Christ, they realized that they would have to find a way to protect themselves. The chief captain of the army told the people of his plan to save them. When they heard him, they put themselves in his hands. They gathered together all their flocks, their herds, their grain, their fruits, and all their other food—enough for seven years. Then they went into Zarahemla and Bountiful and set to work fortifying themselves. When the robbers came to steal their food, they found there was no food left. The Nephites were not sowing their fields, and all the cattle and sheep were kept within the fortifications. Soon the robbers began to grow hungry, and they started preparing for war. It was a terrible war; never before had so many of the people of Lehi been slain. The Nephites prayed constantly for guidance. The Lord heard their prayers, and soon all the robbers were slain or taken prisoner. The Nephites sent men to the prisons to preach to them, and many were converted. The rest were punished for their crimes.

Following this last great war, the people were humble and faithful in keeping God's commandments. They set to work rebuilding their homes and their lands. It was a period of great industry, and soon they were rewarded by prosperity and peace. To be humble and faithful in time of suffering and disaster, and to forget God in time of prosperity, seemed to be a human weakness of the children of Lehi. By the year 30, the people, for the most part, had become proud of their riches and turned to wickedness. It was in this year that they killed the chief judge and overthrew the government.

The Nephites divided themselves into tribes, every man according to his family and friends. Nevertheless, they made an agreement that they would not go to war against each other. Each tribe had a chief and made its own laws. They were very strict in upholdng the laws of the tribe, and because of their strictness, peace continued, even though their hearts were turned away from righteous living. They stoned the prophets and cast them out.

Nephi saw their wickedness and grieved for the hardness of their hearts and the blindness of their minds. With full knowledge of their hatred for the prophets, Nephi went forth preaching and prophesying. God blessed him and made him safe. He performed great miracles among the people. He raised the dead and healed the sick.

Thus began the thirty-third year since the birth of the Savior.

CHAPTER 51

Nephi's wife was in her kitchen, baking, when she heard the door open. Looking up, she was surprised to see her husband. She hadn't expected him until nightfall. It had been his habit to go among the people preaching and prophesying from daylight until dark. Since it was midday, she had thought he wouldn't be home for hours. She studied his face and found him looking more tired and discouraged than he had been for a long time.

"I'm glad you're home early. Perhaps now you can get some rest," she said.

"My words fell upon deaf ears. There are only a few who are willing to repent and prepare themselves for the terrible day that is at hand. These saints are looking, with great earnestness, for the sign that will mark the Savior's death. According to the prophet Samuel, the Lamanite, it is time for darkness to cover the face of the earth. Instead of preparing themselves, so that they might see Christ, the wicked quarrel and doubt that there will be a sign," he said gravely.

"Nephi, I've asked God to let me be by your side when that great and terrible day comes. I'm afraid I couldn't endure it without your strength."

"That's why I came home," said Nephi earnestly.

"What do you mean?"

"This afternoon," he said, "is the time for the sign to be given. I wanted to be with you. Our children have their own families. I know that God will spare their lives, because of their righteousness."

At that moment, he realized that his wife looked strange.

"Come, sit down. Are you ill?" he asked tenderly.

"I'm not ill, but it's a great shock to learn that the great and terrible day is upon us. Perhaps I will be destroyed," she worried.

"No, my dear, you have fed the hungry, clothed the naked, and cared for the sick. God has told us that to serve His people is to serve Him. Besides, you have ever been faithful in keeping His commandments."

Nephi's words reassured her and gave her new courage. He went to the door and looked up at the sky while his wife watched him anxiously.

"Will we stay here?" she asked, so quietly he scarcely heard her.

"No," he said. "We will go to the hills and take refuge in the cave. We will take a little food and warm clothing. I will help you get them ready. We must leave at once. Already, the storm clouds are gathering."

When they reached the cave, a number of the faithful had already arrived. Almost at once, the storm broke in all its fury. First, the rain fell in torrents; then came the wind, slashing and tearing at everything in its wake. The thunder and lightning were more terrible than anyone could imagine. Then came the earthquake. It shook the earth until they thought it would surely tear it asunder.

"Look! Zarahemla has burst into flames," someone cried out above the tumult.

Nephi, standing close to his wife, looked down on the city in sorrow. Great tongues of flame rose almost to the heavens. Never had a fire burned so quickly. It seemed as if the whole city burst into flame at once, destroying the buildings and all the inhabitants. As Nephi watched his beloved Zarahemla being destroyed, great pity filled his heart for the people who were being burned alive. Oh, if they had only listened to the voice of the prophets! But they would not. They stoned them and cast them out, and now God in His anger was fulfilling His warning that unless they repented, they would be destroyed from off the face of the earth.

And it came to pass, on that very day, in the thirty-fourth year, the whole face of the earth was changed. There were mountains where once there had been valleys and valleys where once there had been mountains. Many cities were sunk in the depths of the sea, many were burned, and many others were buried with earth and carried up into high mountains. The inhabitants of these cities were never heard of again. Many people were picked up by the whirlwinds and carried away. Great and terrible was the destruction in the land southward, but there was even greater destruction in the land northward. Thus the face of the whole earth became deformed. And then, after three hours, the lightning and thunder, the wind and the quaking of the earth ceased.

Nephi and the saints who were gathered in the cave were saved, and they thanked God for His mercy and asked for His protection through the darkness that was to come. Then, without warning, darkness fell, thick and black. Many of the people said they could feel it, like a vapor, falling upon them. There could be no light. They tried to light candles and torches, but neither would give light. Then they found wood that was very dry and tried to kindle a fire, but that was of no use either. Neither the flaming cities, nor the sun, nor the moon, nor the stars, gave any light, so great were the mists of darkness on the face of the land. The darkness lasted for three days and the people wept and mourned for their dead constantly.

Through all the long hours of the storm and darkness, Nephi stayed close beside his wife, encouraging and comforting her. All the saints who had gathered in the cave crowded close to him, for they sensed his great faith and felt safe and secure in his presence.

At last, through the blackness, there came a voice that was heard throughout all the land, crying: "Woe, woe, woe unto this people! Woe to all the people of the whole earth for, unless they repent, they shall be destroyed. The devil laughs and his angels rejoice because of the slain of my people, for it is because of their sins that they have fallen."

The voice continued, telling of the destruction of the great cities and how all the earth's surface had changed, and how this terrible disaster was because of the wickedness of the people.

"Oh," came the voice, "all of you whom I have saved because you were more righteous than they, will you now repent and turn to me? Repent of your sins and be converted so that I may heal you. I say to you, if you will come to me, you shall have eternal life. Behold, my arm of mercy is held out to you, and all who come shall be blessed. I am Jesus Christ, the Son of God, and I came to my own and they would not receive me. You shall not offer any more sacrifices of burnt offerings, because I will not accept them. Instead, you shall offer me a broken heart and a repentant spirit. Furthermore, you must come to me as a little child and I will receive you, because of such is the kingdom of God. It was for these that I laid down my life and have taken it up again; therefore, repent, and come to me and be saved."

All the people of the land heard these sayings. After a while the voice stopped speaking, and there was silence in all the land for many hours. So great was the astonishment of the people that they stopped their weeping and mourning. After many hours had passed in silence, the voice came again, saying: "Oh, the house of Israel, whom I have spared, if you will repent and return to me, I will gather you as a hen gathers her chickens under her wings. But if not, your homes shall become desolate, until the time of the fulfilling of the covenant to your fathers."

When the people heard these words, they began to weep and mourn again. They continued in this fashion until three days had passed away. Then, suddenly, the light came. It was morning. The brilliant light flooded the land and filled their hearts with new hope and thanksgiving for being alive. The people discovered that it was only the more righteous who were saved—those who had listened to the prophets and had not cast them out or stoned them or shed the blood of the saints. There were many Lamanites, as well as Nephites, whose lives had been spared. These survivors had great favors shown them and great blessings poured out upon them. But the greatest of these blessings was the fact that soon after the ascension of Christ to heaven, He did truly show himself to them.

CHAPTER 52

When the darkness disappeared and the light came, the people marveled at the wonder of God's creation. Never before had they fully realized what rich, rare gifts had been bestowed upon them—the rain and sun, the moon and stars, the great forests and mighty mountains, the sparkling lakes and clean, fresh air and the fields of golden grain. All these things they had taken for granted, never fully appreciating them until the light was taken away.

A great multitude gathered at the temple in the land of Bountiful. They stood in small groups, talking earnestly with one another. They told of their experiences during the three days of darkness, and marveled at the great change that had taken place. They talked of Jesus, of whom the sign had been given concerning His death. All at once, everyone stopped talking and began to look about, and up at the heavens. They heard a voice. Although they listened carefully, they could not understand what was being said, nor could they see anyone. It was not a harsh voice, neither was it a loud voice. It was a small voice that seemed to pierce their very souls and cause their hearts to burn. It came a second and a third time, and behold, the third time they understood the voice. This is what it said:

"Behold my Beloved Son, in whom I am well pleased, in whom I have glorified my name—hear Him."

The multitude lifted their eyes toward heaven. They saw a man descending. He was clothed in a white robe. It was so white, it fairly sparkled in the sunlight. He came down and down until, at last, His feet touched the ground and He stood in the midst of them. The eyes of the whole multitude were turned upon Him. So great was their amazement, they dared not open their mouths to speak, even to each other. Many of them thought it was an angel standing there, among them.

All at once, He stretched forth His hand and said: "I am Jesus Christ, whom the prophets testified should come into the world. I am the light and the life of the world; and I have drunk from that bitter cup which the Father gave me, and have glorified the Father in taking upon me the sins of the world."

Nephi turned and looked at his wife. High color flooded her cheeks and her eyes were large and bright. She was looking at Christ with a steady earnestness of purpose. The thought came to Nephi that she had the look of an angel, and somehow she looked as young as a girl. Then he looked at the multitude. Their faces had the same shining light about them.

When Christ stopped speaking, the whole multitude fell to the earth. They remembered that it had been prophesied that Christ would show himself to them after he had been taken up to heaven.

"Arise and come to me," he said, "that you may put your hands in my side and also feel the prints of the nails in my hands and feet. I do this that you may know that I am the God of Israel and of the whole earth. I have been slain for the sins of the world."

The multitude arose and went to him, and each one

in his turn did as He had requested, seeing with their own eyes and feeling with their own hands. Now they knew that He was really the one that the prophets had said would come. When they had all touched Him, they cried out in one voice, saying: "Blessed be the name of the Most High God!" They fell to the earth and worshiped Him.

In that moment, Nephi saw that Jesus was searching for someone in the multitude. At last, His eyes found those of Nephi, and a gentle smile touched His lips.

"Nephi, come to me," He commanded.

Nephi arose and went quickly to Him, bowing before the Lord and kissing His feet.

"Arise!" Christ commanded him.

Nephi arose and stood before Him.

Christ spoke again to him, saying, "I give you power to baptize this people when I am again ascended to heaven."

Then He called eleven others and gave them the power to baptize and said to them: "This is the way I want you to baptize; and there shall be no arguments among you. Verily I say unto you, all those who repent of their sins through your words and want to be baptized in my name, then this is the way it shall be done—go down and stand in the water. And these are the words you shall say: 'Having authority given me of Jesus Christ, I baptize you in the name of the Father and of the Son and of the Holy Ghost, Amen.' And then, you shall immerse them in the water and come forth again out of the water."

Jesus turned to the multitude and began speaking to them. He told them that He no longer wanted them to live according to the law of Moses—an eye for an eye and a tooth for a tooth—but, from that moment, if anyone struck them on the right cheek, they were to turn the other cheek also, or if any man sued them at law and took away their coat, they should let him have their cloak also.

"Behold," Jesus said to them, "I say unto you, that you shall love your enemies, bless them that curse you, do good to them that hate you, and pray for them who despitefully use you and persecute you. Therefore, I would that you would be perfect, even as I, or your Father who is in heaven is perfect. Do not lay up treasures upon earth, where moth and rust will corrupt and thieves break through and steal, but lay up your treasure in heaven, where neither moth nor rust can corrupt and where thieves do not break in and steal. For where your treasure is, there will your heart be also."

When Jesus stopped speaking, He turned to the twelve men to whom he had given authority to baptize and preach His gospel throughout the land, and said to them: "Remember the words which I have spoken, for I have chosen you to serve this people. Therefore, I say unto you, take no thought for your life, what you shall eat or what you shall drink, nor of what you shall wear. Behold the birds of the air, for they sow not, neither do they reap, and yet your Heavenly Father feeds them. Consider the lilies of the field, how they grow; they toil not, neither do they spin, and yet, I say unto you, that even Solomon in all his glory was not dressed like one of these. Therefore, do not say, what shall we eat or drink or wear, for your Heavenly Father knows your needs. Seek first the kingdom of God and His righteousness, and all these things will be given to you."

Now, when Jesus had spoken these words, he turned again to the multitude. From the first moment that Jesus had descended to the earth, the people had kept their eyes upon Him, watching and listening to every word He spoke. Their hearts burned with an overpowering desire to serve Him. His mild voice stirred them as nothing else had ever done. They knew that this was the greatest event in all the history of the world. Here was a man who came to earth and gave His life for them. Furthermore, He was buried in the tomb for three days, and on the third day arose from the dead and showed Himself to the people. He then ascended to heaven, and now came to them in the promised land. He did this to convince them that there would be a resurrection and that, by right living, they could gain eternal life.

Now He was speaking again to the people: "Beware of false prophets who come to you in sheep's clothing, but whose souls are like wolves. All who hear these words of mine and do them are like the wise man who built his house upon a rock—the rain and the floods came and the winds blew and beat upon that house, but it was safe, because it was built on the rock. Everyone that hears my words and does not do them, is like the man that built his house upon the sand—when the floods came and the wind blew and beat upon the house, it fell, and great was the fall."

Nephi's wife was a gentle, timid person, and when the Savior called Nephi to come to Him, she let the crowd push her back and back until she was on the outside of the multitude. Here she saw the blind, the deaf, the old, and the sick, who had been brought by their families and friends. Her heart went out to them in pity. She saw a man lying on a cot, close to where she was standing. He had lost the use of his arms and legs. His face was twisted and white with pain, but when the Savior began speaking again, he relaxed and a look of peace spread over his face. Then she looked at the others and saw that they, too, wore the same peaceful expression.

"It is time for me to leave you," said Christ, "and I want you to go to your homes and think over what I have said and ask your Father in heaven, in my name, that you may understand and prepare your minds for tomorrow, when I shall come again. However, now I must go to my Father, for I must show myself to the lost tribes of Israel. They are not really lost to my Father. He knows where He has taken them."

When Jesus had spoken these words, He cast His eyes on the multitude and, at that moment, He saw that they were in tears and that they kept their eyes upon Him, as if they would ask Him to stay a little longer with them.

"Behold, my heart is filled with mercy toward you. Have you any sick or afflicted among you? Bring them here. I will heal them, for your faith is great."

When He had spoken these words, all the multitude went forth with their sick and afflicted, their lame, their blind, and their dumb. He healed them, every one, as they were brought to Him. All those who were healed and all the others, who were whole, bowed down at His feet and worshiped Him. Nephi's wife helped carry the helpless man on the cot to Jesus. She saw Him bend down and touch the man and, instantly, he arose and could walk and use his hands. His joy was boundless! He fell at the Savior's feet and bathed them with his tears. Then Jesus saw Nephi's wife and blessed her, too.

"Bring me your little children," He said.

They brought their children and set them on the ground in a circle about Jesus.

"And now, my people, kneel down upon the ground," Jesus said to the multitude.

They did as He commanded and He, Himself, knelt down and began praying. Now, the eye has never seen, nor the ear heard, such great and marvelous things as they saw and heard. But, from that day forth, no tongue was allowed to speak and no one was permitted to write the Savior's words. The hearts of the multitude were filled with joy.

"Arise," commanded Jesus. "You are blessed because of your faith and my joy is full."

When Jesus spoke these words, He wept and took their little children, one by one, and blessed them. He wept again. Suddenly, a great and marvelous thing happened. The heavens opened up and angels descended, as if in the midst of fire. They came down and encircled the little ones and they were encircled with fire. The angels went among the children while all the multitude watched. There were twenty-five hundred who saw these things.

CHAPTER 53

For several minutes after Christ ascended to heaven, the multitude stood about the temple, talking among themselves. They had seen and heard so many astonishing and wonderful things that they felt compelled to put their thoughts into words. They must know that others had seen what they themselves had seen, in order to trust their senses. Now, the multitude had not seen Christ ascend to heaven; only the disciples had seen Him. Jesus had touched each of the twelve. When He had done this, there came a cloud that overshadowed the multitude and made it impossible for them to see Jesus depart and ascend to heaven.

Nephi's wife waited for Nephi to come, so that they might find lodgings for the night. While she was waiting, she saw a strange man coming toward her, smiling and holding out his hand. She thought she had never seen him and yet, as he came nearer, she had a vague feeling that she had known him before.

"I could not go to my home without first thanking you again for your kindness," said the man, in a friendly voice.

"I don't understand—haven't you mistaken me for someone else?" she asked.

"Have I changed so much? Yes, I guess I have. I am the man who was paralyzed and lay upon the cot. You took me to Jesus when the others had forgotten."

Nephi's wife looked at him in surprise. Years had fallen away from him and his eyes burned with newfound faith. Instantly he had become whole, at one slight touch of the Savior's hand.

"Think," he continued, "how my wife will feel when I go to my home and, instead of being carried through the door, can walk in by myself. What a blessed day this has been! I shall devote all my remaining years to the service of God and His Son Jesus Christ. I shall always remember how, through your efforts, I was taken to my Lord."

"You are truly an example of the glorious miracles performed by Jesus this day. There is no need for you to thank me, for if I had not taken you, someone else would have done. Your faith was great enough to have found a way to reach the Savior. Give Him your praise."

"This is the second miracle that has been given to me. I was once a Lamanite, and through my faith and service to God I was given a white skin and the privilege of calling myself a Nephite. My blessings are great indeed. I hope someday we shall meet again. Should you ever need me, just ask for Nathan of Bountiful and I will serve you with all my heart."

Nephi's wife took his outstretched hand and said, "Good-bye, my friend. I shall remember your promise and, most of all, this great day which made you well again."

She watched him turn and leave the temple grounds. When he was through the gate, he chose the shady lane. There was a spring in his step and his head was held high. Mists clouded her eyes as she thought of the glorious gift the Savior had bestowed upon this man. She knew that no one who had not been deprived of the use of his legs and arms could fully appreciate the richness of this blessing.

At that moment, Nephi's wife discovered that the multitude had nearly all gone from the temple grounds. Each man had taken his wife and children and gone to his home. Immediately, the people began spreading the news that they had seen Jesus—that He had come down to earth while they watched; that they had touched Him; that He had performed wondrous miracles and that, tomorrow, He would be with them again. They told many before it was dark, and when night came, they kept on spreading the news until morning. They labored all night in order that they might gather at the temple the next morning to see Jesus.

When morning came, the multitude gathered at the temple was mighty in number. There was scarcely room enough for them to stand. The multitude was so great that Nephi divided them into twelve bodies. Each of the twelve disciples took charge of one group. They had the people kneel down on the face of the earth and pray to the Father, in the name of Jesus. After they had prayed constantly for many minutes, Nephi and the other disciples went down to the water's edge and the multitude followed them. Nephi went into the water and was baptized. He then began to baptize the disciples and they were filled with the Holy Ghost and with fire. They were even encircled by fire that came down from heaven. The multitude saw it with their own eyes. No sooner had this happened than they saw angels descending, and they came into the midst of the disciples and began ministering unto them.

Suddenly, the people saw a bright light in the heavens, and in the midst of the light they saw a figure descending. Those who had been at the temple the day before knew this man was Jesus Christ, the Savior of the world. All eyes were turned upon Him. When He reached the earth, He stood in the midst of the disciples, but He turned to the multitude and commanded: "Kneel down upon the earth and my disciples will pray."

They did as He commanded, calling Him their Lord and their God. There was a great outpouring of prayers. They opened their hearts to the Savior, confessing their sins and pleading for forgiveness. Their faith was so strong that Christ's soul was filled with joy and He said to them: "Because of your faith, you are more blessed than the people at Jerusalem and I will reveal to you greater miracles than I did to them. Arise!"

Immediately the people stood up, and Jesus told His disciples to eat of the bread. When they had eaten, He bid them feed the multitude.

"Drink of the wine," He commanded them. "Now serve the multitude."

The eyes of the people filled with surprise, for there had been no bread or wine. Furthermore, they knew that neither the disciples nor the people had brought it with them. Yet there it was—great baskets filled with bread and great jars filled with wine—enough to feed the thousands gathered at the temple. Christ told them they were to eat the bread in remembrance of His body and to drink the wine in remembrance of His blood. He told them that when they took this sacrament, their hands and hearts must be clean. He taught them many things and then, turning to Nephi, He said to him: "Bring forth the record which you have kept."

Nephi brought the records to Jesus and laid them before Him. He looked at them carefully.

"I commanded Samuel, the Lamanite, that he testify unto this people, that on the day the Father should glorify His name in me, many saints would arise from the dead and appear unto the living and minister to them. And now, I ask you, did this miracle happen?"

His disciples answered, "Yea, Lord, Samuel did prophesy according to thy words, and they were all fulfilled."

Then Jesus said, "How is it that you have not written that many saints arose and appeared to the people and ministered unto them?"

Now, Nephi was deeply grieved because of his neglect to record this miracle. Jesus commanded him to make a record of it at once, which he did.

The Savior taught the people for three days, and after that He showed Himself to them often. He broke bread many times and blessed it and gave it to them.

On the third day, Nephi's wife was among the multitude, just as she had been the two previous days. She had seen many astonishing miracles. She had seen the sick healed, the lame made to walk, the blind to see, the deaf to hear, and even a man raised from the dead. Yes, Christ had surely shown His power unto them. And now, as she looked at Christ, she said a silent prayer, praising Him and glorifying His name. Suddenly He stopped speaking and turned His eyes toward her, and she knew, in that moment, He had heard the prayer that was in her heart.

"Are you Nephi's wife?"

"Yes," she answered, turning to see who had spoken to her.

It was a young woman, holding a tiny baby in her arms. Her face was thin and pale. Her eyes were large and bright. Instantly, tears formed and went rolling down her cheeks unheeded. Nephi's wife sensed that the young woman was bearing a great sorrow, a burden almost too great for her.

"Is there something I can do for you?" continued Nephi's wife gently.

"It's my baby. I have tried all day to take him to the Savior, but I can't make my way through the crowd. I know that if He touches my child, he will be made whole again." Very tenderly, she unwrapped the baby. He was a beautiful child, except for one arm that was horribly deformed. "The people know you," she continued, "and I thought, for that reason, you could get through to Jesus. Will you do this for me?"

"What is your name?" asked Nephi's wife kindly.

"Mary," the girl answered. "But will you do this thing for me?"

"That's a lovely name. The Savior's mother was named Mary. Yes, indeed, I will help you through the crowd. But you must come with me and carry your baby to Him. Don't be afraid. He will fill your heart with loving kindness and give you strength to be an even better mother than you are now. Come, let us go."

When they reached the Savior, He was waiting for them and immediately took the baby in His arms and blessed him, and he was whole again. There were many children gathered around Him and He taught and ministered unto them. Then, suddenly, a wonderful thing happened—tiny babies began to talk and they said great and marvelous things. The multitude saw and heard these children speak and it was forbidden to write down what they said. But the multitude who saw and heard them could never forget, for it was written deep within their souls.

CHAPTER 54

Nephi reached the summit of a small, windswept hill and made his way to a great black rock that towered some fifty feet above him. The rock was so shaped that it cut off the stinging breeze that seemed always to be blowing across the hill. The rain the night before had washed the rich, green grass and the stately trees to a gleaming brightness. The earth, too, had a clean, washed smell. He reached down and dug his fingers into the ground. When his hand was full, he let the dirt run through his fingers, thinking, as he did, that this was the precious land of his inheritance.

Some weeks had passed since Jesus had ascended to heaven after three days of teaching. The twelve disciples Jesus had chosen began, from that time forth, to baptize and teach as many as would come to them. They had journeyed throughout all the land of promise, each one going his separate way. Now they were to be united in mighty prayer and fasting. They had promised to meet at the temple in Bountiful. Nephi looked down at the white ribbon that was the road he was to travel. It wound down through the rich pasture lands and took its way through the fertile fields of grain, then began to climb the western mountains and down into the city. It was a two-day journey to Bountiful from where he sat sheltered by the big rock.

"Good morning, brother."

Nephi was startled at the sound of a human voice. He got quickly to his feet and, to his surprise, saw that it was his brother, Timothy. Now, this was the brother whom Jesus had chosen as one of His disciples, and the brother whom Nephi had raised from the dead. They loved and respected each other, and it was with a joyful heart that Nephi greeted Timothy. After they had rested, they began their journey to the temple together.

When the disciples met in the temple, they had much to tell each other. All things were common among them. Every man dealt justly with the other, and they did everything Jesus had commanded them to do. While they were fasting and praying, Jesus again showed himself to them. He came and stood in their midst and said: "What do you wish of me?"

They said, "Lord, we would like you to tell us the name that we shall call this church."

Jesus answered, "Since this church is built upon my gospel, it shall be called after me. Behold, my joy is great because of you, and also this generation. Even the Father and the angels rejoice, for none are lost of the ones that are now alive of this generation. But I sorrow because of the fourth generation from this, for they are led away by Satan and will sell me for silver and gold. When that day comes, I will visit them and turn their wickedness upon their own heads."

When Jesus stopped speaking, the twelve disciples kept the silence out of respect for their Lord. At last, He spoke to each of them and asked this question: "What can I do for you when I have gone to my Father?"

Nine of the disciples had the same wish. They said, "We would like to live to the normal age of man and then be taken quickly unto thee in thy kingdom."

When Jesus heard their wish, He smiled and

stretched forth His hand, saying, "Blessed are you because you want this thing of me. Your wish shall be granted, and when you are seventy-two years old, you shall come to my kingdom and there you will find rest."

Then Jesus turned to the other three and asked what He could do for them. Their hearts were full of sorrow, for they were afraid to tell Him what they wanted. The Savior looked at them and said, in a quiet voice that pierced their very souls: "I know your thoughts. More blessed are you, for you shall never taste of death. You shall live to behold all that happens to the children of men, even until I shall come in my glory with the powers of heaven. You shall never endure the pains of death, but, when I come in my glory, you shall be changed in the twinkling of an eye from mortality to immortality. Then you shall be blessed in the kingdom of my Father. You shall never have pain while you live, nor sorrow, except for the sins of the world. All this will I do because you wish to bring the souls of men to me while the world still stands."

When Jesus had spoken these words, He touched each one of them with His finger, except the three who were to stay on earth; then He departed. Just at that moment, the heavens opened and the three were caught up into heaven. They saw and heard unspeakable things, which they were forbidden to tell. A change came over their bodies, to make it possible for them to live forever, without suffering or sorrow, except for the sins of the world. This change was not equal to that which shall take place at the last day. There was a change made upon them so that Satan could have no power over them and could not tempt them. In this state they were to remain until the judgment day, and then they would undergo a greater change, in order that they could enter the kingdom of Heaven.

The Lord forbade anyone from speaking or writing the names of the three disciples. They were to be kept secret, so that the three Nephites could lose themselves in the world. They have been kept secret to this very day, and will continue to be so until the very end.

By the thirty-sixth year, the twelve disciples had established churches of Christ throughout all the land and had converted every living soul. The people shared everything in common. Therefore, there was neither rich nor poor, nor slave nor free. They were all free to partake of the heavenly gifts. The disciples performed great miracles in the name of Christ. They healed the sick, raised the dead, caused the lame to walk, the blind to receive their sight, the deaf to hear, and many other miracles were performed among the children of men.

The Lord made them prosper and they rebuilt many of the cities—even the great city of Zarahemla. A hundred years passed away since Christ's birth, in which there was peace and prosperity. The disciples of Jesus had all gone to God, except the three who were to remain. There were other disciples ordained to take their places.

There was neither envy, nor strife, nor tumult, nor lying, nor murder, nor any manner of wickedness. Surely, there could not be a happier people among all the people who had been created by the hand of God.

Now, Nephi, who was appointed by Christ as one of His disciples, left the records with his son, Nephi the fourth. And it came to pass that he kept this record upon the plates of Nephi. When he died, he turned them over to his son, Amos. Amos kept them for eighty-four years, and all through his days, there was peace. Then at last

Amos died, and the records were turned over to his son, Amos.

Two hundred years had passed away since the birth of the Savior. They were marvelous years, filled with perfect faith in Christ. The people enjoyed complete harmony in all things and perfect devotion to God and to each other. They all shared alike, each one using all he needed to satisfy his wants. It was a time of rare unselfishness—their concern was for the good of others rather than for themselves. It was a period free from want and pain, and joy filled every heart. Sorrow was little known. The Lord was pleased with them, for not a single soul was lost. He blessed them with great riches and they multiplied so fast that they began to fill every nook and corner in the land of their inheritance.

But peace and happiness were destined to end. Black days were ahead for many of them. By 210 A.D., some of the people began to be lifted up in their pride. They dressed in costly clothing and wore precious stones of all kinds. They built churches for themselves, in order to gain riches. They denied the true church of Christ. It was a busy time for Satan. He was constantly reaching out and taking hold of men's hearts. These wicked people began to persecute the three disciples of Jesus who were to live to the end of the world. They cast them into prison, but, by God's power, prisons fell apart and they escaped and performed mighty miracles among the people. But the miracles only made the wicked people hate them more, and they cast them into furnaces of fire. It was of no use, for they walked out unharmed. Then they cast them into dens of wild beasts, but that was of no use, either, for they played with the animals as a child plays with a lamb.

These people, who had been so united, now divided themselves into two great classes. The people who were faithful to the true church of Christ became known as the Nephites, among whom were the three disciples of Jesus. Those who rejected Christ were known as Lamanites. As the years passed, the Lamanites became greater and greater in number and the Nephites smaller and smaller. Those who were still known as Nephites began to be proud and vain, like the Lamanites. From this time, the disciples began to sorrow for the sins of the world.

One afternoon, in early spring of the year 305 A.D., Amos sent for his brother, Ammaron. As Ammaron walked with quick strides toward his brother's house, he thought with regret that it had been several weeks since he had visited him. And now, if anything had happened to Amos, he would never forgive himself. Knowing how independent Amos was, he was sure that something serious had happened or he never would have sent for him. His troubled thoughts made him almost run.

When Ammaron reached his brother's house, he walked in unannounced. He found Amos lying in a great, bare room that smelled musty from the excessive spring rains. He was shocked at the change in Amos. His body was thin and wasted, his face old and tired, and his great, dark eyes could not deny his suffering.

"How good of you to come. Sit down," Amos said, in a thin, weak voice.

"What terrible thing is this that has happened to you?" asked Ammaron, his eyes full of unshed tears.

"Several days ago, the Gadianton robbers broke into my house at midnight and robbed me of my furnishings. Then, after abusing me, they left, thinking I was dead."

"But why didn't you send for me at once?" asked Ammaron. "You might have died, here alone."

"I didn't want to involve you. This band of robbers has spread over all the face of the land, and no one is safe who they think still believes in the true church of Christ.

But now, brother, I am dying. The Lord has commanded me to give the records to you." Amos was forced to rest before he could continue.

"Just wait and see. You will not die. I will get help for you and you will get well. I shall move you to my house and my wife will nurse you back to health," said Ammaron with tender affection.

"No, my dear brother. I have but a few hours to live, and we must plan how you will get the records out of this house and into yours in safety. I am sure they were what the robbers were looking for. I need not tell you how important it is that these records be kept safe for future generations. The Lord has told us He will destroy all of this people if they do not repent, and they will not. Oh, brother, guard the records with your life. Pray for guidance always, and listen for the still, small voice within you. The Lord appointed you because He knew He could depend on you to find a way to preserve these records."

"Brother Amos, the Lord can depend on me. Just tell me what to do and I will do whatever you request," said Ammaron earnestly.

Before night ended, all the records and the other precious things, such as the sword of Laban and the ball, or director, were moved safely to Ammaron's house. At dawn, Amos died and went to his reward.

When 320 years had passed away, Ammaron was told by the Holy Ghost to hide the sacred records that had been handed down from generation to generation. He hid them, with the guidance of the Lord, in order that they could be brought forth again according to the prophecies and promises of the Lord. And thus ended the record of Ammaron.

CHAPTER 55

A ten-year-old boy sat beside a brook fishing. He had cast his net, and now there was nothing to do but wait until it was full of fish. Then he would draw it in and select the biggest and best of the fish to take to his mother for the evening meal.

He thought of many things as he sat there, especially about the mysteries of heaven. Mormon, for that was his name, was not an ordinary boy. He had a quick, keen mind, and already he had mastered the learning of his people. He could read and write in a number of languages, and even at his tender age, he could solve difficult problems. He was, in fact, a very unusual boy.

It was a hot day, but by the brook where he sat the branches of the trees made a dense shade and it was cool and pleasant. Finally, the humming of the bees and the bubble and gurgle of the brook made him drowsy. He tried to keep his eyes open, but his eyelids grew so heavy that at last he gave up and lay back on a grassy knoll, and soon was fast asleep.

A number of small creatures came out of their hiding places to have a look at the intruder. After a while, a tree squirrel came by and, seeing the boy, came closer and closer to get a good look at him. She liked what she saw. Now, the squirrel would never lie down in the forest unprotected. Almost anything could happen, so she decided, then and there, that she would stay and guard the boy. If she saw an enemy approaching, she could warn him with her chattering.

An hour passed and then, to the alert ears of the squirrel, there came a new sound in the forest. She turned her head first to one side and then to the other so as to hear better. Yes, it was someone coming—someone who walked on two legs—a man. Perhaps he would pass by without noticing the boy. But he did not, and the little squirrel made such a chatter that Mormon awoke and sat bolt upright.

"Good morning, Mormon. I see your little friend has warned you of my coming."

Mormon turned quickly and looked into the eyes of a strange man. Through the corner of his eye, he saw the little squirrel disappearing up a nearby tree.

"Good morning," said Mormon. "How do you know my name, sir?"

"It was revealed to me by the Lord our God," said the white-haired man.

Mormon turned quick, searching eyes toward the stranger. In this day, when wickedness was on every hand, men scarcely ever mentioned the Lord. But here was a man who spoke of the Lord with true devotion.

"Who are you, sir?" asked Mormon, observing every detail of the old man's appearance.

"I am Ammaron, but my name means nothing to you, for I do not come from these parts."

"I know your name well," answered the boy. "You are the keeper of the sacred records."

"That is right," said Ammaron, smiling in surprise. "It's about the records that I have come. I went to your house in the village, and your mother gave me directions for finding you."

"You wanted to see me?" questioned Mormon, in bewilderment. "My father's name is Mormon. I am only ten years old. It must be my father whom the Lord told you about."

"No, my boy. Strange as it may seem to you, God made it clear that He referred to you," said Ammaron, coming to sit on the bank beside Mormon.

They talked of many things—of the Savior's visit to the promised land, of the wickedness of the people, and of the sacred records. Ammaron was amazed at the sincerity and learning of this young boy.

"I see," said Ammaron, "that you are a serious child and quick to observe. God trusts you and has called you to perform a great service for Him. And now, I ask you, are you willing?"

"Sir, I shall ever be willing to serve my Lord," replied Mormon.

Ammaron was so impressed with this child—with his great wisdom and sincere faith—that he laid his hands upon him and blessed him. After the prayer, he gave Mormon the following instructions:

"I want you to remember all the things you see and hear concerning this people. And then, when you are twenty-four years old, go to the land Antum, to a hill which shall be called Shim. There I have buried all the sacred records concerning this people."

Mormon repeated the instructions, in order to imprint them on his mind. Then he asked, "Is there anything else I should know?"

"Yes," answered Ammaron. "Behold, you shall take the plates of Nephi with you, but all the rest of the records and sacred things are to be left where they are. You

shall engrave, on the plates of Nephi, all the things you
have seen and heard concerning this people. And now, I
bid you farewell."

"My mother and father will be honored if you will
stay with us a few days," said Mormon politely.

"Now that I have completed my work here on earth
my days are few, and I want to return to my home, to
spend the last few hours with my family and old friends.
So, God bless you with the courage to keep His commandments. Guard the records with your very life. The
danger of losing them grows greater with the increasing
wickedness of the people. They will try every means at
their command to find the records and destroy them. And
now, farewell once again."

Mormon watched Ammaron disappear among the
trees and knew that for a brief space of time he had been
touched by a great spirit and a true man of God. He had
only known him for a few minutes, and yet he had left a
lasting impression upon the life of Mormon.

When Mormon was eleven years old, he went with
his father into the land southward, to the land of Zarahemla. Mormon was astonished to see the whole face of
the land covered with buildings, and people as numerous
as the sands of the sea. Soon after their arrival, war broke
out between the Lamanites and Nephites in the borders
of Zarahemla. After many lives were lost, the war came
to an end and the Nephites were the victors. There was
peace for four years. Although there had been great suffering, yet the people did not repent. They became more
wicked than ever. Now, the Lord was so displeased that
He took away His beloved disciples. There were no gifts
from the Lord—no healings or miracles of any kind.

At fifteen, Mormon was wise and learned far beyond
his years. As a reward for his faithfulness, he was visited
by the Lord and knew of the goodness of Jesus. He
wanted to share the joy of the gospel with other Nephites,

so he began to preach to them. But God commanded him, saying: "I forbid you to preach to this people because they have willfully rebelled against me and my beloved disciples. Because of the hardness of their hearts, I have cursed this land."

When Mormon was sixteen, war broke out again between the Lamanites and the Nephites. Although he was young, yet he was as tall and strong as any man and the people knew of his wisdom and learning. Therefore, they trusted him and appointed him to be the leader of their armies.

Many years passed away and there were wars and rumors of wars with short periods of peace between. The Nephites recognized the threat of complete destruction which hung over them. In spite of this fact, they would not repent of their evil actions. The war spread to every part of the land northward and southward. The country was filled with Lamanites and Gadianton robbers. No man's property was safe from the thieves. Everywhere there was murder, magic art, and witchcraft. Mormon saw thousands of his people cut down in open rebellion against their God.

By 345 A.D., the Nephites began to flee before the Lamanites until they reached the land of Jashon, where it was possible for them to stop their retreat. Now, Mormon had never been to the city of Jashon and so, as soon as the city had been fortified against the Lamanites, he began looking around.

"Do you know the name of the hill north of the city?" he asked one of his soldiers.

The man answered, "Yes, I do, sir. It is the hill Shim."

Suddenly, Mormon remembered Ammaron. He remembered, too, that in this very hill Ammaron had hidden the records unto the Lord, in order to keep them from being destroyed. Furthermore, he remembered his promise to go to the hill and take the plates of Nephi and record on them all the things he should see and hear during his lifetime. He knew that he must take them now. He thought of confiding in one of his men, but a still, small voice inside him told him it was not safe to trust anyone. It was a work he must do alone. He began planning how he could steal away without being noticed. He had learned by experience that there were few, if any, among all the armies that still believed in Jesus the Christ. That night, he knelt down and asked God for guidance.

The next morning, just at break of day, Mormon began climbing the hill Shim. It was still too dark to see clearly, but he felt a strange power within him, guiding his footsteps. It was a strange, wonderful feeling, almost as if he were walking on air or floating through space. He had perfect faith in the power guiding him. At last, he was compelled to stop. He knew this was the spot where the records were hidden. There was a brier bush directly in front of him; pushing its branches aside, he saw that it hid the entrance to a small cave. Once inside the cave, he soon discovered the sacred treasure hidden there so long ago by Ammaron. Remembering the words of his old friend, he took just the plates of Nephi and left everything else.

Mormon set to work making the records of his people. He made an account of all their wickedness and sin, but because of his great love for his people, his heart was filled with sorrow all the days of his life. Nevertheless, he knew that he would be lifted up at the last day.

In 350 A.D., the Lamanites and Nephites made a treaty, giving the land northward to the Nephites and the land southward to the Lamanites.

CHAPTER 56

There never was a time, in all the history of the children of Lehi, when there was such terrible wickedness as at this particular time. It is impossible to give a true description of the horrible scene of destruction among the Nephites and Lamanites. Every heart was hardened, so that they delighted in shedding blood. The Lamanites kept marching forward, taking one city after another. They captured the women and children and offered them as sacrifices to their idol gods. When the Nephites learned of the fate of their women and children, they grew so angry that they came against the Lamanites with such force that they drove them out of their land, although they had only half their number.

After this there was peace for eight years, but in 375 A.D., the Lamanites made war upon the Nephites once again. This time, their armies were so great in number that no one bothered to count them. From this time forth, the Lamanites were victorious. They swept the Nephites before them, even as dew before the sun. They were rapidly pushing the Nephites farther and farther into the northland. Mormon, seeing that the Lamanites were coming dangerously near the hill Shim, became worried for the safety of the sacred records.

Next morning, bright and early, Mormon took his son, Moroni, and began climbing up the hill, first making sure that there were no Lamanites spying on them. The day was cold and bleak and Mormon, who was now in his middle sixties, began to grow weary of the effort required in climbing the stony hill.

"It's been thirty years since I climbed this hill and took away the plates of Nephi," said Mormon.

"Thirty years is a long time. Are you sure you can find the hiding place again?" asked Moroni.

"Yes, my son, for the Spirit of the Lord guides me today, just as it did thirty years ago. This is God's work, Moroni, and as surely as we both live, He will protect us while we find a new hiding place for the sacred records," answered Mormon.

"Where are we going to hide them?" asked Moroni, with deep concern.

"That, I do not know, but God will provide a place. Until then, we will keep them with us. When we get to the hiding place, I will give you a small number of the plates of Nephi. After I have gone to my grave, you will use these plates to record all that you see and hear. May God bless and preserve you, so that you can write the final record of this people." Mormon spoke with deep sorrow in his voice.

Father and son continued to climb up the mountain in silence. At last, as the hill became steeper and more difficult to climb, they were forced to rest. They seated themselves with their backs to the mountain and their faces to the south. As Mormon lifted his eyes and looked out over the vast stretches of the promised land, he instantly caught his breath. Here, from the mountainside, was a complete picture of the destruction of the Nephites and their property.

"What tragic waste of life," said Moroni.

"And all because they hardened their hearts against God. No matter how they suffer, they will not repent. And now, God, in His wrath, will destroy all of us. Your eyes are better than mine. Tell me what you see," requested Mormon.

"Far away, in the distance, I see many fires—"

Moroni's voice trailed on and on, but Mormon didn't hear. He was thinking of the villages and cities being burned by the Lamanites, who were advancing rapidly. In his mind's eye, he saw many of the Nephites trapped in their burning homes, and thousands of others fleeing before the Lamanite armies. Those who were swift would escape; those who were not would be swept down and destroyed. He knew, only too well, the awful fear his people had of death. Their wickedness left them without hope. His thoughts brought him such sharp pain that a groan escaped his lips and Moroni, touched by his father's grief, stretched out a hand to comfort him.

"Is there anything we can do to ease their suffering, or to turn the Lamanites back?" asked Moroni.

"No, there is nothing. They far outnumber us, and without God's help, our cause is hopeless. I have completed my work. Some time ago, God commanded me to make an abridgment of the plates of Nephi. Now I have it completed. Soon I shall finish my own record concerning the destruction of my people. But now we must hurry to the cave, so that we can move the sacred records while there is still time," said Mormon, his voice filled with heartbreak.

A few days later, when a number of the Nephites had retreated to the land of Cumorah, Mormon sent a message to the king of the Lamanites. He asked him if he would grant the Nephites time to gather their people to the land of Cumorah, by a hill which was called Cumorah. There they would give the Lamanites battle. With great promptness, the Lamanite king sent a message granting Mormon's request.

The Nephites began at once to pitch their tents around the hill Cumorah. It was a beautiful land of many waters, rivers, and fountains. Here, hope rose again in the hearts of the Nephites, for they believed their position would give them advantage over the Lamanites.

By 384 A.D., Mormon had gathered all the remainder of his people to the land of Cumorah. He called Moroni to him and said: "My son, I am an old man. I know this will be the last struggle of my people. The Lord has commanded that I should not let the sacred records fall into the hands of the Lamanites, for you know they would destroy them. I made this record, out of the plates of Nephi, and hid it in the hill Cumorah, together with all the records which have been entrusted to me. All, that is, except these few plates, which I give to you, Moroni," said Mormon, his voice trailing off in hopeless despair.

"But, Father, if we are all destroyed and only a remnant of the Lamanites saved, who will bring forth the records?" asked Moroni.

"The prophets have told us that the blessings which we might have received in this great land of promise will go to the Gentiles, who shall possess the land. The Spirit of the Lord has already ceased to strive with the Lamanites. They will be driven by Satan, as chaff is driven before the wind, or as a vessel is tossed upon the waves, without sail or anchor. And in that day, which will be many hundreds of years from now, these sacred records will be brought forth by a Gentile. The remnant of the house of Israel will learn of the children of Lehi through them."

One morning in early spring, just when all God's creation was springing to life, the Nephites waited for death. Many thousands of them who were gathered about the hill Cumorah saw, at last, the thing they most dreaded—the vast armies of the Lamanites advancing upon them. Each man stood with his wife and children. As far as the eye could see, there were Lamanites approaching from all directions. Awful fear of death gripped the Nephites—the kind of fear that fills the breasts of all the wicked. The Lamanites outnumbered them many times over. When they reached the Nephites they fell upon them with the sword, the bow and arrow, and the ax, cutting them down in great slaughter. Mormon fell wounded, and they passed him by for dead. When the Lamanites thought they had killed all the Nephites, they returned to their camps.

When they were gone, Mormon got to his feet and looked about him. It was a horrible sight to behold and his soul was torn with anguish. He cried out: "Oh, my people, how could you have forgotten God? How could you have rejected Jesus, who stood with open arms to receive you? If you had lived according to Christ, you would not have fallen. But, behold, you are gone, and my sorrows cannot bring you back. Oh, that you had repented before this great destruction had come upon you."

While Mormon mourned his dead, night came upon him. Suddenly, from out of the dark, he heard a voice, "You are not alone, my father."

"Moroni!" Mormon's relief was so great that tears streamed down his face unashamed.

All through the night, father and son talked and prayed, and on the morrow, they climbed the hill Cumorah. They found twenty-four souls, in all, that had survived the battle.

Chapter 57

Moroni awakened and stared into the blackness. For a few moments he couldn't remember where he was. Stretching out a hand, he touched something sharp, cold, and hard. At that moment, the awful truth dawned. He was hidden away in a cave among the rocks on the hill Cumorah. He had found this place quite by accident—or, more likely, God had guided his footsteps here. He had gathered food that had belonged to the Nephite armies. So, except for water, he need not venture out and could stay safely hidden from the Lamanites for a long time.

"I am alone. I have neither relative nor friend nor any place to go. Oh, God, how long wilt thou suffer me to live?" whispered Moroni into the darkness.

"You have work to do," came God's answer. "You must finish the record of your father, Mormon."

For a long time Moroni lay awake, thinking about all that had happened. After the great and terrible battle at Cumorah, twenty-three of the twenty-four who had escaped with their lives had been hunted by the Lamanites and destroyed. Mormon had been killed by them, and Moroni alone remained to write the sad tale of the destruction of the Nephite nation.

Before another day passed, Moroni knew that he

would need water, for he remembered that his water jug was all but empty. Many of the streams and small lakes were polluted by the dead. Therefore, he would need to find the headwaters of a spring.

"If it were not so dark," he said to himself, "I would go now, but in this darkness I would become lost."

Suddenly, as if in answer to his thoughts, a tiny stream of light found its way through a small opening in the rocks. Moroni knew the moon had risen. Then, getting on his knees, he prayed: "Father in heaven, guide me to pure water and spare my life yet a little longer, so that I can fulfill the commandments of my father, Mormon. I ask this in the name of Jesus Christ. Amen."

Feeling about in the darkness, he finally found the jug. Then, pulling his coat about him, he went out into the night. The newly risen moon threw long, weird shadows that made Moroni catch his breath. His hands grew wet with perspiration and his heart beat wildly.

"Courage: the Lord your God is with you," said a still, small voice within him, and immediately he became calm.

Moroni circled the brow of the hill, walking noiselessly and keeping to the shadows as much as possible. When he reached the east side of the hill, he saw a clump of trees about halfway down. Thinking that this might be a likely place for a spring, he made his way toward them. He forgot caution and walked boldly through the moonlit space.

A faint sound of gushing water came to his ears and he smiled to himself at his good fortune. When he reached the trees, he discovered that to get to the water he would need to enter from the lower side. It was a beautiful spot, with the tall trees swaying and the moon making fantastic shadows and light among their branches. It all seemed a little unreal. Without looking, he knew he was walking on lush, green grass. When he reached the waterfall, he saw that it fell some twenty feet down a rocky cliff, then came tumbling into a rockbound basin where it boiled and foamed with great tumult.

Washing his jug in the basin, he stood up and filled it before the water had time to reach the pool. He drank long and lustily of the sweet, cold water.

"Dear Lord, I thank thee for this wonderful blessing," breathed Moroni.

All at once, his muscles grew rigid as he sniffed the air. Yes, it was there: the unmistakable scent of a haunting perfume. It was the same perfume he had noticed on the Nephite women. Turning quickly, he fully expected to come face to face with one of them. But there was no one. Then he almost laughed aloud, for he recognized the fragrance. Bending down, he trailed through the grass with his fingers until he found a blossom. Violets were blooming beside the little fall. He would have liked to linger there, but he knew that if he were to get back to his hiding place safely he must go now, while the Lamanites slept.

Next morning, he began to write upon the plates. There was little room and he had no ore with which to make more. Four hundred years had passed away since the coming of the Savior and the prophecies were fulfilled. The Lamanites had hunted the Nephites from city to city and from place to place, until they were no more. When the Lamanites had sought out and killed all of the Nephites, except Moroni, they turned on each other and made war. The whole face of the promised land was one continual round of murder and bloodshed. No one knew when the end of war would come. Over the whole face of the land, there were only Lamanites and robbers. No one knew the true God, except the three disciples of Jesus. But the Lord would not let them remain, because of the wickedness of the people, and where they were, no one knew.

"Behold, my father and I have seen them, and they have ministered unto us," said Moroni to himself. "I will write and hide the records in the earth. And then it will not matter when I go."

Many days passed away and Moroni continued to escape death at the hands of the Lamanites. He stayed hidden up, by day, writing upon the plates. At night, under cover of darkness, he secured food and water. After he had completed his father's record, the Lord commanded him to interpret the record of the Jaredites, taken from the twenty-four plates. These plates were found by the people of Limhi, in the days of King Mosiah. The Jaredites were an ancient people who were brought by the Lord to the promised land and destroyed by Him when they grew wicked. This record was to be known as the book of Ether because it was written by the prophet Ether. The first part of the record told about Adam, but Moroni, knowing that this account was given on the brass plates, did not record it. He began at the time of the great tower, when the Lord confounded the language of the people.

Jared and his brother, together with their families and their friends and their families, came forth from the great tower at the time when the language of the people was changed so that they couldn't understand each other. Now, Jared's brother was a large and mighty man and well favored of the Lord. He cried unto the Lord, asking him not to confuse their language and to guide them out of the land into a place of safety.

The Lord answered the brother of Jared, saying, "Go and gather male and female of your flocks, of the birds and bees, of the fish and of all animals, together with every kind of seed on earth. When you have done this, go to a valley which is northward. There I will meet you and guide you to the land which is choice above all the lands on earth. There I will make you a great nation. I have preserved this land for a righteous people, and those who possess it must serve the true and living God or else be destroyed in their wickedness."

Jared, his brother, and their people did as the Lord commanded. When at last they reached the sea, they pitched their tents and stayed for four years. Then, one day, the Lord came to the brother of Jared and stood in a cloud so that He could not be seen. He was angry with the brother of Jared because he had not remembered to call upon Him. Jared's brother repented and asked forgiveness.

Then the Lord said: "I will forgive you and your brethren. Go to work and build barges."

They set to work immediately and built eight barges, according to the instructions given them by the Lord. Each barge was as long as a tree and built with peaked ends whose sides, bottom and top, were as tight as a dish. They were small and light upon the water.

"Brother," said Jared, "what about our ships? They are tight, which is good to keep the water out, but how will we breathe? And there is no light. How will we steer in darkness?"

The brother of Jared said, "I shall ask God."

The Lord told him how they might get air into the ships. Then Jared's brother went to the top of a high mountain and there he found sixteen small stones. They were white and clear as glass. He carried them in his hands and cried out to the Lord, saying: "Oh, Lord, I know that thou art all-powerful and thou canst do anything to benefit man. Therefore, touch these stones with thy finger and prepare them that they will shine in the darkness."

As soon as the brother of Jared had said these words, a wonderful thing happened—the Lord stretched out his hand and touched each of the stones with His finger. The veil was taken from before the eyes of the brother of Jared and he saw the finger of the Lord. It was like a man's finger, and Jared's brother fell down, struck with fear.

"I saw the finger of the Lord and I am frightened. I didn't know that the Lord had flesh and blood."

Then the Lord said unto him: "Because of your faith, you have seen me. Never before has any man had such great faith. If it were not so, you could not have seen my finger. Did you see more than this?"

"No, Lord, show thyself to me."

"Do you believe the words which I shall speak?" asked the Lord.

"Yes, I know thou speakest the truth, for thou art a God of truth and cannot lie."

Then the Lord showed himself to the brother of Jared and told him He was Jesus Christ.

"Do you see that you are created after my own image? This body, which you see, is the body of my spirit. Even as I appear to you, I will appear to my people in the flesh. And now, because of your perfect faith, the veil is taken from your eyes and you can see all the secrets of heaven."

The brother of Jared saw all the inhabitants of the earth which had been, and also all those who would live in the future. He stood amazed at the things he saw and heard, knowing all and doubting nothing.

Then Jesus spoke again and said, "Go down from the mountain, and write all that you have seen and heard. Then seal up this record and hide it away from the children of men, until after I am lifted up on the cross. You shall write this record in a strange language that man cannot read. Here are two stones. Seal them up with the record and I will show them, in my own due time, to the children of men."

"Oh Lord, what are the stones to be used for?" asked the brother of Jared.

"They are interpreters, which will make clear the things you shall write. Go now and be faithful to my commandments."

The brother of Jared carried out the Lord's wishes and then, taking the sixteen stones that the Lord had touched with His finger, he placed one in each end of the eight barges and they put out to sea. They were driven by the winds toward the promised land. Sometimes great waves, mountain high, forced them into the depths of the sea. But, regardless of whether they were buried beneath the waves or floating on the surface, the stones gave constant light. No monster of the sea had any power over them, and they were driven 344 days upon the water, until they landed on the shore of the promised land.

When their feet touched land, they bowed down on the face of the earth and humbled themselves before the Lord. Tears of joy streamed down their cheeks as they thanked Him for His tender mercy. They went forth and began at once to till the soil.

CHAPTER 58

M oroni got to his feet, stretched, and rubbed his eyes.
It had grown too dark to continue working on the
Jaredite record. At that moment, a puzzled expression
crossed his face and he said, half-aloud: "Why is it so
dark? It's very strange, since it is still early afternoon."

Now, Moroni reckoned time by the amount of engraving he did—not daring to go out of his hiding place
by day. He fell to wondering if the Lamanites had discovered him and were playing some devilish trick. The more
he thought of it, the more restless he became. At last, he
determined to have a look. First, he must put the records
away in their secret place. His first thought was always for
the safety of the sacred records. God had willed it so.

He made his way noiselessly to the mouth of the
cave. All about the entrance were great, giant rocks that
looked like a forest of stone. He walked among them
until he had a clear view of the heavens. A great, black
cloud was lowering itself about the hill Cumorah. While
he watched the wild, rolling clouds, a long finger of lightning lit up the whole mountainside, and in that brief moment, he saw a mighty tree split in two and go crashing to
the earth. The lightning was instantly followed by a
deafening roar of thunder that echoed and reechoed
through the rocks.

"Dear Lord, here I am, all alone—the last of the

Nephite people. If this be the end of me, I pray that I may be worthy to come into thy presence."

Suddenly, without warning, the clouds opened up and the rain fell in great torrents, soaking Moroni to the skin before he could reach the cave. Once inside, he began drying his clothes.

"Ba-a! Ba-a!"

Moroni stopped and listened. Yes, there it was again, the cry of a small lamb. Instantly he grew tense—did it mean danger was near? Or had God sent him the little lamb for company in his loneliness?

God's voice came into his mind, saying, "I have sent you the little lamb to cheer you through the long, lonely hours. Care for the little lamb even as I have cared for you."

Moroni found the lamb without difficulty. It stood among the rocks, its little legs braced against the fierceness of the wind and rain. When it saw Moroni approaching, it went rigid with fear. But then, when it looked into the sad eyes of the man, it was no longer frightened. It knew, instinctively, that Moroni was a man choice above all the men it had known. It sensed, too, the great loneliness of this stranger.

"Don't be frightened," said Moroni, as he lifted the little animal tenderly and carried it into the cave.

All the rest of the day, Moroni cared for the wants of the little lamb and talked to it constantly. Not until now did he realize how lonely he had been. It was so good to talk again, even if he had to whisper. There was always the chance that the Lamanites might discover him, although he had neither seen nor heard any of them for several days.

Early next morning, after he and the lamb had eaten, Moroni put it in the pen he had made for it and set to work engraving on the plates of Nephi the record of the Jaredites. This is what he wrote:

When the Jaredites reached the promised land, they were taught to walk humbly before the Lord. After many years had passed away, they spread out upon the face of the land, for they had become a strong people. Jared and his brother had grown old.

"Jared," said his brother, "we are old, and soon we will go down to our graves. Let us call our people together so that we might number them and find out if there is anything they desire of us before we pass on."

Soon the people were all gathered together. After they had been numbered, the brother of Jared said: "Jared and I would like to grant you some desire you may have before we pass on to our Maker. Tell us your wish."

The people said, "Anoint one of your sons to be king over us."

When Jared and his brother heard these words, they were deeply grieved, and the brother of Jared said, "Surely you do not want a king. Kingship will lead you into captivity."

But Jared said to his brother, "Let them have a king."

Jared's words both shocked and surprised his brother. These two had been very close all the days of their lives, and the brother believed he shared Jared's every thought, especially concerning the freedom of their people. He turned and looked squarely into Jared's eyes, and the protest he was about to make died on his lips. Suddenly he knew that Jared had had a very good reason for saying what he did. Trusting him without question, Jared's brother said to the people, "You shall have a king. Therefore, choose him from among our sons."

"We have chosen your firstborn son," the people said to the brother of Jared. The firstborn son refused to be their king, and they continued to choose all the sons of the brother of Jared. But all of them refused, and all the sons of Jared refused, except one. His name was Orihah.

Now, Orihah made a wonderful king. He walked humbly before the Lord and always remembered the great things the Lord had done for his father, and he taught these things to his people. Soon after Orihah became king, Jared and his brother died. But they lived long enough to see their people prosper and grow very rich under the righteous reign of King Orihah.

Orihah lived to a ripe old age. He had many sons, and at his death, the kingdom passed into the hands of Kib, the son of his old age. Now, Kib had a son named Corihor, and when he was thirty-two years of age, he rebelled against his father and went over into the land of Nehor to live. Corihor was blessed with many sons and daughters. The daughters were very beautiful and their cunning father used them to draw away many of his father's people. When Corihor had gathered a large army, he marched to the land of Moron where his father Kib lived, and took him captive.

Kib lived in captivity until he was very old. But, in his old age, he had a son whose name was Shule, and he became a great blessing to the old king. When Shule grew up, he came to despise his brother Corihor, and determined to help free his father from captivity. Shule became a strong and mighty man, and very quietly began to make swords for himself and his followers. When they were armed, they returned to the city of Nehor and gave battle to his brother. Shule was victorious and restored his father to the kingdom. The old king was very grateful to his son—so grateful that he turned the kingdom over to him.

Many years passed away and the wickedness of the people brought sorrow to Shule. One day, as he rested in his garden, he heard the gate open. Looking up, he saw his son, Omer, coming toward him.

"Good morning, Omer," said King Shule. "What brings you to the palace so early?"

"Have you heard about the prophets? Anyway, they profess to be prophets," said Omer.

Shule looked at his son sharply and said, "I have been a poor teacher, if you do not know the truth when you hear it."

"But, Father, they go about prophesying that our people are bringing a curse upon the land because of their wickedness and their worship of idols. Surely these men cannot foretell the future."

"They come from the Lord, my son, and in His goodness He has sent them to warn us while there is still time for us to be saved."

Now, Omer loved his father, and knowing that he was wise in the ways of God, the youth listened to all he told him and believed in him.

"How are the people receiving the message of the prophets?" asked Shule, almost afraid to hear the answer.

"The people abuse and mock them."

"I will not allow this," roared the king.

He set to work at once to send word throughout all the land that the prophets were to go wherever they wished and not be harmed. Now, because Shule made this law, the people began to listen to the words of the prophets. After a while, they began to believe and were brought to repentance. The Lord spared them and they began to prosper, and there were no more wars in the days of Shule. In his old age, he made Omer king over his people.

Omer was a good man, wise and just in his judgments. He had many sons and daughters, and one of the sons was named Jared. Jared was cruel and wicked and he plotted against his father and took him captive. He kept him in captivity half his days. It so happened that two of Omer's sons became so angry that they raised an army and came against Jared. They were victorious and restored their father to his throne.

Jared pretended to be grateful to his brothers for sparing his life. But, in reality, he was bitter and resentful because of the loss of the kingdom. He had set his heart upon the glory of the world. Jared had many children, and one of his daughters was unusually beautiful. But her lovely face masked a cruel and sinful heart. She was as cunning as she was beautiful, and seeing her father bowed down in sorrow, she decided to use him to further her own desires.

"Father," she said, "why do you sorrow? Am I not lovely to look upon?"

"The vanity of my daughter ill becomes her," Jared answered sourly.

"Don't be angry. I think you can use my beauty to steal away the throne from your father again."

Jared looked at his daughter narrowly and asked, "How?"

"Send for Akish. He is rich and powerful and has many followers. I have long had my eye on him."

"Akish is a friend of my father, Omer. That is a foolish request if I ever heard one. Did you suppose he would help me dethrone his friend?" asked Jared, completely disgusted.

"Send for Akish and let me dance for him. When he sees how lovely I am, he will want to marry me. But when he asks you for my hand in marriage, you must say, 'Destroy my father and bring me the proof of his death; then I will give you my daughter.'"

Now, Jared liked his daughter's plan, and when Akish saw the grace and beauty of the girl, he forgot his friend Omer and could think of nothing else but the fact that he wanted to win her for his wife. Therefore, he readily consented to do as Jared asked.

Akish gathered all his relatives and friends to the house of Jared and made them vow to do whatever he asked of them. If they did not do as he asked, they would be put to death. Therefore, they agreed to support Akish in his attempt to kill the good king, Omer. It was not long after this that, through trickery and cunning, Akish and his friends overthrew the kingdom of Omer.

The Lord had mercy on Omer and his loyal sons and daughters. God warned Omer, in a dream, that he was to go out of the land. As soon as he awakened from his dream he set to work, preparing to leave. Quickly and quietly, he and his family made their way southward. They passed by the hill Shim, and from there they traveled eastward until they came to a place called Ablom. There they pitched their tents.

Jared was anointed king over the people, by the hand of wickedness. As soon as he was king, he gave Akish his beautiful daughter in marriage.

Now, Jared had not been king long before Akish, greedy for power, began thinking that he should be king. Therefore, he called all those sworn to do his bidding and said: "Jared, my father-in-law, is a weakling. We need a strong man to be king. Do you agree with me?"

The friends of Akish knew it was unwise to disagree with him, so they said, "Yes, we agree. We think you should be our king."

"Very well, then," said Akish, "destroy him."

They did his bidding, and Jared was killed as he sat upon the throne talking to his people. So great was the wickedness of Akish that it spread to all the people. No sooner had Akish become king than he grew jealous of the popularity of his son. For this reason, he cast him into prison, where he died. The other sons of Akish grew angry at their father and made war upon him. It was a long, bitter fight that lasted for many years, even until all the people of the kingdom, except thirty, had been destroyed. When this news reached Omer, he and his family returned and he was restored again to the land of his inheritance.

CHAPTER 59

M oroni laid aside the plate he was engraving and bowed his head in the palms of his hands. He was tired, discouraged, and oh, so very lonely. Several years had passed and the little lamb had grown old and died, leaving an aching loneliness. Today, as he sat there, he felt very humble and weak. He was disturbed over the quality of his writing, knowing that these sacred records would be brought forth by the Gentiles. He longed to write with greater skill, in order that it would be impressive and accepted as the word of God. In his troubled heart, he prayed: "Lord, the Gentiles will mock at these things, because of our weakness in writing. We have little skill in writing, due to the awkwardness of our hands. Would that I had words so powerful and great that the Gentiles could not mock us."

The Lord spoke unto Moroni, saying, "Fools mock, but they shall mourn. My grace is enough for the meek and they will take no advantage of your weakness. If they humble themselves before me and have faith, then will I make weak things strong."

When Moroni heard these words, he was comforted and thanked God. He picked up the plate again and began abridging the record of the Jaredites, writing as follows:

Hundreds of years passed away after the reign of the good king, Omer. During this time, the Jaredites had numerous kings. When they grew too wicked, the Lord sent famines and poisonous snakes that killed many and brought great suffering to the people. Each time they saw that their destruction was near, they repented, and God in His great mercy forgave them and poured out rich blessings upon them. But, as soon as they were prosperous again, they forgot the Lord, growing more wicked as time went by.

Finally, in the days when Coriantumr was king over all the land, a great prophet of the Lord came forth. His name was Ether. He began to prophesy to the people, asking them to repent and believe in God.

Ether told them, "Those who believe in God can hope for a better world. This hope comes through faith, making an anchor to the souls of men."

Ether prophesied many great and marvelous things. But many of these things, the Lord forbade Moroni to translate. The people heard Ether's prophecies, but because of their wickedness, they were unimpressed. As a matter of fact, they cast him out and he hid himself in a cavity of a great rock. He spent each day in the rock, making the remainder of this record. At night, he went forth and observed the destruction of the people. In the first year that he lived in the rock, a great war broke out. There were many who were determined to destroy Coriantumr. Now, Coriantumr was learned in the art of making war, so he gave battle to his enemies.

One evening, just at sundown, Coriantumr looked up to see Ether entering the throne room. Over a year had passed since he had seen Ether; he had believed him to be dead. Never had any man pointed out Coriantumr's weaknesses with such daring as this man had done. In spite of his hatred of the prophet, he feared him, knowing in his heart that he spoke the truth.

"This is an unpleasant surprise, to find that you are still alive. I hoped that we were rid of you and your foolish predictions," said Coriantumr, greatly agitated.

"I would not have bothered you, but the Lord commanded me to bring you a message," said Ether meekly.

"You are a brave man to come to me here at the palace. How do you know I will not have you killed?" asked Coriantumr.

"When I have given you God's message, you may do with me as you like," said Ether, without fear.

Coriantumr found himself admiring the courage of this lonely man who stood defenseless before him.

"Very well, I will listen to your message. But if I do not like what you have to say, I will have you flogged and thrown into prison. Speak out!"

"The Lord told me to say to you that if you would repent, and all of your household, He would give you this kingdom and spare the people," said Ether.

"How can your Lord give me what I already have?" roared Coriantumr.

"Because, O King, at His will, He has power over all things," said Ether reverently.

"And if I do not repent, what then?" asked Coriantumr.

"Then God will destroy your household and your people. And you, alone, shall live long enough to see the fulfillment of the prophecies which have been spoken, concerning another people who shall receive this land for their inheritance. Furthermore, you shall be given burial by them."* Ether spoke with authority.

Coriantumr's face grew dark with anger and he

*See Book of Mormon, Omni 1:20-22.

called for his guards to kill Ether. But Ether fled before them and hid again in the cavity of the rock.

Now, Coriantumr, his household, and the people disregarded the warnings of Ether and did not repent. Neither did the war cease. The fighting spread to every nook and corner of the land. Every man in the kingdom joined his own band and fought for the things he wanted. There began to be a great curse upon the land, for the robbers were so numerous that they took whatever they wanted and no one's property was safe. Therefore, every man held tight to the things that were his and would not borrow, neither would he lend. Every man kept the hilt of his sword in his right hand, in defense of his property and his family.

One morning, a messenger came to Coriantumr and said: "O King, I bring you bad news from the battlefield."

This was a morning when Coriantumr was feeling the pains of his many wounds. Bad news was especially distasteful. He began to pluck savagely at his right eyebrow and his scowl grew fierce and black. The messenger, a weak little man, began to shake in his boots and was just looking around for a safe place to run, when the king roared in his most savage voice: "Come here! Tell me the news and be quick about it!"

"Well, sir, you see, sir, a man by the name of Shiz has come forth with a well-trained army and they are killing our men, right and left. Our people fear this man and they speak his name with horror! And they ask, 'Who can stand before the army of Shiz? Behold, he sweeps the earth before him.'"

Coriantumr soon discovered how frightened the people were. They began to flock together in armies. They were divided; part of them fled to the army of Shiz, and part of them to the army of Coriantumr. So great and lasting had been the war, and so long had been the bloodshed, that the whole face of the land was covered with the bodies of the dead.

Coriantumr had killed Lib in battle. Now, Lib was a brother of Shiz, and Shiz vowed, saying: "I shall not rest until I kill Coriantumr with my sword."

"Ether, the prophet, told Coriantumr that he should not fall by the sword," said a soldier.

At the sound of his voice, Shiz turned on him angrily. "What nonsense is this? Do you think it matters what Ether has to say?"

"You, sir," answered the soldier humbly, "are a mighty man with the sword. But Ether, speaking for his Lord, has told us many things that have already come true."

"Tell me everything Ether had to say regarding Coriantumr," demanded Shiz, partly curious and partly afraid.

"He declared that because Coriantumr would not repent, his household and all the people would be destroyed, and that Coriantumr alone should live long enough to see this prophecy fulfilled."

When Shiz heard the words of the prophecy, he became more determined than ever to take the life of Coriantumr. One day, after fierce fighting, he had an opportunity to meet Coriantumr face to face, and Shiz gave him many deep wounds. Coriantumr lost so much blood that he fainted and was carried away as though he were dead. Then Shiz, realizing how great had been the loss on both sides, commanded them not to pursue the armies of Coriantumr. Therefore, they returned to their camp.

When Coriantumr had recovered from his wounds, he began to remember the words Ether had spoken to him. He saw that already nearly two million of his people had been killed. When he came to realize how great had been his loss, he began to sorrow in his heart, and to repeat over and over to himself: "Woe is me! I would that I could stop this mad bloodshed, but I cannot, for the Lord will not heed my words. If only I had listened to Ether and repented of my sins, then the Lord would have spared us."

Coriantumr continued to mourn and refused to be comforted. He wrote a letter to Shiz, asking him if he would spare his people. Coriantumr offered him his kingdom if he would let the people live. But the people themselves were so angry with each other that they went to war for revenge. The fighting was fierce and hard and Coriantumr received another deep wound. This time the armies of Coriantumr were victorious, and Shiz and his army fled before them. The people of Coriantumr pitched their tents by the hill Ramah, which the Nephites later called the hill Cumorah. It was in this same hill where Moroni hid the records unto the Lord.

The next four years were spent in gathering together all the people upon the face of the land, except Ether. But he saw what they were doing—he watched, with deep regret, as Shiz and Coriantumr gathered to themselves the people that were loyal to them. At the end of the fourth year, they marched against each other and continued to fight until all were slain except Coriantumr and Shiz. Then Coriantumr killed Shiz. And it came to pass that Coriantumr fell to the earth and lay as if he were dead.

The Lord spoke to Ether, and said to him, "Go forth! Behold, the words of the Lord have been fulfilled." Ether finished his records and hid them away until the people of Limhi found them.

The last words that Ether wrote are these:

"It does not matter to me whether the Lord takes me up to heaven in the twinkling of an eye, or whether I must suffer death, if only I am saved in the kingdom of God. Amen."

CHAPTER 60

"A t last, I have completed the record of the Jaredites," Moroni whispered to himself. "Oh, God, I am grateful to thee for giving me this task, to fill my empty days and lonely nights."

Moroni had spent so many years interpreting and abridging the Jaredite record that this ancient people had grown very close to him. It was as though they actually lived with him. They seemed more real than his own existence. He fell to thinking of Ether, the great prophet of the Jaredites. He felt a close bond with him. Hadn't they both lived many years in a cave, hidden away from their enemies? Ether, like himself, had made a record of the destruction of his people. He wondered what actually had happened to Ether. Had he been taken up to heaven in the twinkling of an eye, or had he suffered death? Moroni's faith in God told him that, regardless of how Ether had gone to heaven, he was now in God's kingdom. He was cheered by this thought.

Carefully, Moroni began sorting and counting the twenty-four plates which bore the record of the Jaredites. Then he assembled his own abridgment and placed them with the plates of Nephi. When this was done, he carried them to the sacred hiding place and said, "Oh God, the

Eternal Father, I now give these sacred plates into thy keeping."

"Moroni, there is yet work for you," came the voice of the Lord. "You must write as long as you live. I will guide you in the things you shall record."

Now, Moroni was surprised, for he had supposed that this was the end of his writing. Lonely as he was, he was happy to learn that he was to live yet a little longer.

Boldly, he left the cave and made his way through the great rocks. He looked out beyond the hill Cumorah to the valley below. Far in the distance, he saw small bands of Lamanites fighting fiercely among themselves. He knew that their hatred for the Nephites had not lessened and that they would kill him on sight.

Taking note of the destruction of life and property, he said, half-aloud, "This was to have been the land of our inheritance. But, through wickedness, we have been destroyed."

At that moment, Moroni remembered the words of the Lord: "This land of promise is choice above all lands, and my people shall inherit it in righteousness. I will not tolerate wickedness to continue in this, the land of promise. I shall destroy the wicked from off the face of this land and save it for the inheritance of a righteous people."

Moroni thought of how the Jaredites and later the Nephites had been destroyed, because of their wickedness, according to the word of God. He knew, at that moment, that someday the Gentiles would come to this land and that they would possess it as their inheritance.

"Furthermore," said Moroni to himself, "it shall be the Gentiles who shall bring forth the sacred records, and they shall cry, like a voice from the dust, to all the inhabitants of the earth."

For a few moments, Moroni stood viewing what

once had been a rich, lush valley. Now it was the land of desolation, where white bones lay bleaching in the sun. With a heavy heart, he turned and slowly retraced his steps back inside the cave. He threw himself on his bed and, with his hands locked behind his head, lay watching the long ribbons of light that found their way through tiny openings in the rocks. For a long time he lay there, keeping his mind a blank. But then, try as he would, he could not close out the thoughts that were crowding in upon him.

He thought of the constant fighting going on among the Lamanites—of their cruelty to their captives, men, women, and children. They seemed to delight in wickedness. Suddenly, the voice of the Lord came to Moroni, saying: "Moroni, the Lamanites are your brethren and I have promised them that a remnant of their people shall be preserved."

Now, Moroni knew that he and the Lamanites were direct descendants of Lehi, who came out of Jerusalem six hundred years before the birth of Christ. But their dark skins and their wild, savage nature made him often forget that they were related. At that moment, he knew he must write something for their benefit.

"I want the Lamanites to know that more than 420 years have passed away since the sign was given of the coming of Christ. And now, I seal up these records, after I have spoken a few words of warning unto you. I hope that, when you read my words, you shall remember how merciful the Lord has been to the children of men. And when you receive the sacred records, ask God, the Eternal Father, in the name of Christ, if these words are true. If you ask with a sincere heart, having faith in Christ, He will make the truth known to you, through the power of the Holy Ghost.

"Oh, my brethren, do not deny the gifts of God, for

they are many. To one is given the Spirit of God, that he may teach the word of wisdom. To another is given great faith; and to another, gifts of healing by the same Spirit. Some can work mighty miracles, and to some, the power of prophecy is given. Remember that every good gift comes from Christ."

Moroni paused in his writing and sat listening to the sounds of fighting still going on in the valley below. He heard the wild, triumphant cries of the victorious and the pitiable wailing of the captives.

"Oh, my brethren," said Moroni sadly, "why will you continue in this wicked fighting? Why won't you repent and listen to my words? They are the words of Christ, and I do not lie. You will soon know that I tell the truth, for the time comes quickly when you shall see me at the bar of God. And when that time comes, the Lord God will say to you, 'Did I not send you my words, which were written by this man? It is like one crying from the dead, yes, even as one speaking out of the dust.'"

Moroni stopped speaking, his attention drawn to the fact that the battle cries had been blotted out by a new set of sounds. A wind had sprung up and was whining and whistling through the rocks. Wind disturbed Moroni as nothing else could do, and, sighing heavily, he put the records away, thinking he would finish them on the morrow. But he did not. Several days passed and then, one morning, he arose early and hastily ate of dried berries and meat and began immediately engraving the last of Nephi's plates.

"And now," wrote Moroni, "I bid you all farewell. I soon go to rest in the paradise of God. There I shall remain, until my spirit and body shall be reunited again and I am brought forth triumphant through the air, to meet you before the pleasing bar of the great Jehovah, the Eternal Judge of both living and dead. Amen."

For a long time, Moroni sat looking at the last word he had written—"Amen." To him it was a solemn word with deep spiritual meaning. On this particular day, it meant an end to his writing and, perhaps, an end to life itself. His father, Mormon, had taught him to say "Amen" when he agreed with the words of another. At last, he arose and took the plate on which he had written his final farewell, and carefully placed it in the stone box with the other sacred records. Then, with great care, he sealed the box.

That night, he lay upon his bed and stared into the blackness, while his thoughts reviewed his entire life. He thought of his childhood, and a gentle smile touched his lips as he remembered how happy he had been. How tenderly and yet how firmly his parents had led him into the paths of righteousness. He had been secure in their love.

"Ah, yes," said Moroni to himself, "I was happy. Little did I know what sorrow and heartbreak lay ahead for me."

He thought of the wars, the famines, the poison serpents, and the various forms of suffering that the Lord had visited on the people when their wickedness grew too great for Him to endure. He remembered seeing his father sorrowing over the sins of the Nephites and the Lamanites. When he was powerless in his attempt to lead them back to Christ, his grief was boundless. He thought of the last twenty years of his own life, the aching loneliness of days and nights with no one to turn to for comfort or consolation. There was always the threat of being discovered by the Lamanites. Yet, in spite of it all, he decided that life had been very dear to him. Through joy and pain, his soul had been refined and God had trusted him to write His word, which would cry out from the dust and be a source of good for generations yet unborn.

Now, as he lay there, suddenly a great calm settled down upon him. He was old and tired, but at this moment he felt young and new in spirit, and, folding his hands across his chest, he whispered, "Amen." Then, closing his eyes, he drifted away in peaceful sleep.

In 1827 A.D., this same Moroni, then a resurrected personage, delivered the engraved plates to Joseph Smith.